AN
ARTIST'S
JOURNEY

Literary Tea at Madame de Girardin's ca. 1837.
The guests depicted include Dumas, Balzac, Liszt, Jules
Janin, and Victor Hugo. Drawing by J. J. Grandville, 1845.

AN ARTIST'S JOURNEY

Lettres d'un
bachelier ès musique
1835–1841

Franz Liszt

Translated and annotated by
Charles Suttoni

THE UNIVERSITY OF CHICAGO PRESS
Chicago and London

CHARLES SUTTONI has written and lectured extensively
on Liszt's writings. He is a member of the board of
directors of the American Liszt Society.

The University of Chicago Press, Chicago 60637
The University of Chicago Press, Ltd., London
© 1989 by The University of Chicago
All rights reserved. Published 1989
Printed in the United States of America

98 97 96 95 94 93 92 91 90 89   5 4 3 2 1

LIBRARY OF CONGRESS CATALOGING-IN-PUBLICATION DATA

Liszt, Franz, 1811–1886.
[Lettres d'un bachelier ès musique, 1835–1841. English]
An artist's journey : lettres d'un bachelier ès musique, 1835–1841
/ Franz Liszt : translated and annotated by Charles Suttoni.
p. cm.
Bibliography: p.
Includes index.
ISBN 0-226-48510-2 (alk. paper)
1. Liszt, Franz, 1811–1886—Journeys—Europe.   2. Composers—
Biography.   3. Music—Europe—19th century—History and criticism.
4. Europe—Description and travel—1800–1918.   I. Suttoni, Charles.
II. Title.
ML410.L7A3   1989
780'.92'4—dc19   88-34025
[B]   CIP
                                                         MN

CONTENTS

CONTENTS

ACKNOWLEDGMENTS

In the course of working on this volume I incurred a deep debt of gratitude to the late Ted Fagan, an old friend, chief of interpreters at the United Nations, who read the initial draft of the translation and was of great help cutting a sensible path through the sometimes superabundant thicket of prose. In equal measure my gratitude extends to Vera Brodsky Lawrence who, having watched this project grow since its inception and having read several drafts of the text, proved a constant source of sound, adroit advice. I also wish to acknowledge the generosity of the Ingram Merrill Foundation, whose award in 1984–85 helped finance the time and research needed for this work. My thanks as well to the Heyman Center for the Humanities at Columbia University for an opportunity to try out some portions of the translation in a talk I gave on "Liszt the Writer" as part of the Liszt centenary celebrations there in 1986. Finally, I am most appreciative of the lively, sympathetic interest that the University of Chicago Press has taken in these travel article/essays and their transformation from manuscript to finished book.

INTRODUCTION

> There are those ardent souls who are tormented by the need to
> love something and to believe in it; for them art is a religion. . . .
> They have faith in art, a personal faith, a faith which has no logic,
> no rational basis, yet a sincere faith, an instinctive, enthusiastic,
> and almost involuntary faith.
>
> Joseph d'Ortigue, Sainte-Baume (1834)

On 1 June 1835 Franz Liszt left Paris aboard a public coach bound for
Basel, where he was to meet Marie d'Agoult. The pianist, who was
twenty-three years old at the time, and the countess, twenty-nine, had
been lovers, albeit intermittently, for about two years. Now that she,
pregnant with their child, had decided to leave husband and daughter
for him, they were meeting in Switzerland to begin a life together.
This shared period of their lives was to last four years. They settled in
Geneva for something over a year, then returned to France for about
nine months. From there they journeyed south to Italy, where they
visited Milan, Venice, Florence, and Rome, exploring in leisurely
fashion the artistic heritage of this land "wo die Zitronen blühn" and
so beloved of transalpine Romantic travelers. Their Italian sojourn
came to an end two years later in the autumn of 1839 when Liszt, having finally decided to take up a virtuoso's career in earnest, embarked
on his phenomenally successful series of trans-European tours.

For the pianist, this period spent with the countess was not only
a time for travel; it was also an important opportunity for him, freed
from the social and intellectual distractions he had found so vitiating
in Paris, to take stock of himself and his talents. Working diligently at
the keyboard, he filled hundreds of pages with music, and even if
many of the pieces he produced at the time—fantasies on opera
themes, transcriptions of Beethoven symphonies, Schubert lieder and
Rossini songs, or the early version of his *Transcendental Etudes,* etc.—
are little recalled today, they nonetheless represent substantial progress in writing and transcribing music effectively for the piano. In a
more poetic vein, he memorialized his stay in Switzerland with a collection of pieces that explores a new dimension in piano music, his
Album d'un voyageur; the half-dozen pieces that make up its opening

section, aptly entitled *Impressions et poésies*,[1] are a fusion of literature and descriptive landscape rendered at the piano. They mark the beginning of impressionism in music.

All during this time Liszt both supplemented and complemented his musical endeavors by writing a series of articles for the Parisian press. These articles—the ones collected in this volume— were published for the most part in the city's leading musical journal, the *Gazette musicale,* and except for the first of them, which appeared as a *Lettre d'un voyageur* (Letter of a Voyager), they all bore the series title *Lettres d'un bachelier ès musique* (literally, "Letters of a Bachelor of Music").[2] They are grouped here, however, as *An Artist's Journey,* since that general concept not only gives some idea of their content, but is also truer in spirit to the journey, both physical and interior, that they recount.

Madame d'Agoult, we know, took a hand in writing these articles. There have even been those who maintained that she was the sole author of them, as well as of Liszt's other writings of this period, but that view is untenable. They were a collaboration. Also, the fact that they were a joint effort is not, perhaps, to be unexpected; she and Liszt shared the same enthusiasm for art and literature, which indeed was an important factor in bringing them together, and she (the future writer "Daniel Stern") had decided literary aspirations. As for the nature of their collaboration (a matter examined in detail in appendix E, "Liszt as Author"), it is generally agreed that the countess wrote a fair if undeterminable amount of the prose that actually appeared in print, but that it was Liszt who initiated the articles and was basically responsible for the ideas about music and art they express. For all practical purposes, then, the Letters can be regarded and accepted as authentic Liszt, as integral a part of his canon as are his musical compositions.

Written over a span of six years, but mostly from 1837 to 1839, these Letters—much like their direct precedent, George Sand's *Lettres d'un voyageur*—are too broadly and variously based to be easily characterized as a group. Some of them, such as the two Letters to Louis

---

1. This group of pieces is better known in its later, revised form: the *Années de pèlerinage; Première année, Suisse* published in 1855. Continuing the series, Liszt also composed a *Deuxième année, Italie,* although some of these works were not completed until after he had left Italy, and the collection itself not published until 1858.

2. Although Liszt never explained his choice of so patently academic a title, it was apparently connected with his being named "Professeur honoraire" of the Geneva Conservatory in July 1836. Nonetheless, it is ironic that Liszt, who had never received a formal education, would style himself as an academic in print.

de Ronchaud, are essentially travel pieces; some, like the one on musical conditions in Italy or the Letter to Léon Kreutzer, are a music correspondent's reports; some, namely the second and third letters to George Sand, are so personal and autobiographical that they border on being spiritual confessions; and still others, such as those about Cellini's *Perseus* and Raphael's *Saint Cecilia,* are really brief essays on the nature of art. But various as the individual articles may be, when read in sequence they provide a narrative account of Liszt's life, activities, and interests during this journeying period of his mid-twenties. Viewed in that manner, there are two broad, interrelated aspects of them to be considered.

Read simply as travel pieces, they are an especially wide-ranging account of the social, artistic, and musical life that Liszt encountered in the cities he visited, notably in Geneva, Milan, Vienna, Hamburg, or even in Paris. He discusses such things as musical taste, religious music, the opera repertory of the time, and the reigning favorites of the lyric stage. He also gives reports of his own concerts, the works he performed, and the audience's response to them. Still, without slighting the articles' value and interest as a historical source, it is not Liszt writing as a reporter or correspondent who ultimately commends these articles to a reader's attention; we have, after all, similar reports on music in Italy by Berlioz and Mendelssohn, as well as the contemporary press. It is, rather, Liszt himself as reflected in these highly personal writings who is the main source of interest, the center of attraction.

The Letters, the closest he ever came to writing an autobiography, are saturated with his experiences and opinions, both of which are those of an idealistic young musician who was firmly convinced that art and the artist had a high and noble calling in society, but who as a performing pianist had to contend with the exigencies of everyday concert life. The Ideal versus the Real; the disparity between them recurs throughout the writings like the ground theme of a passacaglia. In this sense the Letters can also be seen as something of a continuation of the polemic stance he had taken in his earlier essay "On the Situation of Artists and their Status in Society."[3] In that

---

3. The essay appeared in six installments, plus an epilogue, "Some Further Words on the Subalternity of Musicians," in the *Gazette musicale,* 3 May–15 November 1835. (Note: Although the *Gazette musicale,* founded in 1834 and published by Maurice Schlesinger, theoretically became the *Revue et Gazette musicale* a year later when it subsumed the nearly defunct *Revue musicale,* published by F. J. Fétis, its readers continued to refer to it by its original name (or simply the *Gazette*), and that is the form cited here.)

work he fulminated not only against the Parisian musical establishment for its failure, among other things, to encourage young musicians and their works, but also against modern civilization because it had failed to recognize the vital and comprehensive role that the artist—priest, prophet, seer—could and should play in the betterment of society. Basic as it is to Liszt's thinking, this conception of the artist is reflected in the broad range of topics he discusses in the articles. Music, though primary, is only one subject in a spectrum of themes that includes literature, the visual arts, social justice, the Church, human destiny—in short, everything that stirred his concern and feelings during this questing period of his life.

Viewed as a whole, then, the sixteen Letters present a fascinating amalgam of autobiography, polemic, and social history. As such they are a necessary complement to any account of Liszt's artistic development, particularly since the source of his later activities can be traced back to these crucial years just prior to the start of his virtuoso career: his "mission" as an artist, his strong sense of the underlying unity of the arts, especially literature and music, and his later efforts in Weimar to promote music worthy of the times are all matters that reflect the basic fund of ideas expressed or implied in the writings.

Liszt himself was well aware of this, setting such store by what he had to say that he hoped to assemble the articles and publish them in book form. When that time came, he planned, he said, to "add a number of more private, more personal matters that would be out of place at present."[4] Had that book with his additional comments ever been published, the *Lettres d'un bachelier ès musique* might well have become one of the major firsthand accounts of nineteenth-century musical life, much like Spohr's *Autobiography* or Berlioz's *Memoirs*. The project, however, was abandoned; most likely because his concert tours, for one thing, became ever more extensive and time consuming and, for another, his relationship with Madame d'Agoult deteriorated so completely during the early 1840s—they parted formally in 1844— that almost any reminder of the years they had spent together, including their three children, became a source of contention between them.

In their day the articles enjoyed considerable fame—or notori-

4. Letter 28 August 1839 to Lambert Massart in Jacques Vier, *Franz Liszt, L'Artiste-Le clerc*, p. 56. The following short news item from *La Belgique musicale* is also revealing: "Liszt, they say, has just declared that he considers a pianist's talent a talent of such little importance that he would much prefer to be known as a good writer capable of handling musical matters than a celebrated performer on the piano" (9 March 1843, p. 173).

ety, depending on the reader's point of view. Published first in Paris, they, or various excerpts from them, were also translated for readers throughout Europe, in Vienna, Pest, Milan, and London. But as Liszt himself eventually came to ignore them, these early writings lay neglected in old newspaper files for several decades. It was not until the early 1880s that his biographer Lina Ramann sought them out and included twelve of them in her edition of his *Gesammelte Schriften*.[5] Three decades later, Jean Chantavoine reprinted thirteen in the original French in a collection he called *Pages romantiques*.[6]

When Chantavoine introduced the writings to readers, he observed that they "pertain no less—and one is sometimes tempted to say maybe even more—to their age than to their author,"[7] and it is in this sense that they are presented here without apology. They belong to a time when emotional sensitivity, extravagance, and even hyperbole were the accepted order of the day, when concepts and causes were matters of zealous concern. Of all the great nineteenth-century musical figures, Liszt is the one who, more than any other, asks us to put aside a twentieth-century mentality and see him in his own time.

Just as the writings are firmly linked to their epoch, Liszt himself and the Paris in which he lived are, in a broader sense, also virtually inseparable, in that his own development from prodigy to musician/author paralleled the shift from an *ancien régime* of privilege and patronage to the emerging new and humanistic society envisioned by the liberal social philosophies that came to the fore in intellectual circles during the 1820s and 1830s.

Adulated and pampered as a prodigy, Liszt nonetheless came to resent the aristocratic society that regarded a musician like himself as little more than an artistic servant, an entertainer. "I would sooner have been anything in the world," he writes, "than a musician in the

5. Liszt, *Gesammelte Schriften*, ed. Lina Ramann, in six volumes. The Letters, *Reisebriefe*, appear in vol. 2, pp. 113–257. The volume also includes "On the Situation of Artists" (without the epilogue) and five other articles published in the *Gazette musicale* during these years. All are in German translation.

6. Liszt, *Pages romantiques*, ed. Jean Chantavoine. This collection includes the complete "On the Situation of Artists" and the Letters, but none of the other articles from the period. Further, the text of the Letters as reprinted is not wholly accurate, since a few sentences and brief paragraphs have been overlooked in various places. Both the *Schriften* and the *Pages* are, moreover, incomplete: neither includes the articles "Venice" and "Genoa and Florence" or the Letter to Léon Kreutzer. The *Schriften* also omits the article on Cellini's *Perseus*. (The missing articles were to appear in a seventh, supplementary volume, but it was never published.)

7. Chantavoine, in *Pages romantiques*, pp. v-vi.

service of the Great Lords, patronized and paid by them on a par with a juggler or the performing dog Munito."[8] Upon reaching his mid-teens he began an extensive and eclectic program of self-improvement in order to overcome his lack of any formal education and to make himself into something more than a pianist. As one scholar notes, "Young Liszt 'devoured' at random everything that he heard discussed, everything that fell into his hands, and French literature from Montaigne to Hugo became familiar to him. He was capable of citing La Rochefoucauld, Voltaire, and Chénier to make a point. He not only read the poets (Hugo, Lamartine, Vigny, Musset [and others]), but also the philosophers (Montesquieu, Ballanche, Lamennais) and the historians (Michelet, Mignet, Quinet, Custine)."[9]

All this reading, this insatiable thirst for knowledge, coincided with the emergence of a "New Jerusalem," the liberal political and artistic world of Paris that came into being at the time of the July Revolution of 1830 (an event which Liszt, incidentally, greeted by sketching a Revolutionary symphony). It was the heyday of French Romanticism, a time when Hugo, Dumas, Musset, Delacroix, Balzac, Vigny, Lamartine, Sand, Berlioz, and even Heine and Chopin were living and working in the city. Liszt knew them all—"everyone" in fact. Yet even in such notable artistic company, he cut a singular figure. In the years from 1830 to his departure with Madame d'Agoult in 1835, one could almost hear people whisper "C'est Liszt" wherever he went. He gave concerts. He frequented the salons, the lecture halls, the concert rooms, and they—indeed, Paris herself—became his university. Sand, Heine, and Berlioz have all left illuminating, if differently perceived, portraits of him, what he had become, and how he was regarded at this time. Their published remarks, which prompted Liszt to respond in kind, are given in the articles reprinted in the appendices. To them, one might add this little-known *aperçu* by France's renowned popular poet, Jean-Pierre Béranger (1780–1857):

> If there be pretension about Franz Liszt, it is a pretension borne out by far more varied gifts and acquirements than any other artist whom I have known could boast. In his conversation on all subjects, and from the venerable metaphysics of the Middle Ages to the last production of [dramatist Eugène] Scribe, there was nothing which he had not touched and tried; there was a luminous

8. "To a Poet-Voyager," chap. 2.
9. Léon Guichard, "Liszt et la littérature française," p. 4. The article is an outgrowth of his earlier *La Musique et les lettres au temps du romantisme* (see pp. 83–86).

spirit which enchanted me, whether it rose to fervent and mystical eloquence on the highest themes, or sparkled in the pleasantries of social life. There are two people of genius in the world, [Maria] Malibran and Liszt.[10]

While Liszt certainly enjoyed his social eclat, the more philosophic, speculative, and even religious side of his nature was strongly drawn to the new breed of social thinking which flourished together with the creative air then pervading Paris, the one supporting the other. Seeking out the social philosophers, he took their teachings to heart. Indeed, it was under their influence that he, espousing *le sentiment humanitaire,* found his personal justification for being not just a pianist, but an artist.

In very general terms, this compelling "humanist spirit," along with its implications of liberty, personal achievement, and progress, was born with the French Revolution. Its implementation as a social force, however, met with two broad, intractable obstacles: one was the rapidly increasing political power of the *bourgeoisie,* which was by nature conservative; the other was a Catholic Church whose conception of society and social attitudes were still firmly allied with the *ancien régime* the Revolution had unseated. The societal problem thus posed was one that occupied social thinkers all during the early decades of the nineteenth century as they attempted to develop a philosophic basis for a new and modern world. Their solutions, that is, the types of society they proposed, took on a wide variety of forms, which, in retrospect, make these years an age of "isms"—reformed monarchism, republicanism, neo-Catholicism, socialism, utopianism. Yet, despite the diversity, the social thinkers were all more or less united in advancing the ideas of "liberty, progress, the sanctity of the ideal, the dignity of science, faith in Providence, and a religious belief in the future of mankind."[11] Another characteristic they generally shared was their rejection of the Church and clergy as a spiritual guide, but as they were equally eager to maintain a direct channel of communication between God and Man, they elevated the artist to the priestly role and function. It was, in all, a very optimistic age, and even if the manner of accomplishing its social goals remained unclear in the 1830s, the future itself was a never-ending source of hope.

10. *Norfolk Chronicle,* 26 September 1840, quoted in Adrian Williams, "Liszt's British Tours (II)," p. 12. I have not located the original source of Béranger's remarks, though they can only have been made prior to Malibran's death in 1836 and most likely before Liszt left Paris in 1835.

11. Paul Bénichou, *Le Temps des prophètes,* p. 11.

Liszt, who had "an indefatigable thirst for divinity and enlightenment,"[12] took a lively interest in this type of religio-social speculation, and among the advocates, the prophets of a better world, there
were three who struck an especially responsive chord in him. They
were the Saint-Simonians, and the neo-Catholic thinkers Pierre-
Simon Ballanche and Felicité Lamennais. Though quite different,
they were nonetheless essentially similar in their goals and in the
priest-like role they accorded artists.

In the autumn of 1830 Liszt began to attend the meetings of the
Saint-Simonians, a para-religious sect which preached a doctrine of
benign, elitist Christian socialism and attracted many like-minded
Parisians during its brief existence, roughly from 1828 to 1832.[13] Behind the group stood the figure, or rather the shade, of Henri de
Rouvroi, Comte de Saint-Simon (1760–1825), who, having realized
that society had reached the threshold of a new, industrial age and
that its old aristocratic institutions were inimical to that age, had proposed an entirely new societal structure; that is, a tripartite functional
hierarchy which consisted of the men of industry, those of learning,
and those of imagination and feeling, that is, the artists. The cohesive
force of this novel structure, an antidote to the egoism that plagued
and stifled humanity, was the gospel spirit of brotherly love, or, as it
came to be called, the "principle of association," and the collectivism
such association implied.

When the count died in 1825, shortly after the publication of his
most notable book, *Le Nouveau Christianisme,* his ideas were taken up
by a band of disciples who refined and developed them into a quasi-
philanthropic social doctrine, the gist of which was to be found in the
three maxims printed in their newspaper *Le Globe:* "The aim of all
social institutions should be the alleviation of the moral, physical, and
intellectual lot of the most numerous and poorest class"; "All privileges of birth are, without exception, to be abolished"; and the famous motto which, in one form or another, has resounded through
social thinking ever since—"From each according to his ability, to
each ability according to his works." Given this vision of a responsible, caring society in which any person, regardless of birth, could
function and be rewarded accordingly, it is not difficult to understand
why the Saint-Simonians proved so appealing to talented people.

12. Heinrich Heine, "Confidential Letter," app. B.
13. Although there is a substantial literature on Saint-Simon and the Saint-
Simonians, the most pertinent work in the present context is Ralph P. Locke, *Music,
Musicians, and the Saint-Simonians.*

Attending the group's meetings and socials, as did Heine, Berlioz, and tenor Adolphe Nourrit to varying degrees, Liszt can only have been impressed by what he heard there.[14] The Saint-Simonians assigned the artist a high position in the social hierarchy, recognizing both the emotional power he and his work exercised over people in promoting new ideas and the leadership role he could consequently play in bringing about social change. One of the adepts, Philippe Buchez (1796–1866), expressed the latter point this way: "To sense the illness of the age and express it, to conceive the future, to discover through inspiration what the sciences can only learn, and to indicate to the great number [of people] this path of happiness and immortality—these things fall only to great talents. The artistic genius . . . is no slave destined to follow after society step by step. His function is to rush ahead of it, to serve as its guide. He must march, and it must follow."[15]

The vast literature the Saint-Simonians produced is shot through with similar statements, and even if there is little doubt that they, by extolling the artist, saw him as a propagandist for their own cause, the broader import of their *dicta* was not lost on Liszt.

Although he never formally joined the group, Liszt was convinced of the justice and morality of their teachings. He also seemed particularly drawn to the principle of association: "In music, as in everything else," he writes, "associating with others is the only principle that produces great results. . . . One person is not really effective unless he can gather other individuals around him and communicate his feelings and thoughts to them."[16] He even speculates about a community which would be modeled along the lines of the semi-monastic Saint-Simonian establishment at Menilmontant: "The spirit of association is spreading so among us that I would not be at all surprised to see the formation of a new sort of cloister before too long; that is, groups of artists, thinkers, and workers living together under an agreed-upon rule and sharing their investigations and discoveries in common."[17] It might be a little farfetched to see Weimar as a latter-day Menilmontant, but a feeling for association, a sense of artistic community, was very much part of the atmosphere that Liszt attempted to create during his residence there.

Early in 1833, apparently, Liszt was introduced to the second of

14. For further details see Locke, *Saint-Simonians,* pp. 101–6; also his "Liszt's Saint-Simonian Adventure."

15. Quoted in Locke, *Saint-Simonians,* p. 44.

16. "Musical Conditions in Italy," chap. 9.

17. "To Louis de Ronchaud," chap. 5.

those whose ideas he found particularly sympathetic, Pierre-Simon Ballanche (1776–1847). A devout Catholic, Ballanche was a mystic and a philosopher who sought to develop a theology to support that basic tenet of the era, human progress.[18]

Faith, innate faith, is the foundation of Ballanche's neo-platonic cosmology. "Man has a need to believe," he wrote. "His reason seeks support; his heart seeks solace"—and from the need to believe "in the depths of the soul," there arises "the idea of God," which is "the highest expression of the harmony of beings and the world." This harmony—the "Great All," as another of Liszt's guides, Alphonse de Lamartine (1790–1869), called it[19]—is the unity the soul senses when, losing itself in God, it is gripped by a "dazzling, irreducible essence" manifesting itself in the "intimate, mystic feeling which lies at the bottom of all human experience." But while a sense of harmony with the Creator and Nature is common to all, it is human genius, the artist, who provides it with a voice. "The poet," Ballanche wrote in *Orphée* (1829), "is the living expression of God, of Nature, and of Humanity!", words which prompted Liszt to exclaim, "Lord, what great and marvelous thoughts!"[20]

With regard to progress, Ballanche was convinced he found the answer to it with his theory of *Palingénésie sociale* (1827), literally, "renewed social birth." Starting with his idea of "harmony," he maintained that God is ever and actively present in creation and that, consequently, Man and his social institutions are constantly evolving to ever higher planes as a progressive manifestation of God's will. In order to keep the process moving, God from time to time inflicted a calamity on humanity—a kind of divine purge, such as the French Revolution—and even though the calamity produced temporary disruptions in society, its inevitable result was the further advancement of the social order.

Ballanche was a cosmic optimist. The fact that he chose to present his ideas in the guise of proto-Christian mythical sagas made them difficult to grasp and prompted some to call his thinking "nebulous." Still there were many, Liszt among them, who eagerly em-

---

18. As there is no single work by Ballanche that summarizes his thought, the précis of it that follows is based on the analysis by Oscar A. Haac in Ballanche, *La Théodicée et La virgine romaine*, pp. 9–74. Also see Bénichou, *Les Temps des prophètes*, pp. 74–104.

19. Liszt took the inspiration of his early *Harmonies poétiques et religieuses* (1834) from the similarly titled collection of verse (1830) by Lamartine.

20. Letter to Marie d'Agoult [15 September 1834] in *Correspondance de Liszt et la comtesse d'Agoult*, I: 114.

braced his tenet that human progress was divinely ordained. It is difficult, furthermore, not to detect distinctly Ballanchian overtones in Liszt's discussion of Perseus, an essay that traces the progressive creative stages of an idea from its initial manifestation in words as legend, to its visual representation as Cellini's statue, and then to its musical fulfillment as Berlioz's opera, *Benvenuto Cellini*.[21]

If Ballanche dwelt in mystic realms, there were other Catholics who were more directly involved with reforming a Church whose attitudes reflected nothing of the modern spirit; and no religious leader among them took more active a part in the heady socio-religious currents of post-Revolutionary France than Abbé Félicité-Robert Lamennais (1782–1854), the personification of *le sentiment humanitaire*.

Ordained a priest in 1816, Lamennais had begun his career as a leading spokesman for conservative Catholicism. A theocrat at heart, however, who sensed the import of the rapidly changing political climate during the Restoration, he emerged in the late 1820s as the energetic proponent of a "liberal" Catholicism, one that disavowed its connection to the monarchy and appealed more directly to the people. Soon after the July Revolution he founded *L'Avenir* (The Future), the first crusading Catholic newspaper which, proclaiming "God and Liberty" as its motto, boldly advocated such reforms as separation of church and state, freedom of conscience and of the press, an independent educational system, and universal suffrage. Many believing Catholics and more liberal cleries applauded his efforts. Pope Gregory XVI, however, condemned them in a famous encyclical *Mirari vos* (1832) directed against all forms of "modernism."

Deeply wounded by the blow and totally disillusioned with Rome, Lamennais responded with his apologia *Paroles d'un croyant* (Words of a Believer). He was arranging for its publication when Liszt met him in April 1834 and promptly fell under the sway of the wiry, mesmerizing little abbé.

Lamennais's *Paroles* was an extraordinary little book, a best-seller of the age. Its power lay not only in its simple, evangelical, and hortatory language, but also in its direct appeal to the people. Having rejected the established, traditional order, Lamennais turned to humanity itself as the wellspring of religious sentiment on earth. Humanism and social progress were the key to the religion of the future.

Liszt, reading the *Paroles,* was beside himself with enthusiasm and exclaimed when writing the abbé that "it is incontrovertably clear that Christianity in this nineteenth century, which is to say the entire

21. "The *Perseus* of Benvenuto Cellini," chap. 8.

religious and political future of mankind, lies with YOU!"[22] Having met a true spiritual hero,[23] he also made what can only be called a pilgrimage that September to Lamennais's home at La Chênaie in Brittany. The three weeks he spent there were filled with talk of God, the future, and the social role of art.[24]

Much like Ballanche, Lamennais believed that God is ever-present in creation and that His work is eternally progressive. If science consists in knowing and understanding "the temple of God" that is creation, then the proper sphere of art is to reproduce that temple in material, perceptible form. Yet the beauty art embodies is only a means by which humanity becomes aware of the grandeur of the destiny God has planned for it. Art for art's sake is, therefore, "an absurdity." The true aim of art is to perfect human beings, that is, "to satisfy the dictates of the moral order, to assist the efforts of humanity to fulfill its destiny, to raise it above earthly matters and set it in perpetually ascending motion."[25]

Music occupies a special niche among the arts in this respect, since it is not only "the liaison of the arts that appeal directly to the senses with those that are proper to the spirit," it is, by being analogous to a family in its harmonious combination of disparate elements (melody, harmony, rhythm) also "the complete expression of social and intellectual life."

Given this aesthetic, it follows that artists do not promote the cause of art by devoting themselves to "the servile imitation of the past" or by isolating themselves as just one man among mankind. Art, on the contrary, receives a new impetus when artists, "plumbing the most profound depths of society, gather in themselves the life palpi-

22. Letter to Lamennais [May 1834], in Marc Pincherle, *Musiciens peints par eux-mêmes,* p. 102. "Christianity" in this context means Catholicism. The Protestant tradition, though well established historically in France, was simply too limited to have any appreciable effect on the socio-religious writings of the time.

23. The Abbé Z.'s narrative about the "man who had risen in the bosom of the Catholic Church" in the article on Venice, chap. 7, is a thinly disguised account of Lamennais and Liszt's relations with him. In more general terms, see Bénichou, *Temps des prophètes,* pp. 121–73.

24. Although Lamennais did not publish his views on aesthetics—*De l'Art et du Beau*—until 1840, as part of his *Esquisse d'une philosophie,* his ideas on the subject were formed years earlier; in February 1833 he told a close friend that he was in the process of sketching "the broad outlines of a philosophy of the Beautiful in architecture, sculpture, and music" (quoted in Thérèse Marix-Spire, *Les Romantiques et la musique,* p. 436).

25. Quoted in Jacques Poisson, *Le Romantisme social de Lamennais,* pp. 360–61.

tating there and disseminate it in their works, so that art will give life, just as the Spirit of God animates and fills the universe." Artists, in brief, are the "Apostles of the Spirit" who prepare the way for His coming. "The old world," Lamennais concludes, "is disintegrating, the old doctrines are dying, but amid the confused travail and apparent disorder, one can see the new doctrines that are starting to dawn and give order to a new world. The religion of the future casts its first glimmers of light on an expectant human race and its future destiny. The artist must be the prophet of that future."[26]

The Saint-Simonians, Ballanche, and Lamennais all exerted an influence on Liszt, but he was far too eclectic by nature to be so closely identified with any one of them that we could call him a Saint-Simonian or even a Mennaisian. Each of his guides was, rather, a manifestation of the overriding humanist spirit, which was what mattered most, and it was in this connection that Liszt, who as a youth had often thought of becoming a priest, put aside the Church and became instead a priest, a prophet of Art.

On a more personal level, there is little doubt that it was Lamennais, the crusader of *L'Avenir*, who first inspired Liszt to take up his pen and do battle for art. In the year they met he wrote a ringing essay, a manifesto, on "Religious Music of the Future" in which he anticipates the day when it would move out of the sanctuary and become the property of the people. When that day comes, he adds, art will fulfill itself "by fraternally uniting all mankind in rapturous wonder." The essay, which is given in appendix D, is both a good indication of the attitudes of the young reformer who would soon write these Letters and something of a platform on which he based his later religious compositions.

For all their wide-ranging choice of topics and their historical and anecdotal interest, Liszt's articles are basically concerned with two broad, interrelated subjects, but as his discussion of them was never intended to be systematic, it might be helpful to give the general outlines of each here. The first is Liszt's own role as an artist, which is a particularly pressing matter in the early Letters written before his journey to Italy. The second, a little cooler, a little more detached, is the nature of music, and it tends to be discussed in the later Letters.

The Saint-Simonians, Lamennais, and others had described the artist in the abstract as a priestly social force, an intermediary between

26. Quoted in Poisson, *Romantisme social*, p. 364.

God and Man. Liszt, however, writes as one who for better or worse was actively trying to live that role. His views on the subject are far from dispassionate.

In the neo-platonic universe of the Ideal and the Real, the Good, True, and Beautiful is, of course, God—in Liszt's words, "that great and sublime artist who, by creating the universe and man, had shown that He was at one and the same time an all-powerful, eternal, and infinite poet, architect, musician, and sculptor."[27] And in the Real world of earth there are the artists, whom Liszt extols as "these elite men who appear to be chosen by God Himself to bear witness to the greatest emotions of humanity—these predestined, thunderstruck, enthralled men who have carried off the sacred flame from heaven, who have given life to matter, form to ideas, and by attaining the Ideal raise us by an invincible bond of understanding to excitement and celestial visions—these priests of an ineffable, mystical, and eternal religion which takes root and grows incessantly in all our hearts."[28] Divinely gifted though they be artists are also isolated by the nature of their gift; they are "men who have no brothers among men . . . children of God . . . exiles from heaven who suffer and sing and whom the world calls 'poets.'"[29]

"What a sad and great destiny it is to be an artist!" Liszt exclaims. "He certainly does not choose his vocation; it takes possession of him and drives him on." He is, moreover, rootless, "alone," and even when circumstances force him into society, "he creates an impenetrable solitude within his soul," where he "contemplates and worships the ideal that his entire being will seek to reproduce."[30]

Artists, in effect, exist "within the confines of two different worlds," where they "contemplate the things of the one as illuminated by the divine light of the other."[31] Their calling is to convert the light into Art, which is "the apprehensible reproduction of that which is mystically divine in man and in creation."[32] The task, however, is difficult and discouraging, for an artist also realizes that he "will not be able to give . . . an account of the celestial banquet to which he had been invited."[33] This is a source of extreme frustration for Liszt:

27. "To George Sand, chap. 1.
28. "On the Situation of Artists" *Gazette musicale,* 3 May 1835; in *Pages romantiques,* p. 4.
29. "To a Poet-Voyager," chap. 2.
30. "To George Sand," chap. 3.
31. "Venice," chap. 7.
32. "To George Sand," chap. 3.
33. "The *Saint Cecilia* of Raphael," chap. 8.

"How wretched, how truly wretched we artists are! We experience momentary flashes when we seem to have an intuitive grasp of the divine . . . a mystical insight, a supernatural understanding of the harmony of the universe; but as soon as we want to flesh out our sensations, to capture these evanescent flights of the soul, the vision vanishes."[34]

Liszt's frustration takes on an especially bitter edge at a concert when he assumes the double role of a pianist who earns his living by the trade and a musician who is actively presenting a work of art to his hearers. On these occasions the artist usually "must prostitute himself to an unresponsive audience . . . scoff at his most intimate feelings and toss his soul out . . . to stir up some applause from the inattentive crowd. Even then, a tremendous effort is required if the flame of his fervor is . . . to strike a few sparks from those loveless, apathetic hearts."[35] Still, these direct contacts with the public are not always so irritating and devoid of satisfaction: "I will not deny," he writes, "that there is an indescribably powerful enchantment, a proud yet loving delight, in exercising a faculty that draws the thoughts and hearts of others to us, that causes other people's souls to break into the fiery sparks that consume our own and to shine with that mutual enthusiasm that sweeps them irresistibly along with us toward the realm of the beautiful and ideal—toward God. Sometimes an artist . . . senses an infinitely small particle of creative force inside him because he has created emotions, feelings, and ideas with his sounds. It is a dream that ennobles his existence."[36] This comment—coupled with the earlier ones he made about the artist "attaining the Ideal" and religious music "uniting all mankind in rapturous wonder"—indicate that Liszt the artist lived for, and quite possibly on, the shared feeling of emotional and spiritual exaltation which lifts Man closer to God.

About halfway through the journey of these years Liszt reached the point where he could regard his emotional role of artist/performer with some degree of detachment. Writing from Milan, he makes this

34. "Lake Como," chap. 5.
35. "To George Sand," chap. 3. Given Liszt's reputation as a virtuoso, it may seem surprising that he reacted so negatively to his audience. Marie d'Agoult nonetheless noted: "An artist's life is so miserably agitated. The direct contact with the public . . . [is] so bruising, so irritating. He [Liszt] would have renounced his career as a performer a long time ago had he not wanted to assure his complete independence and his mother's bread." (Letter to Sand, 4 July 1838, in Jacques Vier, *La Comtesse d'Agoult et son temps*, 1: 300.)
36. "To Lambert Massart," chap. 6.

brave if ironic comment about his life: "I continue on my way, carrying my annoyances like so much necessary baggage and very cleverly steering a course between the Ideal and the Real, without allowing myself to be overly seduced by the former, nor ever to be crushed by the latter."[37] He did in time adjust, and rather easily, to the practicalities of performing in the real world, and even though his youthful, uncompromising fervor naturally abated in the process, his commitment to art as a means of drawing mankind closer to God remained a guiding principle of his life.

During his sojourn in Italy Liszt evidently gained considerable insight into the nature of music, that is, as *he* saw and was to conceive the art. "The beautiful in this special land," he writes, "became evident to me in its purest and most sublime form. Art in all its splendor disclosed itself to my eyes. It revealed its universality and unity to me. Day by day my feelings and thoughts gave me a better insight into the hidden relationship that unites all works of genius. Raphael and Michelangelo increased my understanding of Mozart and Beethoven; Giovanni Pisano, Fra Beato, and Il Francia explained Allegri, Marcello, and Palestrina to me. . . . The Colosseum and the Campo Santo are not as foreign as one thinks to the Eroica Symphony and the Requiem."[38] He also mentions one particular instance of this insight in his discussion of Raphael's *Saint Cecilia:* It "made an immediate and twofold impression on my soul: first, as a ravishing portrayal of . . . the human form . . . and [then] as an admirable and perfect symbol of [music]. The poetry and philosophy of the canvas were actually so visible to me that its abstract sense of line and its IDEAL beauty gripped me as forcefully as did its beauty as a painting."[39]

In each of these cases, Liszt is really presenting two points. One is the neo-platonic tenet that all forms of art, or at least works of genius, are intrinsically related since they are but different manifestations of their common source, which is God. The other—and the more consequential as far as the musician is concerned—is that the more realistic, representational arts (painting, sculpture) can help someone understand music, which is the most ideal and least overtly representational form of art. To restate this in another, and negative, way, the "ideality [of music] is perceptible only by cultivated minds," while virtually everyone can appreciate and be stirred by the reality of a statue. But music "does not imitate [as a statue does], it expresses";

37. "To Lambert Massart," chap. 6.
38. "To Hector Berlioz," chap. 10.
39. "The *Saint Cecilia* of Raphael," chap. 8.

it "has no reality, so to speak." As a result, "music remains almost entirely inaccessible to the crowd,"[40] and this, certainly, is where the other arts can come to its aid.

Liszt never generalizes beyond his own experience, although he alludes to the problem that people can have with understanding abstract or absolute music when he writes: "The musician . . . exhales the most personal mysteries of his destiny in sounds. . . . But as his language, more arbitrary and *less explicit* [emphasis added] than any other, lends itself to a multitude of different interpretations . . . is it not without value . . . for [him] to state the fundamental idea of his composition?"[41]

Music, in other words, is too Ideal of itself to be truly understood by any but the select few. If it is to flourish, therefore, in the world of the Real, it should have a more comprehensible point of reference for the ideas and/or feelings it means to convey. One way of achieving this is to relate it to another form of art, visual or literary; this is the underlying concept of the symphonic poems or the discussion of program music in Liszt's 1855 essay "Berlioz and His 'Harold' Symphony." Actually, though, the concept is broader than that, since there is scarcely a published work by Liszt that does not include some extra-musical, or call it para-musical, guide to its "fundamental idea." *Il Pensieroso,* for example, was published with an engraving of the Michelangelo statue that inspired it; there is the Dante Symphony; the *Album d'un voyageur* includes a preface, and the pieces in it have both descriptive titles and poetic mottoes; all the symphonic poems have prefaces; and so on through the catalogue of Liszt's works.

His high-minded conception of music and the artist was considerably at odds with the prevailing level of musical taste, especially in Paris and Italy. Music history may look glowingly back to the time of Beethoven or Berlioz or Chopin, but such men counted for very little in the typical music fare of the 1830s. It was a time when the lyric theater, the opera, was the unrivaled queen of cultural life, catering by and large to a musically uneducated public, while instrumental music, the more abstract form, was still the exception. Liszt wanted to change that. He wanted to elevate the public's taste and appreciation for music by exposing it to more serious instrumental works as well as better opera, and his complaints about the situation combined with pleas for reform run like a refrain through the articles. He was not, of course, unique in this respect, as there were a number of other musi-

40. "The *Perseus* of Benvenuto Cellini," chap. 8.
41. "To a Poet-Voyager," chap. 2.

cians and critics—Schumann, Berlioz, or Fétis, for example—who were also concerned with molding public taste for the better. Still, it is difficult not to believe that these Letters, given Liszt's reputation, did not spark a special interest in better music among their readers.

NOTES ON THE TRANSLATION

This complete collection of the *Lettres d'un bachelier ès musique,* coming as it does some 150 years after they were written, is the first to be published in English, allowing for brief excerpts that have appeared in various biographies. It is also the first to include three articles— "Venice," "Genoa and Florence," and the one addressed to Léon Kreutzer—that were omitted from the earlier German and French editions.[42] Further, as three of the Letters—the first one to Sand and those to Heine and Berlioz—were prompted by articles that these individuals had addressed to Liszt, their articles are also included here as appendices so that the reader will know what he was responding to; such personal exchanges in public print were a feature of the lively press scene that prevailed at the time.

The translation of the Letters follows the French texts as first published in the *Gazette musicale* and *L'Artiste,* an elegantly styled journal devoted to literature and the fine arts. Similarly, the translations of the Sand, Heine, and Berlioz articles are also based on their first appearance in periodicals. Except for Sand's Letter, portions of which not pertaining to Liszt have been summarized, all the other articles are given in complete form, including their footnotes. (Note: All the original footnotes are marked with asterisks. Editorial annotations are numbered.)

Completeness may seem an obvious point, but it is worth stressing here in order to alert the reader that the ellipses (the row of periods extending across a page) which are scattered throughout the text of Liszt's articles indicate deletions that were made when they were first published. Just what the editors chose to omit at that time, we shall probably never know, since none of the manuscript copy Liszt submitted for publication has ever been found. All that survives of the articles are the printed versions.

As for the translation, its aim has been to give today's reader an accurate but not doggedly literal version of the French, while retain-

---

42. All the letters are to be reprinted in the new and critical edition of Liszt's writings, in French and German, that is being prepared under the general editorship of Detlef Altenburg (Padeborn).

ing as much flavor of the Romantic prose as possible. Clarity is paramount, and to this end some long paragraphs have been divided into shorter ones; punctuation has generally been modernized to conform to English usage, although two favorite practices of the period have been retained—that is, the use of a dash before a sentence opening and the ubiquitous use of suspension points (. . .) for dramatic effect; dashes also have occasionally been inserted into the text to set off the long subsidiary and qualifying clauses that are characteristic of the prose style; and last, typographical errors in the names of people and places have been tacitly corrected—proofreading, as Liszt complained more than once, was not one of the *Gazette*'s strong points.

The dating and the chronological sequence of the articles present a problem that also deserves a few words. When the Letters, particularly those from Italy, are read in conjunction with Liszt's remarks about them in his private correspondence, a confusing mass of editorial considerations becomes apparent. First, the date Liszt assigns to an article, if indeed it carries one, cannot be taken too literally since it usually indicates the time when the writing was begun, not when it was finished. Second, the articles, dated or not, were written sporadically; some were completed and sent off for publication within a week or two of the events they describe, while others were as long as four to six months in the writing. Third, Liszt had no control over when any given article appeared, and in some cases its publication was considerably delayed. Given this tangle of circumstances—the details of which will be discussed, as necessary, in the notes to the individual Letters—it seemed best to ignore the publication dates and present the Letters in a topical sequence that conforms to Liszt's itinerary. This procedure has also meant that two of the articles are presented not as a unit, but as separate halves fitted into their proper chronological order. Those affected are the Letter to Massart, which is itself divided into two sections dealing separately with Milan and Vienna, and the one devoted to Genoa and Florence.

Further, as the Letters are basically *oeuvres de circonstances,* articles produced when and where Liszt was prompted to write them, each Letter or small group of them is preceded by a brief introduction which discusses and chronicles the journey that he and Marie d'Agoult took, highlighting its more notable events. In this connection, however, there has been no attempt to give a complete accounting of all the music, mostly arrangements, that Liszt produced during these years; only those works that pertain to the articles or the events relating to them are taken into consideration.

THE LETTERS

Note

All the original footnotes to the letters are marked with asterisks. Editorial annotations are numbered.

I

GENEVA

CHRONICLE

4 June 1835. Liszt and Marie d'Agoult, having quietly left Paris several
days apart, rendezvous in Basel to begin their life and travels together.

14 June–18 July. Moving in a clockwise direction, they make a grand
circular tour of Switzerland, including the Falls of the Rhine,
Saint Gall, Einsiedeln, Lake of Lucerne, the Furka Pass, and
Grand-Saint-Bernard.[1]

19 July. They arrive in Geneva. Liszt, who has friends and former pupils living in the area, insists that they settle there for a time,[2]
despite the countess's misgivings about their social acceptance in
the rather small, Calvinistically straitlaced community. Liszt pre-
vails, and they move into comfortable quarters on Rue Tabazan
on 28 July.

1 September. George Sand's "Letter of a Voyager" to Liszt appears in
the *Revue des deux mondes*.

1 October. Liszt gives his first public performance in Geneva, appearing at a charity concert.

9 November. The newly founded Geneva Conservatory opens its
doors. The piano faculty of three includes Liszt, who teaches a
class of ten students—gratis.

15 November. The *Gazette musicale* publishes the last installment of
Liszt's "On the Situation of Artists." This essay, though begun
in Paris, was written mostly in Switzerland.

1. A daily account of the tour through Switzerland, based on Liszt's pocket cal-
endar, is found in Maria P. Eckhardt, "Diary of a Wayfarer."
2. Liszt, writing to Sand, had told her to "address General Delivery in Geneva.
I'll be there about 20 July—and won't budge until the spring" ([27 June 1835], in
Marix-Spire, *Romantiques,* p. 611).

Three weeks later the *Gazette* also published the first of his travel articles. It is the "Letter of a Voyager" addressed to George Sand, written in direct response to the Letter she had directed to him (Appendix A).

To George Sand[1]

Geneva, 23 November [1835]

Not having in my capacity as a musician a citizen's rights to the *Revue des deux mondes,* I am taking advantage of the columns of the *Gazette musicale,* which I regret having burdened so often with my terrible prose, to remember myself to you, my dear George.

Arriving here after a long tour through the mountains, I found your brotherly letter,[2] for which I thank you a thousand times over, even though it does seem to retract the promise you made to me about coming to join us soon.—And yet, how I would still love to lure you—you, the most capricious and whimsical of travelers—to the flank of the black Jura, which with its mantle of clouds appears to me in the uncertain light of dusk like a sad and gloomy spectre standing forever between me and my dearest friends! . . . But what can I say to rouse your curiosity to a point that it will overcome your inertia?— During my travels in the Alps I did not have an opportunity "to fathom the treasures of the snow." The wall-nettles, bindweeds, and harts' tongues, with whom you love to talk since they whisper harmonious secrets in your ear that they surely do not reveal to us, have not ventured to suspend themselves on the smooth, uncracked walls of my white house. The republic of music, already established by a leap of your young imagination, is still only a dream for me, a hope which the gracious laws of intimidation have fortunately not thought to threaten so far with prison or exile.[3] And when I reflect seriously on my life, I blush with shame and confusion to pit your dreams against my realities;—the heavenly flames with which your poetic fancy encircled my brow, against the earthly dust my steps raise on the mundane road I travel;—your noble presentiments, your beautiful illusions about the social effects of the art to which I have dedicated my life,

1. *Gazette musicale,* 6 December 1835, pp. 397–400.
2. "See the Letter of a Voyager (On Lavater and a deserted house, addressed to F. Liszt) that appeared in the *Revue des deux mondes,* 1 Sept. 1835" (note in the *Gazette musicale*).
3. Evidently the "September Laws." See Sand's Letter to Liszt, app. A.

against the gloomy discouragement that sometimes seizes me when I compare the impotence of the *effort* with the eagerness of the *desire*, the nothingness of the *work* with the limitlessness of the *idea*;—those miracles of understanding and regeneration wrought by the thrice-blessed lyre of ancient times, against the sad and sterile role to which it is seemingly confined today.

But since you are among those who do not despair of the future, however shabby the present might be, and since you have asked me to give you my travel impressions, such as they are, and considering that the special interest of the *Revue* that serves as my intermediary bars those political and metaphysical digressions that entertained us so by the fireside amid the incense of your glory and Turkish tobacco, I would like (that is, until I am able to tell you about Pergolesi's *Stabat Mater* and the Sistine Chapel) to keep you abreast of a few interesting facts pertaining to the musical chronicle of Geneva, the Protestant Rome.

I arrived here right on the eve of a secular celebration which is held to honor Calvin's Reformation.[4] That celebration lasts for three full days. The first, in accordance with the canton's paternal authority, is dedicated to the children. I felt my heart swell as I watched them scampering about the gardens like a swarm of grasshoppers—running, laughing, leaping, turning somersaults and doing their best to repudiate Catholic abstinence by gulping down quantities of meringue tarts and almond pastries.

The second day, more religious in nature, is celebrated inside the temple of Saint Peter. That temple, until August 1535 when Minister Farel first preached the Reformation there, was a cathedral dedicated to the Prince of the Apostles. Hence, it is due to one of those vicissitudes which abound in the drama of humanity—whose unity, discerned by God alone, will not be revealed to us until the last man has had his last say about it—that the founder of the papacy, the great Fisher of Men, presides today over the celebration and assembly of those who would wrest the major portion of his heritage from his successors and shake the vast Catholic edifice to the very foundations for which Peter himself had served as the first stone. *Tu es Petrus, et super hanc petram aedificabo ecclesiam meam.*

At the time when Geneva was still orthodox the cathedral contained twenty-four altars. It was adorned with many paintings, statues, and bas-reliefs. The stalls where the plump canons piously reposed

4. The commemoration took place 22–24 August, a month after Liszt had settled in Geneva.

were curiously carved and embellished with figures of the apostles and prophets. Among these latter, some artist, weary no doubt of so many venerable and solemn countenances, had had the happy inspiration to place the Roman sibyl Erythrea, believing that he was authorized to take such a liberty by the legend which tells us that the inspired woman announced the coming of the Messiah to the emperor at the very moment He was born in Bethlehem.

Today the walls are stripped bare. The sculptures and bas-reliefs have been mutilated by reformers' hands, and the old gothic facade has yielded to a modern front; an emaciated, shabby, and impoverished imitation of the Pantheon, an abortive monument to the moribund faith of the eighteenth century.

My blood ran cold as I entered that denuded church, where the commemoration of Calvin's work and a fragment of one of Handel's oratorios had both summoned me.

In the section of the choir where a gilded grill had once marked the sacred precincts, in that most specially consecrated area where entry was forbidden to all those not participating directly in the celebration of the divine mysteries, in that very place where God the Redeemer descended at the priest's call to a flower-covered altar amid the perfumed clouds of incense, they had placed all the singers.

No doubt, as God Himself informs us, the altar to which He would truly prefer to descend is a pure heart, a pious and chaste soul; no doubt the most gorgeous flowers, the rarest and most precious perfumes, do not possess in His eyes the splendor of a virginal face and the agreeable sweetness of an innocent prayer; yet who, after being present at this Jubilee celebration of the Reformation, would not acknowledge that the grandeur, the solemnity, the immense and mysterious profundity of the Catholic sacrifice had found but a very poor substitute in these ladies and gentlemen of the Protestant society of sacred chant, most of whom "protested" with a fanatic's zeal against keeping in time or in tune? . . . Who would not be tempted to think that this very dubious harmony of voice and instruments implies a far more problematic harmony between mind and will? . . . Further, by what strange inconsistency do the reformers who banish painting and sculpture from their temples continue to allow music and eloquence, "the first of the fine arts"?[5] How can their preoccupations and narrow-

5. Both Saint-Simon (*Le Nouveau Christianisme*) and Lamennais (*De l'Art et du Beau*) held that eloquence was "first of the fine arts" since it was an artistic accomplishment whose essential purpose was to remind Man of his wretched condition and of God's compassion.

minded prejudices make them forget that the beautiful is only the splendor of truth, and art the radiance of thought? . . . How, in sum, do they fail to realize that by wanting to spiritualize religion to the point that it exists deprived of all its outward manifestations, they are, in a sense, actually reforming the works of God, that great and sublime artist who, by creating the universe and man, had shown that He was at one and the same time an all-powerful, eternal, and infinite poet, architect, musician, and sculptor?

I will not expand further on the endeavors, quite laudable in some respects, of the sacred chant society;* and without stopping to give you an epically styled description of the rejoicings and enlightenments of the Jubilee's third day, I will move on to another musical gathering, one that was more profane and for that reason more entertaining: the concert given for the poor and the refugees by Prince Belgiojoso⁶ and F. Liszt.

How you would have laughed to see our two names printed in huge letters on monstrous, bright yellow posters,** which for several days attracted many groups of idlers who were anxious to know by what right we had had the audacity to ask *five* francs from them, when from time immemorial they had been able, for *three* francs or less, to obtain all the music they could want to while away a pleasant evening and then go off to sleep with no fear of a nightmare or bad dreams.

Whether it was for curiosity or charity—or that "Some devil was also pushing them"⁷—a large, affluent crowd attended our concert, and it offered the attentive observer an extremely interesting and *socially picturesque* spectacle.

The canton of Geneva, hardly noticeable in an atlas and lost, as it were, in the shadows of the two mountain chains encircling it, is con-

---

*No matter how mediocre the results were during the Jubilee, the society still renders a service to art by performing the religious compositions of great composers. It would be desirable to see similar societies established in France, if only to chase the troop of ignoble bellowers, commonly called singers, from our churches.

**In order to give you an idea of the skill with which artists who are to appear in Geneva pique the public's curiosity, here is the literal wording of a notice I read at the bottom of a program that was pasted up everywhere when I arrived, one which makes me despair of ever being able to attain such poetry of style and such elegant editing: "*Notice.* The public, which is frequently distrustful of ostentatious announcements, can be misled at times by a deliberate deception. Here, what one sees, what one hears is still beyond the artist's promises and the amateurs' hopes."

6. Emilio Barbiano Belgiojoso. A gifted amateur tenor, estranged husband of Liszt's friend Princess Cristina Belgiojoso.

7. "Quelque diable aussi les [sic, me] poussant" (La Fontaine, "The Animals Stricken with the Plague," book 7, fable 1, line 52).

stantly having its territory occupied by a host of obliterated grandeurs, fallen majesties, and snuffed-out powers. Every day sees an increase in the number of such high-ranking persons—kings, ministers, generals of the army—who, driven before the wind, wander from land to land, forming a kind of nation without a country—branded like the Jews and struck like them too by a mysterious curse for having failed to understand the Word of God—liberty!

Among those gathered in the concert hall one could see the ex-king of Westphalia, Jerome Bonaparte, and his ravishing daughter, with her blond hair and sweet, sad face, looking like a dove poised upon a ruin; a minster to Charles X who, being neither despondent nor bitter, retains the cruelty he has always had and now regards his fall from grace with derision; a woman who honored her name and had been seen on the battlefields of the Vendée,[8] a hundred others whom I forget or who are too numerous to name here; and, lastly, that companion of Bourmont's at Waterloo, dishonored by victory and rehabilitated by suffering, who dedicates his exile's leisure to a work of art which he pursues with untiring zeal.

General C____, a passionate lover of old music and Handel's in particular, which he sings with captivating warmth, has undertaken the publication of a "Collection of Classical Airs" in order to contrast what he terms the decadence of modern music with a model of historical purity and to erect the names of Handel and Palestrina, with their august legitimacy and undefiled majesty, as a kind of sacred dike against the flood of Italian *fioriture* and stiff French ornamentation. Thus he dedicates himself in art, as he did in politics, to the worship of the past, which is all that he admires, without considering the present, which he unwittingly serves with his collection.

Just as soon as I know precisely where on earth my illustrious friend George is now living, he will receive the five or six volumes that have already appeared of this interesting publication by the old Vendéan.

But let us return to the details of the concert.[9]

---

8. The counterrevolution in the Vendée (western France) following the execution of Louis XVI. Its fierce battles raged intermittently from 1793 to 1796.
9. The concert, organized by Belgiojoso, took place 1 October 1835 in the Casino of St. Peter. The complete program included: Boïeldieu's Overture to *La Dame blanche;* Carl Maria von Weber's *Conzertstück* played by Liszt; a duet from Bellini's *La Straniera* sung by Belgiojoso and Bonoldi; a fantasy on themes from Auber's *Léocadie* performed by violinist Lafont; an aria from Bellini's *La Sonnambula* sung by Belgiojoso; the Grand Fantasy on the Tyrolienne from Auber's *La Fiancée,* composed and performed by Liszt; a group of songs and airs sung by Belgiojoso; a Duo concertante

Behind a balustrade skirted in white and decorated like a first-communion altar with festoons and flowers, there rose a bank of platforms for the battalions of violins, oboes, bassoons, and double basses that performed the popular Overture to *La Dame blanche,* while an enormous chandelier of Argand lamps, regularly and in a kind of cadence, dropped large globules of oil on the rose and white hats of the elegant Genevan ladies. Then Prince Belgiojoso, so appreciated and pampered in the salons of Paris, most tastefully sang several pieces by Bellini, Schubert's ravishing Serenade, and an Italian romance ("L'Addio") whose words and music he had composed in honor of the charming Countess M ____. His pure and vibrant voice, his simple and open method of singing, caused a sensation, and a great burst of applause followed him as he moved away from the piano. All the talk throughout Geneva today is about that princely artist, whose liberal views are expressed in liberal works, and who, without disavowing the hereditary crown of his ancestors, is fashioning his own glory by surmounting it with the plebeian crown that is only bestowed on the aristocracy of intelligence and talent.

It was our "old" comrade and disciple, young Hermann from Hamburg (whom you have made famous under the name Puzzi)[10] who accompanied him. Hermann's pale and melancholy appearance, his beautiful dark hair and frail physique, provided a poetic contrast to the prince's confident manner, blond hair, and open and ruddy face. The dear boy gave further proof of that precocious understanding and profound feeling for art which already set him apart from the ordinary run of pianists and lead me to predict a brilliant, fruitful future for him. He was roundly applauded after a piece for four pianos performed by Messers Wolff, Bonoldi, him, and me. I would not be surprised to learn that more than one pretty young lass was tenderly drawn to him by some naive and ardent passion, and I don't doubt that many a grammar or ancient history textbook has had its classic pages embellished with Hermann's romantic monogram symbolically interlaced in a garland of forget-me-nots with that of a fresh, young Julie or a fourteen-year-old Delphine.

Lafont was kind enough to contribute all his great talent to make

---

performed by Lafont and Liszt; and a Brilliant Potpourri on Folk Airs for Four Pianos by Carl Czerny performed by Liszt, Pierre Wolff, Francesco Bonoldi, and Hermann. It is a typical program for this period, when concerts regularly featured several performers, relied on opera to provide most of the selections, and mixed orchestral, instrumental, and vocal pieces.

10. See Sand's letter to Liszt, app. A, p. 214.

the evening more successful. His brilliant, thirty-year career leaves me nothing to add about this artist who is so universally admired and justly esteemed.[11]

As for your friend Franz, dear George, he will not tax you with his success, nor with his songs, and since you have many far better things to do than read my words, I will end my Genevan narrative at this point, except for the promise of possibly continuing it another day. As I was hoping to persuade your well-known indolence to exchange a Parisian chaise for a Helvetic armchair, I would have liked to talk to you in some detail about the contemporary notables whom Geneva takes pride in sheltering within its walls* and about the many fine friends who often gather on the Rue Tabazan; among whom I will name only Fazy, the Atlas of *l'Europe centrale*,[12] and Alphonse Denis, geologist, archaeologist, orientalist, metaphysician, artist, and, above all, an infinitely amiable and clever man. But I am terribly afraid of anything that might seem indiscreet.

Come visit us, therefore, and do so as soon as possible. Puzzi has already bought a "peace pipe" in your honor; your garret is furnished and ready for you; and my mother-of-pearl piano, silent for more than three months now, is only awaiting your arrival to make the nearby mountains resound with discordant echoes.

Adieu, and au revoir.

*Mr. de Sismondi, Mr. de Candolle, etc. [i.e., Jean de Sismondi (1773–1842), political economist, and Augustin Pyrame de Candolle (1778–1841), botanist].

11. Charles-Philippe Lafont (1781–1839), a violinist whose fame earlier in the century had rivaled that of Paganini.

12. Swiss statesman James Fazy (1794–1878) was the publisher of the *Journal de l'Europe centrale,* better known as the *Journal de Genève.*

2

RETURN TO PARIS

The fourteen months that separate the publication of the first and second of Liszt's articles were an unsettled time during which he and Madame d'Agoult came to realize that they were not as detached from Paris as they might have thought.

CHRONICLE

18 December 1835. The child Marie and Liszt are expecting is born in Geneva, a daughter who is christened Blandine-Rachel. Like many aristocratic infants of the time, she is quickly given over to the care of a foster family, with whom she will remain for the next three years.

22 February 1836. Liszt performs at a concert given by Hermann.

6 April. Liszt gives a concert of his own at the casino, which is not well attended. The program includes Hummel's D-minor Septet Op. 74, the first performance of Liszt's Fantasy on a Cavatina by Pacini "I tuoi frequenti palpiti,"[1] and a potpourri for six hands at two pianos by Czerny.

13 April. He appears for a fee of 500 francs at a concert of the Société de Musique. The featured number is the Hummel Septet, repeated by request.

21 April–11 May. Liszt travels alone to Lyons and gives three concerts there—2, 5, and 7 May—again for his own benefit.

13 May. He arrives back in Paris, where he is eager to check on the

---

1. Also known as the *Grande Fantaisie sur des motifs de Niobe*, this piece which Liszt composed in Geneva was a warhorse he included in nearly every concert during this period. The work itself is a caprice, a loosely structured set of variations—mixing bravura with percussive and lyric episodes—on an eccentric but attractive and very popular cavatina from *Niobe* (1826) by Giovanni Pacini (1796–1867).

reports of Sigismund Thalberg, an extraordinary pianist who had unexpectedly appeared in the French capital during his absence. (See the following chapter.) He also sounds out his mother, Madame d'Agoult's brother, friends, and colleagues to determine if his surreptitious, scandalous flight with the countess had permanently tarnished their reputations. Apparently not.

Mid-May. He gives two semi-private matinees, which are very successful.

Early June. He rejoins Marie in Switzerland.

13 July. The Directors of the Geneva Conservatory decide to recognize Liszt's services to the institution by naming him "Professeur honoraire"—a distinction he proudly accepts.

Late July. He gives concerts in Lausanne and Dijon.

5–28 September. Keeping her long-standing promise, George Sand arrives in Switzerland with her children and joins Liszt, Marie, Puzzi, and a Genevan friend, Adolphe Pictet, for a delightful if manic excursion to Chamonix and Freiburg, plus a brief stay in Geneva. Sand promptly writes a spirited account of the visit, her "Letter of a Voyager" to Didier, which is published in the *Revue des deux mondes* on 15 November.[2]

26 September. Liszt performs at another concert given by Hermann. Sand attends.

3 October. Liszt gives his farewell concert in Geneva. The program features two of his solo works and Beethoven's Trio, Op. 97.

16 October. Liszt and Marie d'Agoult arrive back in Paris, taking rooms at the elegant Hôtel de France. Marie asks Sand to share their salon, which she does. In no time at all the salon is frequented by all the artistic lions of Paris and acquires a reputation for its humanist views.

ca. 1 November. Liszt, at Sand's request, introduces her to Chopin. Chopin is put off by her manner and appearance, considering her a bluestocking. (Their famous affair does not actually begin until mid-1838.)

18 December. Liszt joins Berlioz in giving a concert at the conservatory, his first public concert in Paris in a year and a half. He performs his Grand Fantasy for Piano and Orchestra on Themes from [Berlioz's] *Lélio,* two excerpts from his piano transcription of the *Symphonie fantastique,* and his Fantasy on "Frequenti palpiti." The concert is a tremendous success.

---

2. Readdressed "To Herbert," Sand's description of the Alpine holiday appears as no. 10 in the collected edition of the *Lettres.*

It is against this rather unsettled background that Liszt, relying heavily in this particular case on his collaborator, wrote the article that follows. The second one addressed to Sand, it was the first to bear the series title *Lettres d'un bachelier ès musique*.

To a Poet-Voyager [George Sand][1]

Paris, January 1837

You ask me to write to you. Why not? Zelter[2] certainly wrote to Goethe. Yet, even though a kind of timidity restrains me, I would still be strongly tempted to ask you the same question that I did during my childhood of a wonderful woman—a most generous purveyor of pralines and puppets—who had extracted the same promise from me: "Supposing I don't know what to tell you, must I write anyway?"[3]— And another reason, perhaps. Who would venture to speak explicitly about anything today? It would be in poor taste and set a bad example. What, let me ask, would become of the concocters of books and articles if the book shops and readers suddenly took it into their heads to demand that they have something to say? Good Lord, we never say anything, yet we write about everything. Besides, what would I chat with you about? Politics? Every morning the newspapers print a hundred thousand copies of everything that they can print without being sent to Conciergerie Prison. I, however, greatly love being out-of-doors, and my homeopath orders me to exercise to overcome my fatigue.—Poetry? To you, beloved of the flowers, brother to the stars . . . that would be as appropriate as offering a gold piece to Baron Rothschild or a handshake to His Majesty Louis-Philippe.— Science? I know nothing about it.—German philosophy? Barchou de Penhoën[4] makes you sick.—About you and me, then? Let me again ask, why not?

In the past, as a matter of fact, it would have been considered

---

1. *Gazette musicale*, 12 February 1837, pp. 53–56.

2. Carl Friedrich Zelter (1758–1832), Berlin-based teacher and composer, especially of songs and men's choruses. His correspondence with Goethe was published in Berlin, 1834–35, in six vols.

3. Liszt recounts the same story in a letter to Marie d'Agoult written in the spring of 1833 (*Corres. Liszt-d'Agoult* 1:27).

4. August-Théodore-Hilaire Barchou de Penhoën (1801–1855), a historian-philosopher known for his studies of German philosophy and translation of Fichte. Sand and Liszt humorously regarded him as the personification of abstruse pedantry.

improper to speak openly about oneself, or one's affections, tastes, and foibles. But in our time the public takes the initiative and asks for all the family secrets, all the details of one's private life. Do you have the semblance of a reputation? Then people want to know the color of your bedroom slippers, the cut of your dressing gown, the kind of tobacco you prefer, and what you call your favorite greyhound. The newspapers, eager to profit from this pitiable curiosity, heap anecdote upon anecdote, falsehood upon falsehood, and cater to the idle amusement of the salons with such items as "The conversations of one of Madame de Lamartine's chambermaids with a steamship passenger," "The condition of the bathrooms in Mr. Jules Janin's house,"[5] or "The topography of Mr. de Balzac's walking stick," etc., etc. And the public never says, "Enough!" And the social world, which should at least have a well-developed sense of propriety, even if it is lacking in excellence, welcomes the vilest gossip, the silliest slander, with unprecedented alacrity.

But I do not know why I am telling you all this. You do not bother much with stupid speeches, and that is good. You do not read the newspapers, and that is even better. Let us, in any case, decide that I will write to you for as long as it amuses you, and myself too, and that I will tell you a little less than nothing or a little more than everything, depending upon my mental state or the state of my barometer that day.

I should be writing to you from Rome, and my letter is dated from Paris. Why? How did that come about? What happened? I do not know. To speak of fate, one would have to be a direct descendant of the family of Atreus or at least deem it an honor to claim distant kinship with the impious monk who was struck down by an inexorable Divinity in the forecourt of Notre Dame. Yet there was really something like that in the unknown force that suddenly gripped me on the southern slopes of the Alps the moment I gazed down on the plains of Lombardy and rapturously inhaled the scented breezes that that heaven-blessed land gives off like a sigh of love, a confident and serene prayer.

Italy! Italy! The foreigner's steel has scattered your noblest children far and wide.[6] They wander among the nations, their brows

5. Jules Janin (1804–1874), a leading drama and literary critic who wrote for such publications as the *Journal des debats* and *L'Artiste*.

6. Italy was, of course, a very divided nation at this time, and Paris a center for expatriates who were working for the cause of Italian unification and independence.

branded with a sacred curse. Yet no matter how implacable your oppressors might be, you will not be forsaken, because you were and will always be the land of choice for those men who have no brothers among men, for those children of God, those exiles from heaven who suffer and sing and whom the world calls "poets."

Yes, the inspired man—philosopher, artist, or poet—will always be tormented by a secret misfortune, a burning hope in your regard. Italy's misfortune will always be the misfortune of noble souls, and all of them will exclaim, along with Goethe's mysterious child: DAHIN! DAHIN![7]

Instead of the Alps, it is the somber Jura that I cross. Three days of monotonous traveling bring me back to Paris, where a misty atmosphere envelops my head once more. How different these dense, low clouds mingled with foul-smelling fog from the beautiful, star-lit sky reflected so chastely in the waters of Lake Geneva! That blue, transparent sky invites a man's attention and elevates his thoughts, while the mist in which I now walk seems incessantly to say: "Abandon yourself to your vilest instincts. Disgrace yourself with the most sordid debauchery. The day is dismal, I shall hide you from God Himself. Wallow in degradation, you will find gold and pleasure there."—

For the third time in my life, here I am tossing around in this living chaos where brutal passions, hypocritical vices, and shameless ambition tumble and hurl themselves about pell-mell, hellbent on destroying each other.[8] And yet, every now and then startling moments of clarity seem to burst from the tumultuous clash of evil passions,

---

Liszt, in more specific terms, seems to be thinking of Lombardy-Venetia, which was then a province of the Austrian empire.

7. Mignon's song from Goethe's *Wilhelm Meister:* "Kennst du das land, wo die Zitronen blühn? . . . Dahin! Dahin! Möcht' ich mit dir, o mein Geliebter, ziehn." (Do you know the land where the lemon trees bloom? . . . There! There! I would go with you, my beloved.)

8. This is neither Liszt's first nor his last diatribe against Parisian life, at least as he found it to be. Nearly four years earlier, for example, in May 1833 he had written his pupil Valérie Boissier: "This winter has been particularly exhausting for me. Scarcely realizing how, and Lord knows by what chance, I found myself hurled and launched into a world that had nothing to say to me and that did not understand what I said, as Chateaubriand put it. For over four months now I have had neither sleep nor rest.—The aristocracy of birth, the aristocracy of talent, the aristocracy of wealth, the elegant flirtations of the boudoir, the sultry and mephitic atmosphere of the diplomatic salons, the stupid scrambling of the *rout,* the yawns and bravos earned at the literary and artistic soirées, the egotistic joys and effronteries of the ball, the prattle and nonsense of the tea parties, the embarrassments and remorse of the night

liberating voices rise from the depths of the accursed chaos, and in this city, which could be said to be dedicated to the worship of hell, a sacred flame suddenly breaks through the shower of brimstone and the torrent of lava restoring life to the stupified world and dispelling the darkness completely with its vast light. Thus it is always with a holy feeling, a mixture of profound sadness and vague hope, that I plunge into Paris, where I have already lived out two phases of my life.

The first occurred when my father's hopes and expectations tore me from the Hungarian plains, where I was growing up free and un-tamed among the wild herds, and threw me, poor lad, into the midst of a brilliant society that applauded the feats of those whom it honored with that glorious and infamous stigma of CHILD PRODIGY. Thence-forth a premature melancholy weighed upon me, and I submitted with an instinctive sense of repulsion to the thinly disguised degradation of being an artistic servant. Later, when death had carried off my father and I returned alone to Paris, where I began to have an inkling of what art could be and what an artist should be, I was crushed, as it were, by the insurmountable difficulties that loomed up all along the path my thoughts were taking. As I did not, moreover, receive any sympathetic understanding—neither from those in society, nor even from artists, who were slumbering in comfortable indifference and showed no con-cern for me, for the aims that I had set for myself, or for the talents with which I was endowed—I was overcome by a bitter disgust for art, which had been reduced in my view to a more or less lucrative occupation, a diversion for polite society, and I would sooner have been anything in the world than a musician in the service of the Great Lords, patronized and paid by them on a par with a juggler or the performing dog Munito. May he rest in peace!

But I am getting carried away like an old man in telling you about my childhood. Memories crowd my brain, the objective "Me" observes itself, as the new philosophers say. What does it matter? Let us con-tinue. . . .

In those years, I was struck by a malaise that lasted for two years, following which my compelling need for faith and self-sacrifice, not having any other outlet, was given entirely over to the austere practices of Catholicism. My fevered brow bent low over the damp flagstones

---

before and the morning after, the triumphs of the salon, the wildly exaggerated re-views and praises in the press, the artistic disappointments, the public success—I have been through all that! I have lived it all! I have felt, seen, sneered, cursed , and wept!" (Robert Bory, "Diverses lettres inédites de Liszt," p. 12).

in the Church of Saint Vincent de Paul.[9] I drained my heart and sub-jugated my thoughts. The vision of a woman, as chaste and pure as the alabaster of sacred vessels, was the sacrifice I tearfully offered to the Christian God.[10] The renunciation of all earthy things was the sole force, the only watchword of my life. . . .

. . . .

But such total isolation could not last forever. Poverty, that old intermediary between man and misfortune, wrested me from my con-templative solitude and frequently sent me back to appear before the public, upon whom my mother and I partially depended for our exis-tence. Young and excessive as I was then, I suffered painfully from the impact of those everyday, extraneous concerns that I, as a practicing musician, had to face constantly and that severely impaired the mystic feeling of love and devotion which filled my heart. The worldly— those who have no time to think of the man's sufferings when they come to hear the artist perform and for whom the easy life is always bounded by those compass points known as PROPRIETY and DECO-RUM—had no idea of the conflicts and strange behavior that necessar-ily resulted from my double life. Tormented by a thousand confused instincts and a need for unlimited development, too young to distrust my feelings, too ingenuous to suppress anything inside me, I aban-doned myself to my own impressions, admirations, and loathings. I acquired a reputation for playing the comedian, even though I had no idea of how to pretend and had let myself be seen for what I was—an enthusiastic young man, a congenial artist, a religious ascetic, in short, everything that a person is at eighteen, when one loves God and Men with an ardent, passionate heart that has not yet been dulled by the brutal crush of egocentric society.

During that time, both at public concerts and in private salons (where people never failed to observe that I had selected my pieces very badly), I often performed the works of Beethoven, Weber, and Hummel, and let me confess to my shame that in order to wring bra-vos from a public that is always slow, in its awesome simplicity, to comprehend beautiful things, I had no qualms about changing the tempos of the pieces or the composers' intentions. In my arrogance I

9. Liszt's parish church in those years. It was located near the apartment he shared with his mother on Rue de Montholon in Montmartre.

10. Young Liszt's first love, Countess Caroline Saint-Cricq (ca. 1811–1872). Their hopes of marrying were dashed when her father dismissed Liszt as an unsuitable match for the daughter of a Peer of France. In the count's defense, however, be it said that Liszt was a mere seventeen-year-old *professeur du piano* at the time.

even went so far as to add a host of rapid runs and cadenzas, which, by securing ignorant applause for me, sent me off in the wrong direction—one that I fortunately knew enough to abandon quickly. You cannot believe, dear friend, how I deplore those concessions to bad taste, those sacrilegious violations of the SPIRIT and the LETTER, because the most profound respect for the masterpieces of great composers has, for me, replaced the need that a young man barely out of childhood once felt for novelty and individuality.

Now I no longer divorce a composition from the era in which it was written, and any claim to embellish or modernize the works of earlier periods seems just as absurd for a musician to make as it would be for an architect, for example, to place a Corinthian capital on the columns of an Egyptian temple.

About that time I wrote a number of pieces that inevitably reflected the kind of fever that was consuming me. The public found them strange and incomprehensible, and even you, my friend, have criticized me at times for being vague and diffuse.[11]

I am so far from protesting that twofold condemnation that my first thought was to throw them into the fire. Nevertheless I would like permission to say a few words on their behalf, in the guise of a funeral oration.

The work of some artists is their life. Inseparably identified one with the other, they are like those mythical divinities whose being was inextricably linked to that of a tree in the forest. The blood pulsing through their heart is also the sap that spreads through the leaves and fruit of their branches, and the precious balm that collects on the bark forms the silent tears which drop one by one from their eyes. The musician, especially, as one who is inspired by nature but does not copy it, exhales the most personal mysteries of his destiny in sounds. He thinks, feels, and speaks in music. But as his language, more arbitrary and less explicit than any other, lends itself to a multitude of different interpretations—rather like those beautiful clouds gilded by the setting sun that willingly assume all the shapes that a solitary walker's imagination assigns to them—is it not without value, and certainly not as ridiculous as some have repeatedly stated, for the composer to give a brief psychological sketch of his work, for him to say what he

11. It is difficult even to hazard a guess as to which early pieces Liszt had in mind—perhaps his *Harmonies poétiques et religieuses* after Lamartine. It is also possible that he was thinking of his more recent Fantasy on "Frequenti palpiti," a work which one reviewer had criticized for being vague and lacking both in form and a clear sequence of ideas (*Le Fédéral*, 8 April 1836; in Henri Kling, "Franz Liszt pendant son séjour à Genève en 1835–1836," p. 245).

intended, and, without going into childish explanations or minute details, for him to state the fundamental idea of his composition? Criticism is then free to step in so as to censure or praise the more or less
beautiful and adroit statement of that idea. By working in this manner,
it would avoid not only a host of erroneous interpretations, speculative
explanations, and useless paraphrases of an intention that the musician
never had, but also the interminable commentaries that have no basis
in fact.

Few books are published today that are not preceded by a long
preface, which in some ways is a second book written about the book.
Isn't the same precaution, superfluous in many ways when dealing
with a book written in the vernacular, an absolute necessity—not, it is
true, for instrumental music as it has been conceived until now (Beethoven and Weber excepted), music that has been directly regulated by
a symmetrical scheme and that could be measured in cubic feet, so to
speak—for the compositions of the modern school, works that generally aspire to be the expression of a distinct personality? Isn't it regret-
table, for instance, that Beethoven—who is so hard to comprehend
and whose intentions are so difficult for people to agree upon—didn't
briefly indicate the inner, intimate thought behind many of his great
works and the principal modifications of that thought?

I am firmly convinced that there is a philosophic form of art criticism that no one can do better than the artist himself. Don't make fun
of my idea, however odd it might seem at first. Don't you think that a
musician of good faith, after a time during which the fever of inspiration has abated and he has recovered from the elation of triumph or
the irritation of failure, knows better than all the aristarchs in the
world where he went wrong—what the flaws of his composition are
and how they came about? All he needs is a sense of pride that is so
free from vanity that he will dare to admit them to the public frankly
and courageously. Is that courage so difficult to find?

But please note the admirable loquacity that has carried me cross-
country in the realm of hypothesis, while you are sitting peacefully by
the fireside asking yourself where I am heading and when I will get to
telling you a few things about Paris, since I could have written all this
to you just as easily from Peking or Buenos Aires.

Thus, let us get back to Paris. Immediately upon my arrival I
stumbled across a marvel, a glory of wood and straw, across Mr. Gusikow,[12] the musical juggler who plays an infinite number of notes in an

12. Michael Joseph Gusikow (1806–1837). Dressed in traditional Polish-Jewish
garb, he and his instrument—a homemade xylophone constructed of wood and

infinitely short time and draws the greatest possible sonority from the two least sonorous bodies. It is a prodigious example of "the difficulty overcome" which all Paris is applauding right now. But what a pity it is that Gusikow, the Paganini of the Boulevards, did not apply his gift, one might even say his genius, to inventing an agricultural instrument or to introducing some new form of husbandry to his country. In which case, he might have enriched an entire nation; whereas his talent, being misguided, has produced nothing but musical inanities to which the charlatans who write feature articles for the newspapers will ascribe incalculable value. In this connection don't you deplore, as I do, that mania for hyperbole that has seized so many people, that rage to BYRONIZE and WERTHERIZE everyone and bestow laurel wreaths on the most fleeting brows, the flattest heads? Criticism has adopted Law's system[13]; the paper money of praise is printed and accepted with incredible ease. But woe to the artist or writer who accepts payment in these false values. He goes to sleep complacent in his artificial celebrity and wakes up face to face with some hollow, empty newspaper articles, completely astonished that the public no longer pays him in those pretty, redundant phrases, those beautiful, shiny words which have nothing but ridicule behind them.

The elegant world, which entertains itself with Gusikow's truly amazing performance, exhausting all its enthusiasm to admire the rapid play of his wooden mallets on a bed of straw, hardly condescends as yet to look into the fine and noble attempt at progress by the dedicated and conscientious Professor Mainzer.[14] Several times a week for the past four months or so he has been holding meetings for humble men, poor workers who, after the day's labor, come to sit on school benches and listen docilely to the lessons of a professor filled with zeal and patience. He imparts the benefits of music to these half-tutored, uncultivated minds and introduces these men—fatally brutalized by

---

straw—were a sensational novelty on the European stage for a short time. He first appeared in Paris at the Opéra-comique on 30 November 1836 and then gave several more concerts during the following months, including an especially well attended one at the Salle Pleyel on 27 December.

13. John Law (1671–1729), Scottish financier and speculator. He founded France's first public bank and persuaded the government to adopt the use of paper currency.

14. Joseph Mainzer (1801–1851), a German-born priest who devoted his career to teaching singing. He had settled in Paris in 1834, establishing a singing school there. In 1841 he moved to England, where he continued his work with considerable success.

the coarse and only pleasures possible for them—to sweet and simple emotions that elevate them without their being aware of it and return them by an indirect but non-threatening path to the thoughts of a lost God, to a devout and comforting feeling which the pharisaical Christianity of the potentates and the contemptuous teachings of a clergy feudalized by earthly powers had caused them to lose. Oh! what a wonderful thing it would be, my friend, to see the musical education of the people cultivated and disseminated throughout France. The beautiful myth of Orpheus's lyre, pared down to suit our prosaically middle-class age, could still be partially realized. Music, though stripped of its ancient prerogatives, could itself become a benign and civilizing deity, and its children would then circle their brows with the noblest of crowns, the crown that the people award to the one who has been their liberator, friend, and prophet.

But adieu. This letter is far too long. I shall wait for another time to tell you about all the marvels, musical and otherwise, whose existence the posters of Paris never cease revealing to us. In the meantime, do plant your cabbages, write fine books, tell S.[15] the story of "Princess Donkey-Skin" . . . and love me always as you have done in the past.

15. Solange, Sand's eight-year-old daughter.

3

STRIFE IN PARIS

All during the spring of 1837 Liszt was preoccupied with the so-called "rivalry" that arose between him and Thalberg. Not that there was any real animosity between the pianists—the two twenty-five-year-old combatants scarcely knew each other—but many in the Paris press and musical establishment had seized upon the accomplished Austrian, championing him both as the master of an impressively novel manner of piano playing and as a counterfoil to the unbridled style of Liszt.

Sigismund Thalberg (1812–1871) was born in Geneva, the natural son of the Austrian Prince Franz-Joseph von Dietrichstein and a Baroness Wetzlar.[1] When he was about ten years old his mother took him

---

1. This assertion is plainly at odds with the standard music reference works, which identify Thalberg's father not as Prince Franz-Joseph (1767–1854) but as his better-known younger brother, the sometime patron of Beethoven and Schubert, Count—or at times "Prince"—Moritz von Dietrichstein (1775–1864). This consensus, however, is open to question on several grounds. First, the identity of the pianist's father was no mystery in Vienna, and when Liszt called upon the family in April 1838 he sent Marie this unequivocal report of the visit: "Dietrichstein, Thalberg's father, is a white-haired old man with a princely, courteous air about him and was extremely polite and obliging toward me. . . . He told me that Thalberg had written him some time ago asking him to put his [Thalberg's] piano at my disposal when I came to Vienna. . . . The brother, Count Moritz D[ietrichstein] impressed me as a very distinguished man. [But] I think we will have very little to do with each other" (*Corres. Liszt–d'Agoult,* 1:216). Second, nineteenth-century sources agree in identifying the father as Prince Dietrichstein, but Moritz never held princely rank; when Franz-Joseph died the family's *Fürstenstand* passed to his legitimate son Joseph-Franz. A third and perhaps peripheral point, Count Moritz was the official tutor of the Duke of Reich-Stadt (the son of Napoleon and Archduchess Marie-Louise), and it seems most unlikely that the ultra-conservative Imperial Court would, if only for appearances' sake, entrust that position to a man who was openly raising an illegitimate son in Viennese society. Finally, the identity of Thalberg's parents is further complicated by the fact

to Vienna, where he received an excellent education and all the polish of a gentleman. He first studied music with a bassoonist in the court orchestra named Mittag, and later piano with Johann Nepomuk Hummel (1778–1837) and composition with the renowned Simon Sechter (1788–1867). At thirteen he began to perform at aristocratic soirées, an experience he evidently did not find as distasteful and socially demeaning as young Liszt had. During the next decade he acquired a very respectable but modest reputation,[2] and then toward the end of 1835 he went to Paris.

Although he was virtually unknown and unheralded when he arrived, his quiet demeanor at the keyboard, his dazzling technique, and the unprecedented sonorities he drew from the instrument soon sent the press into paroxysms of praise: "Moscheles, Kalkbrenner, Chopin, Liszt, and Herz are and will always be for me great artists," proclaimed the critic of *Le Ménestrel* on 13 March 1836, "but Thalberg is the creator of a new art which I do not know how to compare to anything that existed before him. . . . Thalberg is not only the premier pianist of the world, he is also an extremely distinguished composer."

It is small wonder that reports such as this reaching Liszt in Geneva would draw him back to Paris.[3] Thalberg had already departed

---

that his birth certificate in Geneva lists them as Joseph Thalberg and Fortunée Stein. But who, in fact, was this Joseph Thalberg? The answer, I submit, is to be found in Dietrichstein line of succession: the founder of the princely dynasty (d. 1533) was Sigmund von Dietrichstein, Freiherr von Hollenburg, Finkenstein und Thalberg. Thalberg, in other words, was actually one of Franz-Joseph's minor hereditary titles, and it is not unlikely that he, like many a high-ranking nobleman in similar circumstances, might allude to such a title when registering the birth of a natural son, viz., [Franz] Joseph [Baron von] Thalberg. It is also possible that he chose to accent the boy's oblique connection to the family by giving him the rather unusual name Sigismund, after his ancestor. Despite the present consensus, then, there seems to be a good case that can be made *contra* Moritz and *pro* Franz-Joseph. (See W. K. Isenburg et al., *Europäische Stammtafeln* 3: tables 22 and 23.) Thalberg's mother has been further identified as a Baroness Julie Bidescuty d'Eyb, who bore the child before she married Baron Ludwig Wetzlar in 1820 (Mary Lutyens, *Effie in Venice*, p. 127).

2. It was during this period that Chopin met him and pronounced his familiar judgment: "Thalberg plays famously but he is not my man; he is younger than I, popular with the ladies, writes Pot-pourris on themes from *Masaniello*, produces *piano* with the pedal instead of the hand, takes tenths as easily as I do octaves and wears diamond shirt studs" (letter to Matuszynski, Christmas Day [1830], in Chopin, *Selected Correspondence*, p. 76).

3. Liszt was no doubt also disturbed that his publisher Schlesinger had asked Thalberg to compose the more or less "official" piano fantasy on Meyerbeer's new and

when he arrived in May 1836, but Liszt, reestablishing his own presence, gave two private matinées at the Salle Erard which were packed to overflowing.[4] And there the whole matter rested until Liszt moved back to Paris that fall and waited for Thalberg's return.

All Liszt biographies give a more or less complete account of the Thalberg episode, concentrating in the main upon the three major concerts—Thalberg, then Liszt, then both at the same concert—but few seem to convey Liszt's exasperated obsession with the new pianist—his compulsion, call it that, to keep himself in the public eye all during the time that Thalberg was in Paris. An outline of the pertinent events[5] indicates, among other things, that Liszt appeared on the concert stage no fewer than fifteen times in one guise or another during these three months of early 1837.

CHRONICLE

8 January 1837. Liszt's review of Thalberg's compositions (the Fantasy Op. 22 and Caprices Opp. 15 and 19) appears in the *Gazette*. Berlioz (presumably), then its acting editor, adds a notice disassociating the publication from the views expressed in the article, which is indeed a mean-spirited piece. Liszt belittles Thalberg's reputation and his position as chamber virtuoso to the Austrian emperor, and he snidely suggests that Thalberg's "indirect connection to a noble family" is the real reason for his success. Thalberg's Fantasy, in Liszt's words, is "pretentiously empty and mediocre," lacking in all "invention, color, character, verve, and inspiration." The Austrian, he concludes, offers nothing but

---

immensely successful opera *Les Huguenots*. (Thalberg's resulting Op. 20 was first performed and published in April 1836.)

4. Berlioz, writing in the *Gazette musicale* (12 June 1836, pp. 198–200), discussed Liszt's reappearance in glowing terms, more of a puff than an objective review. The basic thrust of his remarks was that a new Liszt had returned, one who so surpassed even his old self that no comparisons or rivalries were possible. At the close of the article he singled out Liszt's performance of Beethoven's Hammerklavier Sonata, Op. 106 (its first known public performance in Paris) for special praise: "It was the ideal performance of a work that was thought to be unplayable. Liszt, in recreating a work that is still not understood, has proven that he is the pianist of the future. Honor to him." (Lina Ramann, *Franz Liszt* 2: 229–34, gives Berlioz's essay in its entirety.)

5. I am indebted to Geraldine Keeling for her assistance in sorting out the plethora of Liszt performances during this time. See her "Liszt's Appearances in Parisian Concerts, 1824–1844."

"sterility and boredom." A promised sequel in which Liszt was to discuss Thalberg's opera fantasies never appears.

28 January. Liszt, together with violist-violinist Christian Urhan (1790–1845) and cellist Alexander Batta (1816–1902), begins a series of concerts devoted for the most part to Beethoven's chamber music. It proves a great success with both audience and critics.

4 February. The second concert in the chamber music series.

5 February. Leaving Paris, Marie d'Agoult begins a long visit with George Sand at Nohant, the novelist's estate and manor house near La Châtre in Berri. That day the *Gazette* notes that Thalberg has returned to Paris and plans to perform, adding that "it is not impossible that we will soon witness a grand musical tournament." Thalberg attends at least one of the Beethoven concerts.

11 February. The third chamber music concert.

12 February. The Letter to Sand (chap. 2) appears in the *Gazette,* causing quite a stir. Liszt also learns that one of his more severe critics, the redoubtable François-Joseph Fétis (1784–1871), is to write an answer to his Thalberg article.

18 February. The fourth and last of the chamber music concerts.

ca. 19 February. Thalberg plays at the studio of Pierre Zimmerman (1785–1853), a renowned professor at the conservatory. Liszt attends and remarks to Chopin that Thalberg is "a failed aristocrat who is even more a failed artist."

27 February–5 March. As Thalberg keeps postponing his announced concert, Liszt pays a short visit to Nohant, his first.

9 March. Liszt, back in Paris, performs at a concert by violinist Lambert Massart (1811–1892). He also puts in an unscheduled appearance, playing at a concert by harpist Theodore Labarre (1805–1870).

12 March. Thalberg finally gives his concert, which takes place at the conservatory; the program includes his Fantasy on "God Save the King," the Fantasy Op. 22, and his Fantasy on Themes from Rossini's *Moses,* Op. 33, by far his most successful composition.[6]

---

6. Although it is nearly forgotten today, Thalberg's Fantasy was for the 1830s a startlingly innovative work, with respect to both its figuration and its overall structure in presenting the famous prayer "Dal tuo stellato soglio." It was the first piano composition to popularize the "thumb melody"; that is, the technique of presenting the theme divided between the hands in the tenor register while arpeggio figuration

ca. 15 March. Marie returns to Paris to be with Liszt.

18 March. Liszt performs at a concert given by Batta.

19 March. Liszt gives his concert at the Opéra. The program features his two most successful concert pieces: Weber's *Conzertstück* and his own Fantasy on Pacini's "Frequenti palpiti."

28 March. Liszt plays at a concert by bass Just Géraldy (1808–1869).

31 March. Both pianists appear at a gala charity benefit for Italian émigrés given by Princess Cristina Belgiojoso.[7] Thalberg plays his *Moses* fantasy, Liszt his on "Frequenti palpiti." Neither pianist bests the other. Both are declared victors, by the audience and press alike, in the highly publicized confrontation.

2 April. Thalberg plays at the Salle des Bouffes.

9 April. Liszt gives a concert at the Salle Erard. The program includes Hummel's D-minor Septet and Beethoven's Quintet for Piano and Winds Op. 16. Liszt also plays his Reminiscenses of [Meyer-beer's] *Les Huguenots* (a first performance?) and several Chopin etudes. As a finale, Liszt and Chopin play Liszt's *Grande valse di bravura*.

13 April. Liszt performs at a concert given by his pupil Puzzi. That day he also plays at a charity benefit for the workers in Lyons, sponsored by Countess Merlin.

15 April. Liszt takes part in a concert at the Théâtre Italien benefitting an emergency fund for dramatic authors.

23 April. Liszt performs in the showroom of the piano manufacturer Henri Pape.

That same day the *Gazette* publishes Fétis's long-awaited article "Thalberg and Liszt." After opening with a long and solid review of the evolution of piano playing, Fétis goes on to distinguish between two basic schools of pianism: one is the singing school best exemplified by Chopin, the other is the bril-

---

ranges above and below it over the length of the keyboard. More significantly, it was also the first composition of its sort to do away with the fast, brilliant finale with which pieces of the period typically ended and to replace it with a big, climactic per-oration of the melody: "Little by little," wrote Ernest Legouvé, "the movement quick-ened, the expression became more accentuated, and by a series of gradual crescendos he [Thalberg] held one breathless until a final explosion swept the audience with an emotion indescribable" (quoted in James Huneker, *Franz Liszt*, p. 286).

7. Cristina Belgiojoso-Trivulzio (1808–1871) was a dear friend of Liszt's, an ar-dent Italian patriot, and one of the most fascinating, seductive women in Paris. See Heine's "Confidential Letter" (app. B), which gives a fanciful account of Liszt's play-ing at the concert and a judicious summary of the entire Liszt-Thalberg affair.

liant school for whom the piano is "an arena for cleverness and dexterity." Liszt, both as performer and composer, belongs firmly to the brilliant school, for while he has conquered difficulties with incredible ease, there is little "creative" or "truly personal" about his playing, marvelous though it is. Thalberg, on the other hand, is an innovator who combines the best of both schools with a variety of pianistic means. Then, after taking Liszt severely to task for his ill-tempered Thalberg article, which he blames on bad advice from "imprudent friends," Fétis concludes: "You [Liszt] are the transcendent man of a school that has passed and has nothing more to offer, but you are not the man of the new school. That man is Thalberg—and this is the whole difference between you."[8]

30 April. Liszt completes the article that follows: or at least it carries this date. The *Gazette*, however, does not rush to print it.

ca. 4 May. Liszt and the countess leave for Nohant.

14 May. The *Gazette* publishes Liszt's response, "To Professor Fétis," an article which is more notable for its special pleading and sarcasm than the substance of its remarks.

21 May. Fétis, in a letter to the *Gazette*, complains of the shabby treatment he has received from Liszt. And with that the *Gazette* firmly declares that so far as it is concerned the whole matter is closed.

Liszt's article written during these hectic months follows; it is the third and last addressed to George Sand.

---

8. If one considers only the pieces Liszt had published by 1837, Fétis's conclusion is an eminently fair one. Works such as the early fantasies on Paganini's "La Clochette" (1834), Halévy's *La Juive* (1835), or even *Niobe,* are overladen with shallow, almost senseless brilliance and bravura; one can only wince, for example, when the gentle, haunting bolero from *La Juive* is hammered out in octaves for the sake of a showy finale. Yet Fétis was a poor prophet. Liszt was not only slow to develop and find his authentic voice as a composer, but he also, despite flashes of extreme annoyance, evidently took Fétis's words to heart and did in time weed the purely extraneous glitter from his own "Lisztian" style of writing for the piano. Thalberg, as it turned out, also confounded the prophet in Fétis. Having forged his early innovations, he seemed quite content to repeat the same pianistic effects over and over again (see n. 14 below concerning Thalberg.) Four years after the altercation, Fétis, in an article prompted by the earlier version of the *Transcendental Etudes,* modified his opinion. Less enthusiastic then about Thalberg, he praised Liszt warmly for his innovations in the "progress of musical art" (i.e., performance, pianistic sonority, harmony, etc.) as evidenced by the *Etudes* and the yet unpublished *Années de pèlerinage* (*Gazette musicale,* 9 May 1841, pp. 261–64).

[To George Sand][1]

Paris, 30 April 1837

One more day and I depart. Finally free of the thousand obligations, more imagined than real, that a man so childishly allows to fetter his will, I am now leaving for the unknown lands where my hopes and expectations have already resided for a long time.[2]

Like a bird that has just broken free of its narrow cage, the imagination shakes the weight from its wings and lo! takes flight across the distance. How fortunate, how very fortunate is the voyager! How fortunate is he who never travels the same path twice and who never retraces his own footsteps. Cutting across reality without ever stopping, he sees things only for what they appear to be and people for what they show themselves to be. How fortunate is he who knows when shaking a friend's hand to release it before he feels it grow cold in his own, and who does not wait for the day when his beloved's burning gaze will turn to placid indifference. How fortunate, then, is he who knows enough to break with things before he is broken by them!

It behooves an artist more than anyone else to pitch a tent only for an hour and not to build anything like a permanent residence. Isn't he always a stranger among men? Isn't his homeland somewhere else? Whatever he does, wherever he goes, he always feels himself an exile. He feels that he has known a purer sky, a warmer sun, and nobler beings. What then can he do to escape his vague sadness and undefined regrets? He must sing and move on, pass through the crowd, scattering his works to it without caring where they land, without listening to the clamor with which people stifle them, and without paying attention to the contemptible laurels with which they crown them. What a sad and great destiny it is to be an artist! He is born marked with the seal of predestination. He certainly does not choose his vocation; it takes possession of him and drives him on. Whatever the adverse circumstances might be—the opposition of his family or the world, the grim bonds of poverty or any apparently insurmountable obstacle—his ever-active determination points steadfastly toward the pole, and that pole for him is art, the apprehensible reproduction of that which is mystically divine in man and in creation.

The artist lives alone, and when circumstances throw him into

---

1. *Gazette musicale,* 16 July 1837, pp. 339–43. A note in the *Gazette* stated: "The publication of this letter has been delayed by an abundance of other materials."

2. Italy ostensibly, though Liszt and Marie d'Agoult stopped at Nohant to visit George Sand for three months before they actually departed.

the middle of society, he, in the midst of discordant distractions, creates an impenetrable solitude within his soul that no human voice can breach. Vanity, ambition, greed, jealousy, and love itself, all the passions that arouse mankind, remain outside the magic circle he has drawn about his ideas. There, as though in a sanctuary, he contemplates and worships the ideal that his entire being will seek to reproduce. There he can envision divine, incredible forms and the colors that the most gorgeous flowers in the brilliance of springtime have never presented to his eyes. There he hears the eternal, harmonious music whose cadence regulates the universe, and all the voices of creation are united for him in a marvelous concert. A burning fever then seizes him, his blood courses impetuously through his veins, filling his brain with a thousand compelling concepts from which there is no escape except by the holy labor of art. He feels himself prey to a nameless misery; an unknown power demands to be brought to light in words, colors, or sounds, that ideal which takes possession of him and forces him to endure a thirst of desire, a rage to possess such as no man has ever felt for the object of an earthly passion. But once a work of his is completed—one that the whole world may acclaim enthusiastically—he is still only partially satisfied, still discontent, and would perhaps destroy the work if a new vision did not arise to shift his gaze from the thing accomplished to the heavenly and sorrowful raptures that turn his life into a perpetual pursuit of an unattainable goal, the mind's unceasing effort to rise to the accomplishment of those things it had conceived during the extraordinary time when eternal, unclouded beauty made itself known to him.

Today's artist exists outside the social community because the poetic component, that is, the religious component, of mankind has disappeared from modern governments. What have they to do with an artist or poet, with those who believe that they can resolve the problem of human happiness by the liberalization of certain privileges, by the unbounded growth of industry and personal well-being? What do they care about these men, *useless* to the mechanics of government, who travel the world reviving the sacred flame of noble sentiments and sublime exaltations? Or about those whose works satisfy the indefinable need for beauty and grandeur that exists, albeit smothered to some degree, in the depths of all human souls? The happy times have passed when art spread its flowering branches over all of Greece, intoxicating the land with its perfume. In those days every citizen was an artist, because all the people—legislators, warriors, or philosophers—were concerned with the idea of moral, intellectual, and physical beauty. No one was astonished by the sublime, and great deeds were as common as the great works that simultaneously inspired and celebrated them. The forceful, austere art of the Middle Ages, which erected cathedrals and summoned an enthralled populace to them with the sound of the organ, has been extinguished along with the faith that gave it life. Today we have broken that sympathetic bond, which, by uniting art and society, gave force and brilliance to the former and provided the latter with the multifarious excitement that gives birth to great things.

Social art is no more and has yet to return. What, then, do we usually see these days? Sculptors? No, just statue makers. Painters? No, just picture makers. Composers? No, just music makers. *Artisans* everywhere, and not an *artist* to be seen. And this state of affairs also imposes cruel suffering on one who was born with the pride and fierce independence of a true son of art. All about him he sees a mob of those who manufacture art paying heed to the public's caprice, striving assiduously to gratify the fantasies of rich simpletons, and obeying the slightest whim of fashion. So eager are they to bow their heads and abase themselves that it seems difficult to believe that they could stoop so low! He must accept these people as brothers and watch the crowd, confusing him with them, offer him the same coarse appreciation, the same childish, dazed admiration. And don't let anyone tell you that this is the suffering of injured vanity and self-esteem. No, no, you know it well, you who are so highly placed that no rival can touch you. The bitter tears that fall at times from our eyelids are those of one who, adoring the True God, sees His temple invaded by idols and the gullible populace kneeling before the gods of mud and stone for which they have abandoned the Madonna's altar and the worship of the Living God.

Perhaps you find me in a very somber mood today. For you, perhaps, the nightingale's song accompanied the transition from a delightful night to a splendid day. Perhaps you took a nap beneath the flowering lilacs and dreamed of a beautiful, golden-haired angel, whom you saw upon awakening in the smiling features of your dear daughter standing at your side. Perhaps you commanded your fiery Andalusian dog, quivering beneath the hand that trained him, to bound speedingly across the distance that separated you from your best friend. Perhaps—no, surely—you once met the gaze of an unhappy man upon whom you called down the blessings of Providence. . . . As for myself, I have just spent the past six months living a life of shabby squabbles and virtually sterile endeavors. I willingly laid my artist's heart open to all the bruises of an active public life. Day by day, hour by hour, I have endured the silent tortures of the perpetual *misunderstanding* that apparently must still continue to exist for some time yet between the public and the artist.

In this sort of relationship it is the musician, without doubt, who suffers the worst fate of all. The poet, painter, or sculptor, left to himself in his study or studio, completes the task that he has set for himself; and once his work is done, he has bookshops to distribute it or museums to exhibit it. There is no intermediary between him and his judges, whereas the composer is necessarily forced to have recourse to inept or indifferent interpreters who make him suffer through interpretations that are often literal, it is true, but which are quite imperfect when it comes to presenting the work's ideas or the composer's genius. If, on the other hand, the musician is himself a performer, how many times, compared to those rare occasions when he is understood, must he prostitute himself to an unresponsive audience, must he scoff at his own most intimate feelings and toss his soul out, so to speak, to stir up some applause from the inattentive crowd. Even then, a tremendous effort is required if the flame of his fervor is to reflect even a pale glimmer on those icy faces or to strike a few sparks from those loveless, apathetic hearts.

I have often been told that I have less right than anyone to voice such complaints, as the success I have enjoyed since childhood was far greater than my talent or aspirations deserved. But it was precisely at those times when the applause was loudest that I was sadly able to convince myself that it was to the inexplicable vagaries of fashion, the authority of an important name, or a vigorous style of interpretation, much more than to a feeling for the True and the Beautiful, that most of the success was due. There are more than enough instances of this.

When I was a boy I often amused myself with a schoolboy's prank which never failed to dupe my audiences. I would play the same piece, presenting it at various times as one written by Beethoven, or by Czerny, or by myself. At those times when I was thought to be the composer, I was patronized and encouraged, "Really, that wasn't too bad for your age!" At those times when I played it under Czerny's name, no one listened to me. But when I played it as a work of Beethoven, I could inevitably count on bravos from the entire hall.[3]

The mention of Beethoven reminds me of another, more recent

3. One instance of Liszt's "prank" took place in Bordeaux in 1826 when he was fourteen years old. He played one of his own sonatas at a gathering of musical amateurs, telling them that it was by Beethoven. Needless to say, the assembly found the piece "sublime" (Joseph d'Ortigue, "Études biographiques I: Franz Liszt," p. 199).

incident which only served to confirm my notion about the artistic competence of dilettantes. You know that for some years now the Conservatory orchestra has undertaken to present his symphonies to the public.[4] Today his glory is sacred; the most ignorant of the ignorant take cover behind his colossal name, and impotent, envious people have already used it as a club to crush all our contemporaries who appear to be asserting themselves. Since I wanted to try and supplement the conservatory's efforts (quite imperfectly, however, because my time was limited), I devoted a number of musical evenings this past winter almost exclusively to performances of Beethoven's duos, trios, and quintets.[5] I was almost convinced that the evenings would bore people, but I was also certain that no one would dare to admit it. Actually, the audience's enthusiasm ran very high; one could easily have been fooled by it, believing that the power of genius had vanquished the crowd, but a change in the order of the program given at one of the last concerts put an end to that illusion. Without alerting the audience, we substituted a trio by Pixis for the programmed work by Beethoven.[6] The bravos were more numerous and vigorous than ever, but then when the Beethoven trio was performed in place of Pixis's piece, the audience found it cold, mediocre, and even boring to the point that many people became incensed, declaring that it was most impertinent of Pixis to present his composition to an audience

4. The annual series of concerts, the first of its kind in France devoted to propagating the orchestral works of Beethoven, was initiated in March 1828 by François-Antoine Habeneck (1781–1849). Habeneck conducted performances of two or three of the symphonies per year, and even though Liszt does not mention it, the conservatory programs also included Beethoven's overtures, concertos, and even choral works.

5. Although Beethoven was the featured composer, the series also presented other composers' works. The program at the first of the Beethoven evenings, for instance, included: Beethoven's Trio in B-flat, Op. 97, performed by Urhan, Batta, and Liszt; Liszt's own *Rondo fantastique* on "El Contrabandista" (a work dedicated to George Sand and based on a song by Manuel Garcia); excerpts from *Les Huguenots* sung by bass Just Géraldy; an "air varié" composed and performed by Batta; and to close, Beethoven's Violin Sonata in A major, Op. 47, performed by Urhan and Liszt. (See the listing for 18 Jan. 1837 in Keeling "Liszt's Appearances" for further details.)

6. Johann-Peter Pixis (1788–1874), a highly regarded composer-pianist and an old close friend of Liszt's. The change in program order was made at the third concert, 11 February. Here is Liszt's original report of the incident to Marie d'Agoult two days later: "A charming blunder by the public, who with incredible assurance mistook Pixis's style for Beethoven's last Saturday. The program listed the trio by Beethoven as the opening number and the one by Pixis as the last. But, as Pixis implored me not to sacrifice him so, we agreed to reverse the order, and everyone applauded the supposed Beethoven trio—and said that the other seemed so vapid beside it!—Isn't that something!"(*Corres. Liszt-d'Agoult* 1: 186–87).

who had come to admire the great composer's masterpieces. By telling you this story I do not mean to imply that it would have been wrong for them to applaud Pixis's trio, but even he could only manage a smile of pity when he heard the bravos of an audience capable of confusing two such completely different compositions and styles, because it is certain that people who can make such a crass error are totally unqualified to appreciate the true beauties of his own works.[7] Even Goethe— who, as is commonly thought, took more *pleasure* than anyone in his fame, in being the *honored* poet of his day, acknowledged a king by his contemporaries—exclaimed: "Oh! do not speak to me of that motley rabble, the sight of which alone can make our rapture vanish. Protect me from that human whirlpool that can sweep us against our will into the torrent. Lead me to one of those quiet retreats where a poet's true joy flourishes, and where the love and friendship sent by the hand of God spread their blessings through our hearts."[8]

It is a fact that very few people today are destined to receive some education in music. The majority do not know the rudiments of music, and nothing is rarer, even among the better classes of society, than the serious study of the masters. Most of the time people are content to listen every now and then—and without the opportunity of making a

---

7. Although Liszt seems to have had a low opinion of those who attended the concerts, it was not actually so. When the series ended he asked Marie d'Agoult to write an article about it for him and sent her an outline to follow. Apparently the article was never written, but this is what Liszt had told her to say: "Despite the public's predilection for frivolous things, its passion for gaudy mediocrities, etc., etc., there are, nonetheless, a very considerable number of people in Paris who have dedicated themselves to the serious veneration of art and who work conscientiously at their musical education. . . . Had we been at all skeptical about the existence of such a group, the elite crowd of people who flocked to four concerts [séances] whose programs were not of the sort to beguile the dilettantes or the dandies in the dress circle at the Théâtre-Italien would have changed our skepticism to affirmation.—Then one or two sentences about the powerlessness of obstacles and the necessity for the progress of musical art in France. When you get to the four concerts, say that the audience listened with religious attention and fervent interest to things that probably would have had people yawning at most concerts. [Liszt then indicates what she is to praise about Urhan and Batta.] Close, then, with this: These four concerts are, in a sense, only preparatory. Although we have already performed five trios by Beethoven, there is still a great number of [chamber] works that are not performed, and it is important to make the public familiar with them. . . . The final sentence I leave to you; I would not be displeased if you were to say that it is time for highly placed artists to abandon once and for all the field of public amusement and make it their business to teach the public and introduce them to great and noble things" (*Corres. Liszt-d'Agoult* 1: 193–94).

8. Goethe, *Faust,* part 1, "Prologue on the Stage," lines 59–66.

choice—not to some few beautiful morsels, but to a raft of pitiable things that pervert good taste and accustom the ear to the most thread-bare nonsense. In contrast to the poet who speaks a language common to all and who, moreover, addresses himself to those whose minds have been shaped to some extent by the required study of the classics, the musician speaks a mysterious language that can only be understood after special study or, at the very least, extensive exposure. He is also at a disadvantage compared with the painter and sculptor, in that they address themselves to a feeling for form, which is far more widespread than the intimate understanding of nature and the feeling for the infi-nite that are the very essence of music. Can this state of affairs be im-proved? I believe so, and I also believe that we are moving in that direction in every way. People never stop repeating that we are living in an age of transition, and that is truer for music than for anything else. It is sad, no doubt, to be born into these times of thankless labors, when he who sows will not reap, when he who gathers will not enjoy, when he who conceives beneficial ideas will not see them come alive, but must, like a woman who dies in childbirth, bequeath them weak and naked to a generation that will trample on his grave. But for those who have faith, what do these long days of waiting matter?

Among all the progressive ideas I *dream* about, there is one that should be easy to implement and that came to me a few days ago when, strolling silently through the galleries of the Louvre, I was able to sur-vey, one after the other, the profoundly poetic brushstrokes of Scheffer, the gorgeous colors of Delacroix, the pure lines of Flandrin, of Leh-mann, and the vigorous nature scenes of Brascassat.[9] Why, I asked myself, isn't music invited to participate in these annual festivals?[10] Why do the Louvre's vast halls remain silent? How is it that composers do not bring the finest flowers of their calling here as do the painters, their brothers? Why shouldn't Meyerbeer, Halévy, Berlioz, Onslow, Chopin, and others—less famous and impatiently awaiting their day and place in the sun—want to have the symphonies, choruses, and compositions of every sort, which stay buried in portfolios for the

9. Ary Scheffer (1795–1858), Dutch-born painter, active in Paris; he painted Liszt's portrait some three years later. Eugène Delacroix (1798–1863), the leading Ro-mantic. Hippolyte Flandrin (1809–1864), known mostly for his religious canvasses conceived in simple, early Renaissance style. Henri Lehmann (1814–1882), German-born follower of Ingres; he would later paint portraits of both Liszt and Marie d'Agoult. Jacques-Raymond Brascassat (1804–1867), known for his still lifes and ani-mal scenes.

10. The Paris "Salon," a government-sponsored exhibit of the works of living French artists. Its origins reach back to the late seventeenth century.

want of a means to perform them, heard in these stately surroundings under the aegis of Scheffer's *Christ* or Delaroche's[11] *Saint Cecilia?*

The theaters, which in any case represent only one aspect of art, are in the hands of administrators who do not and cannot have art as their purpose. Forced to *succeed* or face bankruptcy, they shun obscure composers and difficult works. The concert hall at the conservatory is open only to a highly restricted audience, and its orchestra barely suffices for the performances of the great composers. Isn't there, therefore, an urgent need for the government to fill this gap by sponsoring an orchestra and a trained chorus for the performance of modern compositions selected by a special committee? The public, invited over the course of several months to hear this superior music, would develop a taste for it, and young, talented artists, who are rebuffed by innumerable obstacles constantly arising between them and public exposure, would be rescued from obscurity and neglect. Surely by extending its support to music in this way, by according musicians the same privilege it grants painters, the government would be accomplishing something truly national in scope and deserving of as much attention, perhaps, as many a weighty debate in the Chamber of Deputies or many a weighty quarrel in the Ministry.—The National Convention, meeting during the Terror, did not disdain founding the Conservatory.[12]

But I realize that I am behaving like one of those timid, pious souls at confession who hold back the most painful things to say until the end. I have avoided talking to you about a musical altercation that has occupied the public far too much, seeing that it troubles you even in your retreat and that you yourself have asked me to explain this matter—one that began as the simplest thing in the world but became totally incomprehensible to the public because of the articles in the press and a most painful source of irritation for me because of the interpretations put upon it. I want to talk about the matter that some people were pleased to call my "rivalry" with Thalberg.

You know that when I left Geneva at the beginning of last winter I was not acquainted with Thalberg. Even the word of his fame had reached us only in a very faint way,[13] as the echoes of the Faulhorn and

---

11. Paul Delaroche (1797–1856), an especially popular painter, known for his portraits and historical scenes.

12. The Paris Conservatory was founded 3 August 1795. It was the outgrowth of the *École Royale de Chant* and the *Institut National de Musique.*

13. Liszt, in reality, had written his mother as early as March 1836 to say: "I should like to meet Thalberg. Those compositions of his that I have seen seem mediocre to me. The praise in the newspapers doesn't impress me much" (Liszt, *Briefe an seine Mutter,* p. 31).

Saint Gotthard, which seem to have retained the first words of creation, have truly far better things to do than to repeat the names of our poor little current celebrities. When I arrived in Paris the only talk in the musical world was about the marvelous sudden appearance of a pianist the likes of which had never been heard before, one who was to regenerate the art while simultaneously blazing a new path, as both performer and composer, that we all were to endeavor to follow.

Since you have always known me to be attuned to the faintest rumor and fly to the vanguard of each new development with all my sympathetic encouragement, you can imagine how my soul trembled at the prospect of a great and powerful new impetus that was to be given to an entire generation of contemporary pianists. Only one thing aroused my distrust, and that was the speed with which the votaries of the new messiah forgot or rejected that which had come before him.

I was less sanguine, I admit, about Thalberg's compositions when I heard them vaunted so absolutely and by people who seemed to say that everything that had preceded them—Hummel, Moscheles, Kalkbrenner, [Henri] Bertini, Chopin—was reduced to nothing by the simple fact of his arrival. Thus I was eager to see and acquaint myself with these pieces, so new and profound that they would reveal a genius to me. I shut myself in for a whole morning in order to study them conscientiously. The result of that study was diametrically opposed to what I had expected. One thing, however, did surprise me, and that was the effect that these empty, mediocre works had produced everywhere. From that I concluded that the composer's talent as a performer must have been prodigious, and having thus formulated my opinion,[14] I expressed it in the *Gazette musi-*

14. Liszt was not the only one to have reservations about Thalberg. The critic "S" (Sir George Smart?) writing for the musically astute London weekly *The Atlas*, for example, noted: "Our opinion of Thalberg as a musician of exquisite taste, refinement, and expression, and as a performer who has carried certain effects of his own invention to the highest perfection in execution remains unchanged. His mechanism is of a new kind, and the most brilliant conceivable, especially in its first impressions. But there is this deficiency in him which prolonged acquaintance only can detect—namely, a want of variety. Having heard a few of his pieces you have heard all—the same round of bravura passages, the same arpeggios, the same rapid octaves, the same double notes serve for every one of them. . . . He has invented some *magnificent* difficulties, which he executes with a truly astonishing precision, and which it appears to be his object to introduce in every composition. But this constant reference to one sort of passage or effect ends in monotony, and the hearer becomes convinced that the sphere of Thalberg's excellence is far more contracted than he took it to be" (21 May 1837).

cale,[15] with no other intention than that of doing what I had done on many previous occasions; that is, to state my opinion, good or bad, about the piano pieces that I had taken the trouble to examine. Under these particular circumstances more than any other, I certainly had no intention of reprimanding or lording it over public opinion. I am far from claiming such an arrogant privilege for myself. But I did think that I could say to no one's detriment that if this was the new school, I was not part of that new school; that if this was the direction Thalberg was taking, I had virtually no interest in traveling the same route; and finally that I did not believe his thinking contained a single germ of the future that others should strive to cultivate.

What I said, I said with regret and also to caution the public, so to speak, since they had made a point of pitting us against each other and of depicting us as competitors in the same arena, contenders for the same crown. I was, perhaps, also induced to take up my pen and give my sincere opinion by the innate need that men of a certain disposition feel to respond to injustice and to protest against error and bad faith even in the most inconsequential of circumstances. After I had stated my opinion to the public, I said the same thing to the composer when we had occasion to meet some time later. I was happy to do full justice to his fine talent as a performer, and he, better than others, seemed to understand the honesty and frankness of my behavior. This led to an announcement that we were "reconciled," and that provided a new theme to be varied just as lengthily and tiresomely as our "enmity" had been. In fact there had been neither enmity nor reconciliation. If one artist does not grant a colleague a level of artistic merit that has been exaggerated, in his opinion, by the crowd, are they necessarily enemies? Are they reconciled when, putting questions of art aside, they appreciate and esteem each other?

You can well understand how painful these never-ending explanations of my words and actions in this connection have been for me.

Writing that article about Thalberg's compositions, I realized only too well that I was going to stir up some indignation and that storms would gather about my head. Yet, let me confess that I believed a thousand precedents would protect me from the odious suspicion of envy. I believed—oh blessed innocence! you will say—that the truth could and should always be told and that an artist under any circumstance, even the seemingly most insignificant one, should not sacrifice his opinions to carefully calculated self-interest. The experience has en-

15. *Gazette musicale,* 8 January 1837.

lightened me, but it will not benefit me. I, unfortunately, do not have one of those *pliable* natures that the Marquis of Mirabeau[16] spoke about, and I love truth far more than I love myself. Besides, among the harsh lessons I was not spared, I received some little slaps that were so gracious and adorable that I am strongly tempted to incur such punishment again. Little, ladylike slaps! What am I saying—slaps from the muse, which do so little harm and are so sweet to receive that one drops to one's knees and pleads—Again! The lessons in propriety and modesty given me by the ex-muse of the country[17] were priceless, and I am quite sure that there is no one who does not envy me for them.

But I am truly ashamed of writing to you at such length about these childish matters. Let us forget this recent confusion in a world where a viable atmosphere is still lacking for an artist. Somewhere, far away in a land that I know, there is a limpid spring that lovingly bathes the roots of a lone palm tree. The palm tree raises its fronds above the spring, sheltering it from the sun's rays. I want to drink from that spring. I want to rest in that shade—a touching symbol of that holy and indestructible affection which supplants all earthly concerns and will doubtless flourish in heaven.

16. Victor de Riquette (1715–1789), father of the Revolutionary statesman and orator; a landed aristocrat, yet an ardent advocate of social reform.

17. It is difficult to ascertain whom Liszt meant here; Marie d'Agoult perhaps, or possibly Cristina Belgiojoso.

4

NOHANT AND LYONS

CHRONICLE

Ca. 6 May 1837. Liszt and Marie d'Agoult arrive in Nohant for a visit
with George Sand, which lasts nearly three months. While
there, Liszt completes his work on the *Hexameron*[1] and tran-
scribes a small collection of Schubert lieder.[2] Most of his energies, however, go into transcribing Beethoven's symphonies for
the piano, an undertaking he discusses in the Letter that follows.

5 June. Marie begins a journal that she will keep intermittently
throughout the coming sojourn in Italy and which will form the
basis of some mainly descriptive portions of the ensuing articles.[3]

24 July. Leaving Nohant, Liszt and Marie start on their way to Italy.
Their departure is in one sense a repetition of their first flight

1. The piece was an ingenious fund-raising effort devised by Princess Belgiojoso. She persuaded six leading pianists—Liszt, Thalberg, Pixis, Henri Herz, Chopin,
and Czerny (then in Paris)—to write a variation each on the March from Bellini's *I
Puritani*. Liszt then provided the introduction, transitions, and a finale, and the resulting *Hexameron* (his title) was sold to a publisher for the benefit of Italian émigrés.
Even though Liszt performed the work at his later concerts, it has never enjoyed a
lasting success; the words of the March may well have roused the Italian patriots of
the time—"Let the trumpet sound, and I will fight fearlessly with all my might. It is a
noble thing to face death crying 'Freedom!'"—but the musical basis of the work is
one of the most banal, costive tunes Bellini ever wrote.

2. Although these transcriptions were, in part, an attempt to promote Schubert's music at a time when the Viennese master was still barely known, they also
proved such a great commercial success that Liszt transcribed more than fifty songs by
Schubert over the next decade to satisfy the publishers' demands for them.

3. The journal, including occasional comments by Liszt, forms the bulk of Marie d'Agoult's published *Mémoires* and is examined in some detail in Appendix E.

from Paris, as she is pregnant again. On route to Lyons, Liszt
pays a brief visit to Lamartine at the poet's country home,
Saint–Point.

3 August. Liszt and tenor Adolphe Nourrit (1802–1839) give a benefit
concert in Lyons for indigent workers.

The following Letter to Pictet is especially notable for Liszt's own account of his relationship to the piano, and there is hardly a Liszt biography extant that does not cite the pertinent passages.

To Adolphe Pictet[1]

Chambéry, September 1837[2]

Where am I going? What will I become? I do not know. I will always
go straight ahead, as the peasants say, because the straight roads are
the best roads. I will become whatever God pleases, and nothing else
troubles me. No matter what happens, I will rely on Providence.

Today, however, let us talk about what has become of me since
we last conversed with our feet propped up before the fire and our
elbows resting on your Vedas. When I say "conversed," I am actually
thinking of myself, which is to say that you who know everything and
I who know nothing somehow managed to find a common fund of
ideas and to live off that metaphysical fund for days on end. Briefly, no
matter what people make of that, after we last talked and you left Paris
to return to your beautiful lake, I went to find refuge in the farthest
corner of Berri, that prosaic province so divinely steeped in poetry by
George Sand. Staying at our illustrious friend's home there, I lived a

---

1. *Gazette musicale,* 11 February 1838, pp. 57–62. Adolphe Pictet de Rochemont
(1799–1875), a friend from Liszt's Geneva days, was a member of one of that city's
oldest and most socially prominent families. An eclectic and gifted polymath, he was
not only an accomplished linguist, philologist, and Sanskrit scholar but also a ballis-
tics expert and a major in the Swiss artillery. Pictet had also accompanied Liszt, Sand,
et al. on the famous excursion to Chamonix, but he was so upset by the high- and
heavy-handed way Sand had treated him in her *Lettre d'un voyageur* no. 10 that he
wrote his own account of the holiday, *Une Course à Chamonix* (Paris, 1838; reprinted
Geneva, 1930).

2. The place and date cannot be taken literally, since Liszt and Marie d'Agoult
had already arrived in Italy by September. The itinerary in the d'Agoult *Mémoires* (pp.
105–6) indicates that they passed through Chambéry on their way from the *Grande
Chartreuse* to Geneva about the 7th or 8th of August. The article may well have been
begun at that time, but it was most likely completed during their stay at Lake Como.

full and rewarding life for three months, every hour of which I have devoutly stored away in my memory. Our days were simple and easy to fill. We did not have to kill time, to stage hunts in the royal forests, to give amateur theatricals or those so-called "country parties," to which the rich and fashionable bring their own boredom, adding it to the general stock of high spirits. Our activities and diversions were simply these: reading the works of some ingenious thinker or profound poet (Montaigne or Dante, Hoffmann or Shakespeare); reading a letter from an absent friend; taking long walks along the secluded banks of the Indre and then, upon returning, playing a melody to recapture the emotions of the walk; or listening to the joyful cries of the children who had just caught a beautiful sphinx moth with diaphanous wings or a poor, overly curious little warbler who had fallen from its nest onto the lawn. Is that all? Yes, truly everything. But, as you know, the joys of the soul are not measured by their surface but by their depth.

When night fell we gathered on the garden terrace. The last human sounds gradually faded in the distance. Nature seemed to retake possession of herself and to rejoice in man's absence by wafting all her voices and scents heavenwards. The distant murmur of the Indre reached us faintly. The nightingale sang its splendid love song, and the most humble creature of the countryside sounded its own clear, rich note to celebrate its part in Universal Being. A barely perceptible breeze brought us the linden's gentle scent and the larch's savage odor one after the other. The glimmer of our lamps cast fantastic hues on the trees, and then the woman whom I will not name, since she prefers, as Obermann said, not to be named,[3] came to us trailing her long white veil, her feet scarcely seeming to touch the ground,[4] and gently chided: "You incorrigible artists, there you are, still dreaming. Don't

---

3. Obermann is the hero of an 1804 novel of that name by Etienne Pivert de Senancour (1770–1846). A then-famous and influential book, set mostly in a remote Alpine valley, it is permeated by a brooding, listless melancholy and the hero's unrequited love for a Madame Del ——— who remains unnamed. The work was an inspiration for Liszt's *Vallée d'Obermann*.

4. George Sand described an almost identical scene in her diary for 12 June 1837: "This evening, while Franz was playing fantastic melodies of Schubert, the Princess [Marie d'Agoult] walked in the shadows that fall across the terrace. She was wearing a dress of an indefinite color. Her head and tall, slender body were swathed in a long white veil. As I watched her move back and forth with a light tread which scarcely touched the ground, the circle she described was cut across by rays from my lamp around which all the moths of the garden were dancing a delirious sarabande. The moon behind the lindens threw into high relief black specters of pine trees that stood immobile in the blue-gray air" (Sand, *The Intimate Journal of George Sand*, p. 69).

you know that the time for work has come." We yielded to her words, as though they came from an angel of peace and light. George, without giving it too much thought, wrote a beautiful book, and I went to reopen my old scores for the fifth time and to search the legacy of the masters for some traces of their various secrets.

But, as a truly safe retreat no longer exists for anyone who has become something of a celebrity and as everyone today tries to overcome his lack of personal merit by associating himself with the attainments and, above all, the fame of others, imagining that some of it will rub off on him, the château Nohant had become a lodestone for those people who have the misfortune to be consumed by this insatiable illusion. From the depths of their provincialism, they have plumbed the abysses of learning, and having found nothing there but the vacuity and emptiness of their own heads, they have gone about the world parading their big phrases and little persons, all with the aim of playing the Childe Harold with some middle-class sweetheart or the Don Juan to some flirtatious chambermaid. You can just imagine how my friend has fended off these troublesome pilgrims. The strictest orders about them were given and obeyed.

One day, nevertheless, one of them did succeed in outwitting the dogs' noses and the watchmen's vigilance. He had entered the grounds unobserved and reached the inside of the house itself, determined not to move a step or offer an apology. He knew that the mistress of the house, having guests, could not be absent for very long. He immediately announced his unshakable intention of waiting for her, even though it might be far into the night. He was an attorney without clients, and as we were standing there in full moonlight, nothing could keep him from carrying out his threat. We had to invent a strategem, one that would deliver us from these Byronian-styled pilgrims once and for all. It did not take very long.

The gardener was enjoying a visit at the time from his sister-in-law, a former chambermaid to the once-celebrated Madame S.G. During her long service in an artistic residence, this Celestine Cramer had become a very special individual who merged and summed up many diverse types of people within herself. She was as well read as the young lady in a lending library, as majestic as a lady-in-waiting to a Hildburghausen princess, as personable as a match seller, and as crafty as a concierge. In short, she was perfect for the role we wanted her to play. We had her don a satanic dressing gown, a Greek bonnet, and Persian slippers, and installed her at George Sand's desk, which we covered with an enormous pile of papers to represent her unpublished works. Nearby we put a monstrous inkstand, four or five of those pedantic books our friend George never reads, and, to complete the illusion and add a bit of local color, a small package of little cigars. We hid behind a screen, from which we could see and hear everything. The provincial attorney was then presented to the author of *Indiana*. With that the comedy began—one you cannot imagine and which you would find very difficult to believe, since I who was there even had to ask myself if I was really witnessing the bizarre proceedings with my own eyes. The attorney stepped forward in the half-lit room, visibly moved, but nonetheless more proud than embarassed with himself. Madame Cramer put him at ease by telling him with all the grace of a well-bred lady of the manor that word of his fame had long ago reached her in her solitude and that she considered herself fortunate to make the personal acquaintance of such a man as he. Sensing the importance of his position, he got right into the swim of things and broached literary matters straightaway without any circumlocutions. He strongly approved of the marriage of Simon and Fiammina, and that of Bernard Mauprat and Edmée. He stated that Jacques was a true portrait of himself, which he had recognized on every page. He admitted that he did not quite grasp the symbol of Lélia and asked the author how it could have eluded him.[5]

Madame Cramer, realizing that she was dealing with an unmitigated dunce, put him off with the promise of further explanations at their next meeting and then took charge of the conversation. She praised the novels of Balzac very highly, regretting, nonetheless, that they were not quite as moral as they should be. Then, with a sudden, scornfully assured air which almost made us burst out laughing, she launched into a diatribe against the weekly drivel written by the Viscount de Launay,[6] a would-be gentleman, declaring that neither his

5. All those mentioned are characters in Sand's novels. In reverse order: Lélia is a self-portrait of Sand, a despondent, poetic woman in search of herself in an 1833 autobiographical novel of that name. Jacques is the hero of an 1834 novel bearing his name, a noble and understanding husband who is so opposed to the institution of marriage that he sacrifices himself by leaping into a crevasse so that his young wife can find happiness with her lover. Bernard, the title character in *Mauprat* (1837), is a brute of a man who is thoroughly transformed and domesticated by the patient love of the charming, vivacious Edmée. Fiammina is the aristocratic heroine of *Simon* (1836), a noble woman who forsakes both her position and fortune to marry her true love, Simon, a rising young attorney of peasant stock. Generally regarded as the first of Sand's "socially conscious" novels, *Simon* is dedicated, almost ironically it would seem, to Marie d'Agoult.

6. The printed text reads "d'Hantuez," but as this individual has resisted all attempts at identification, it seems reasonable that the name is a misprint for "de Launay." Charles de Launay was the pen name of Madame Emile de Giradin—i.e., Del-

prose nor his poetry was worth reading since it was, after all, nothing but chambermaid literature. At this point the children entered. Their tutor gave an account of the morning's studies. Madame Cramer portioned out praise and blame, finishing with a very fine speech on the advantages of applying oneself and the need for obedience.

Awestruck by such eloquence, the attorney stood there with his mouth open. He remarked that two or three missing teeth and a few grey locks were not at all unbecoming to the author of *Lélia* and that her face—aged with fatigue, drawn and wrinkled by the passions and storms of life—had far more character than the serene and beautiful features that Delacroix and Calamatta[7] had flatteringly given to George Sand, and he departed, happy in the fondness they had come to declare for each other. I leave it to you to imagine how we complimented Madame Cramer on the way she carried off the deception. Puffed up like a bullfrog, the attorney hurried off to recount the impressive welcome he had received. But it was not long before the whole countryside learned the true story and our ill-fated visitor became the butt of countless jokes. People like him have vanished from Nohant since that day, and by now the whole race has apparently been exterminated.

But I keep forgetting that I am speaking to a most serious man who, deeply immersed in Sanskrit, regards Bach's fugues and the books of Barchou de Penhoën as light pastimes which never engage the truly serious portions of his intellect. Above all I forget that, as a good and faithful friend, you are solicitously following the very slow and so far rather halting progress of my musical labors, that you want an account of my working hours, and that you are surprised—yes, you too—to see me occupied so exclusively with the piano, so disinclined to attack the far broader fields of symphonic and operatic composition. Have no doubt about it, you have touched a very sensitive spot. By talking to me about forsaking the piano, you have no idea how you force me to face a day of sadness, a day that will obliterate[8] all of a foremost portion of my life linked inextricably to it. Because, you see,

---

phine Gay (1804–1855)—who wrote a very successful column of literary and salon gossip for her husband's newspaper *La Presse*. These columns, 1836–1839, were collected and published as the *Lettres parisiennes* in 1843.

7. Luigi Calamatta (1802–1869), an Italian engraver, pupil of Ingres, who was active for a time in Paris and known mostly for his portraits.

8. In the printed text of this important passage the verb is "éclaira" (will illuminate, enlighten) which, being totally contrary to the tenor of the thought, is quite possibly a misreading of "écrasera" (will crush, overwhelm, obliterate), and that is the reading adopted here.

my piano is to me what a ship is to the sailor, what a steed is to the Arab, and perhaps more because even now my piano is myself, my speech, and my life. It is the intimate personal depository of everything that stirred wildly in my brain during the most impassioned days of my youth. It was there that all my wishes, all my dreams, all my joys, and all my sorrows lay. Its strings quivered under all my passions, its docile keys obeyed my every whim. And you, my friend, would have me hurry to forsake it in order to chase after the more brilliant, resounding success of the operatic and symphonic worlds? Oh! no. Even if I concede that which you no doubt acknowledge too easily, namely, that I am already too old for a pact of this sort, I have definitely made up my mind not to abandon the study and cultivation of the piano until I have done everything possible or, at least, everything that I can possibly do for it today.

Perhaps this sort of mysterious feeling which binds me to the piano is a delusion, yet I consider the piano extremely important. In my opinion it ranks highest in the instrumental hierarchy. It is the most widely cultivated and popular of all instruments. Its importance and popularity are due in part to the harmonic capability that it alone possesses, and consequently to its ability to recapitulate and concentrate all of musical art within itself. Within the span of its seven octaves it encompasses the audible range of an orchestra, and the ten fingers of a single person are enough to render the harmonies produced by the union of over a hundred concerted instruments. The piano is a means of disseminating works that would otherwise remain unknown or unfamiliar to the general public because of the difficulty involved in assembling an orchestra. Thus it bears the same relation to an orchestral work that an engraving bears to a painting; it multiplies the original and makes it available to everyone, and even if it does not reproduce the colors, it at least reproduces the light and shadow.

Thanks to improvements that have already been made and those that the diligent efforts of pianists add every day, the piano is continuing to expand its assimilative capability. We play arpeggios like a harp, sustained notes like the wind instruments, and staccatos and a thousand other passages that one time seemed to be the special province of one instrument or another. The improvements forecast in piano making will undoubtedly provide us before long with the variety of sonority we still lack. Pianos with a *pedal bass,* the polyplectron, the claviharp,[9] and several other as yet tentative endeavors, all call attention

9. Both the claviharp and the polyplectron were invented by the Parisian instrument maker Joh. Christian Dietz or his son. The claviharp (1814), a keyed harp, had

to a widely felt need for the instrument's further development. The expressive keyboard of the organ will naturally lead to the creation of pianos with two or three keyboards, and with this advance the piano will complete its peaceful conquest.

Even though we still lack the essential element of varied sonority, we have nonetheless managed to produce symphonic effects that are satisfactory and which were completely beyond the ken of our predecessors, because the *arrangements* made up to now of great vocal and instrumental compositions betray, in their poverty and uniform emptiness, the lack of confidence that they had in the instrument's resources. The fainthearted accompaniments, poorly distributed melodies, truncated passages, and meager chords were more of a *traduction* than a *translation* of the ideas of Mozart and Beethoven. If I am not mistaken, I am the one who first proposed a new method of transcription in my piano score of the *Symphonie fantastique*. I applied myself as scrupulously as if I were translating a sacred text to transferring, not only the symphony's musical framework, but also its detailed effects and the multiplicity of its instrumental and rhythmic combinations to the piano. The difficulty did not faze me, as my feeling for art and my love of it gave me double courage. I may not have succeeded completely, but that first attempt has at least demonstrated that the way is open and that it will no longer be acceptable to *arrange* the masters' works as contemptibly as has been done to this point. I called my work a *partition de piano* [piano score] in order to make clear my intention of following the orchestra step by step and of giving it no special treatment beyond the mass and variety of its sound.[10] The procedure I followed for Berlioz's symphony I am currently applying to those by Beethoven. The serious study of his works, a profound feeling for their virtually infinite beauty and for the piano's resources, which have be-

---

silk-covered strings and a keyboard mechanism to pluck them with a gentle, side-swiping motion. The later polyplectron was designed to reproduce the sound of a string orchestra or quartet. It consisted of several bows attached to a spindle and set in motion by a keyboard. Liszt was among the musicians present when Dietz introduced the instrument at a special concert given in January 1833 (*L'Artiste*, 27 January 1833, p. 316).

10. Maurice Schlesinger published the score in November 1834 (Liszt himself had underwritten the cost of it). It was through the piano score that many musicians first came to know Berlioz's work, since it was not performed orchestrally outside Paris until October 1842 (nearly twelve years after its premiere) and Berlioz's own orchestral score was not published until 1845. Robert Schumann, for instance, used the Liszt score for his perceptive analysis of the *Symphonie* in the *Neue Zeitschrift für Musik*, July-August 1835.

come familiar to me through constant practice, have perhaps made me less unfit than anyone for this laborious task. The first four symphonies are already transcribed, and the others will be completed shortly.[11] I will then put this type of work aside because, while it was important for someone to do it conscientiously at first, there are others in the future who will no doubt do it as well or better than I did.

Once the "arrangements," or, more to the point, the usual "derangements," are no longer possible, that title will properly revert to the infinite number of "caprices" and "fantasies" that inundate us and which consist of nothing but motifs pilfered from all types of music stitched together for better or for worse. When I see a composer's name pompously attached to these types of compositions, which, for the most part, have no value except what is imparted to them by the relative popularity of the opera from which the motifs are taken,[12] I am always reminded of what Pascal said: "Certain authors when speaking of their works say: my book, my commentary, my account, etc. They are like worthy citizens with a town house of their own and an everlasting 'my house' on their lips. They would do better to say: our book, our commentary, our account, etc., seeing that there is usually more of other people's work than their own therein."[13]

Thus the piano has, on one hand, the capacity to assimilate, to concentrate all musical life within itself and, on the other, its own existence, its own growth and individual development. It is simultaneously, as an ancient Greek might say, a *microcosm* and a *microthea* (a miniature world and a miniature god). As to its own development, its preeminence is unquestionably assured by both the number and the quality of the pieces written for it. Historical research would show us since its beginnings an uninterrupted succession not only of famous

11. Liszt's wording is ambiguous; he actually means that Symphonies nos. 5, 6, and 7, and possibly a part of Symphony no. 3 were transcribed. In corresponding with Lambert Massart (then acting as his agent in Paris) about the scores' publication, Liszt also sent him a brief preface to the Symphonies which summarizes all the points he makes in this article about the piano (see Vier, *Liszt-Artiste*, pp. 149–50).

12. Since opera fantasies—combining as they did pianistic display with melodies that the unsophisticated audiences of the day would find familiar—were the *sine qua non* of virtually every practicing virtuoso of the time, Liszt composed and performed his fair share of them. The best of his works in this genre—e.g., the Fantasies on *Norma, Don Juan,* or *Robert le diable*—do, however, show a far greater respect for the dramatic integrity of the parent opera than do the works of his contemporaries (see Charles Suttoni, Introduction to Liszt, *Piano Transcriptions from French and Italian Operas*).

13. *Pascal's Pensées,* p. 504. The editor, H. F. Stewart, credits the thought to Jacques-Bénigne Bossuet.

performers but also of transcendant composers who cultivated this instrument in preference to all others. The piano works of Mozart, Beethoven, and Weber are not their least important claims to glory; they are an essential part of the legacy that has been left to us. These masters were remarkable pianists in their own day, and they never stopped composing for their preferred instrument. I do not know but that there is as much passion in some of Weber's piano pieces as there is in *Euryanthe* and *Der Freischütz;* as much learning, depth, and poetry in Beethoven's sonatas as in some of his symphonies. Do not be surprised, then, that I, their humble disciple, should aspire to follow them—at a considerable distance, alas—and that my first course, my dearest ambition, would be to leave to pianists who come after me some useful lessons, an outline of some advancements that I made—a work, in short, that worthily represents my studies and diligent efforts as a young pianist.[14] And, mind you, I must also confess that I am still not that far removed from the time when I had to learn La Fontaine's verses by heart and have never forgotten the tale of the overly greedy dog who dropped the succulent bone he held in his mouth to chase after a phantom reflected in the river, where he ultimately drowned.[15] Let me, therefore, gnaw on my bone in peace; the day will come soon enough, perhaps, when I will drown in the pursuit of some immense and unattainable phantom.

Upon leaving Berri—where I had lived within a small circle of those warm personal attachments one is tempted to describe as selfish, such was the contentment they offered—I went to Lyons and found myself in the midst of such horrible suffering, such cruel distress, that a sense of injustice rose within me and brought on a feeling of inexpressible sadness. What torture, my friend, to stand there with your arms folded and watch an entire population struggle vainly with suffering that preys upon the soul as well as the body! To see old age without peace, youth without hope, childhood without joy! To see everyone

14. Liszt is reputed to have written a piano method for the Geneva Conservatory, which was lost [?] when the printing plates were inadvertently destroyed (Claude Tappolet, *La vie musicale à Genève au dix-neuvième siècle,* p. 42). Nevertheless, rumors of a Liszt method, fueled by this statement, persisted for years. But late in life Liszt himself flatly stated: "I have never written such a work and never thought of doing so, because a number of praiseworthy works of this sort have been published, and I have no talent for discussing the rules of performance, interpretation, and expression in pedagogic terms. I can only communicate something of them on a personal basis" (Lina Ramann, *Lisztiana,* p. 39).

15. La Fontaine, "The Dog who Dropped his Mouthful for a Shadow," book 6, fable 17.

huddled together in foul little hovels envying those among them who work for next to nothing to embellish opulence and idleness! . . . Because—oh, the cruel irony of fate!—those who do not have a pillow on which to lay their heads use their hands to fashion the luxurious spreads on which the indolent rich will rest; those who have nothing but rags to cover their own nakedness weave the gold brocades that will clothe queens; and little children, who never know a mother's smile, bend over the looms, staring blankly at the arabesques and flowers that take shape beneath their fingers and that will become the playthings for the children of the high and mighty.

Oh, merciless law of social fatality! when will your brazen tablets be shattered by the Angel of Wrath? Oh, you tears, sighs, and groans of the people! when will you bridge the abyss that still separates us from the reign of justice?

For want of the benevolence that has found no place in our hearts, the giving of alms has, at least, become one of our habits. In Lyons, as in Paris and elsewhere, when human suffering exceeds the limits set by some sort of tacit agreement, a general appeal is made to people in all walks of life. A praiseworthy zeal then takes hold of all the social classes, and a thousand ingenious ways are devised to confound greed. The appeal takes a thousand different forms and does not shrink from the shocking contrast between the gala charity balls and the misery of the poor, so that an appeal to vanity and pleasure seeking will yield the alms that the love for humanity had failed to produce. The most elegant ladies employ their charms, turning flirtation into a Christian virtue; maidens, obeying the two-fold precept of work and charity, scatter golden pearls from cashmere purses; men form committees and spend days gravely discussing the number of chandeliers or the color of the hangings which are to decorate the gala. For God's sake, kind Sirs, do hurry your philanthropic discussions a bit, because an old man has fallen dead on your doorstep at this very moment and a mother has just sold her daughter.

This, however, is not to say that these actions are not good, very good. To desire the good is already a good thing; to tell a needy person that you are thinking about him is to comfort him to some extent; to give a thought to humanity amid self-centered pleasures is an accomplishment—and that, perhaps, is all that we are able to do at present. Accordingly, I have always considered it a duty to associate myself with charitable societies at every opportunity—except that on the day following those concerts in which I had taken part, I have seen the patrons of the gala praising and congratulating themselves on the amount raised, while I continued on my way, my head lowered, pondering the fact that when the alms are distributed each family might receive one loaf of bread to eat and one stick of wood for the fire.

Eighteen centuries have passed since Christ preached the Brotherhood of Man, and His Word is still not really understood! It burns like a sacred flame in the hearts of some men, but it does not illuminate others, and this generation which has risen to the most enlightened concepts of the mind still remains plunged in the darkest ignorance of the heart. Much like a doctor who thinks he can heal a sick person by keeping the pestilential matter suppressed inside him, society vainly thinks it can cure a deep wound by applying a palliative that does not go below the surface. Those who hold the fate of nations in their hands too often forget that submissive compliance will not remain the virtue of the masses for very long and that when the people have moaned long enough, they will suddenly be heard to roar.

What is art, the artist to do in these terrible times? The painters exhibit pictures and the musicians give concerts for the benefit of the poor. No doubt they do well to be concerned in this way, if only to demonstrate their ever-present desire to serve the cause of the working class. But should they really limit themselves to something as partial or as incomplete as that? For too long they have been regarded as courtiers and parasites of the palace. For too long they have celebrated the affairs of the great and the pleasures of the rich. The time has come for them to restore courage to the weak and to ease the suffering of the oppressed. Art must remind the people of the beautiful self-sacrifice, the heroic determination, the fortitude, and the humanity of their peers. The Providence of God must be announced anew to the people. The dawn of a better day must be shown to them so that they can hold themselves in readiness for it and hope can inspire noble virtues in them. Above all, the Light must flood their spirit from all sides, the sweet joy of art must take its place in people's homes, so that they too will come to know life's prize and never turn barbaric in their vengeance or merciless in their frustration.

I had the good fortune in Lyons to see Nourrit again, that eminent artist whose talent is now lost to the Paris Opéra,[16] but who is

16. An uncommonly sensitive person, Nourrit had left the Paris Opéra in 1837 rather than contend with the rivalry that would have inevitably developed between him and the Opéra's newly acquired tenor, Gilbert-Louis Duprez. Although Liszt does not mention it, he and Nourrit gave a benefit at Lyons's Grand Théâtre on 3 August that produced some 4,500 francs for needy workers. Liszt played his Fantasies on "Frequenti palpiti" and La Juive. Nourrit sang Schubert songs—including "Erlkönig"—with Liszt accompanying.

destined to exercise a great and positive influence wherever he appears, no matter what he chooses to do. Given his beliefs and sympathies, it was inevitable that we would meet one day traveling the same path, and I regard the chance I had to shake his hand at the farthest French limits of my journey as a good omen. A mutual friend, Madame Montgolfier,[17] brought us together every day. Schubert's lieder, which Nourrit sings with considerable power, produced a spate of excitement in us which gradually spread to our little audience. One evening while he was rendering "Erlkönig," M ——,[18] who understands the full depth and sublimity of Schubert and Goethe, took a pencil and on an album leaf wrote a kind of free translation, a paraphrase of the song, which I am now sending you to make amends for the trouble of reading this overly long letter.

Farewell

"Erlkönig" while Nourrit was singing it

Do you hear in the terrifying shadows the galloping of a horse, its flanks bloodied by spurs? Do you hear the roaring wind, the rustling leaves? Do you see the father holding in his arms a child who grows pale and presses close to his breast?

"Oh my father, do you see the Erlking down there?"

The horse gallops, gallops on. It devours the distance. Its hooves, flashing over the stones, kick up a thousand sparks that intensify the terror of the shadows.

"Have no fear, my son, it is only a passing cloud."

But a suave, soft voice is heard from behind the curtain of leaves. Heed it not, for it is as treacherous and false as a siren's call.

"Father, my father, did you not hear what the Erlking told me so softly?"

The horse gallops, gallops on. It devours the distance. Its hooves, flashing over the stones, kick up a thousand sparks that intensify the terror of the shadows.

"Calm yourself, my son, it is nothing. Just dry leaves rustling in the wind."

---

17. Jenny Montgolfier (ca. 1790–1879), an accomplished pianist, was a leader in Lyons's social and musical life. Liszt had first met her when he was a boy of fourteen in May 1826, and the two remained close friends.

18. Marie d'Agoult. A bit of poetic license here, as her paraphrase of Goethe's text was actually written in June at Nohant (d'Agoult, *Mémoires,* p. 86).

The voice resumes—sweeter, more endearing, more seductive. It promises the child perfumed flowers, games along the river banks, dances to the sound of joyful instruments.

"Oh father, my father, do you not see the Erlking's daughters down there, dancing strange dances?"

"My child, I see them now. They are the trunks of old willows. From afar they look like gray phantoms."

Still sweet and suave, the voice resumes. Then suddenly it threatens! The child gives a tortured cry. . . .

"Father, my father, the Erlking has seized me."

The father feels a cold sweat flood his face. He spurs the horse's flanks and presses his moaning son to his breast. At last he reaches his destination. He breathes. His anguish is over. In his arms he holds his child . . . dead.

Do you see the dreams of your youth pass before your eyes? Do you hear the voice of experience? Are you watching the struggle between the Ideal and the Real? Oh poets, poets, and you women who are all poets at heart, hearken to the dark and desperate words of genius: beware the Erlking; he is constantly seeking new victims.[19]

19. Although this closing paragraph is, of course, Marie d'Agoult's gloss and not part of Goethe's text, the whole paraphrase is indicative of the potent spell the song cast over its hearers. One Lyons critic who attended the Nourrit-Liszt benefit had this to say: "To fully understand all that is moving, terrifying, and uncanny in "Erlkönig," one has to hear that celebrated ballad by Goethe and Schubert performed by Liszt and Adolphe Nourrit. Who but Nourrit would be able to convey in such a precise and distinct manner the three totally different voices of the father, the child, and the Erlking? . . . Who but Nourrit could excite such feelings of pity and terror and move the audience so profoundly? . . . But then, who but Liszt could follow the singer through all the nuances of his interpretation and instill his playing with an energy and power that doubled the terror the audience felt when hearing the cries of the doomed child? Who but Liszt, taking those many rapid scales, whose thunder-like rumblings make us shudder with fear, would have dared to intensify their reverberations by playing them in octaves?" (*Courrier de Lyon,* 7 August 1837, cited in Jacques-Gabriel Prod'homme, "Les Oeuvres des Schubert en France," p. 19).

5

FROM SAVOY TO THE ITALIAN LAKES

CHRONICLE

5 August 1837. Having resumed their way to Italy, Liszt and Marie
d'Agoult make the almost unavoidable pilgrimage to the monastery *Grande Chartreuse* near Grenoble.

6–10 August. They stop to see Blandine at the Savoy town of Etram-
bière. Satisfied that she is in good hands and flourishing, they
continue on to Geneva to visit friends and prepare for their
journey through the Bernese Alps and the Simplon Pass down
into Italy.[1]

17 August. The travelers reach their first stop in Italy; Baveno on the
shore of Lake Maggiore. They spend about a week exploring the
area, including neighboring Lake Como.

End of August. They arrive in Milan, and Liszt quickly presents himself to the music publisher Giovanni Ricordi.

3 September. Liszt performs at Ricordi's.

6 September. He and Marie return to Lake Como, where they settle
for about two months in the lakeside town of Bellagio. Liszt
works diligently at the piano in the isolated, idyllic setting and

---

1. In view of Liszt's comments in some of the following articles, it is well to
recall that Italy was still a collection of separate small states and duchies, many of
which were under Austrian control: the Lombardy-Venetia area extending across
most of northern Italy was, in fact, an Austrian province; a Habsburg archduchess,
Marie-Louise, ruled in Parma; and the grand duke of Tuscany was also a German
prince. The Austrians kept a rather close watch over political matters, and censorship
was strict.

completes several pieces of his *Impressions et poésies*[2] and his set of *Grandes études*[3] there.

Early November. They leave Bellagio and move to Como, which is closer to Milan, so that Marie can await her coming confinement.

The two articles written in the fall of 1837, both addressed to Louis de Ronchaud, are devoted for the most part to describing the lovers' travel experiences.

To Louis de Ronchaud[1]

[September 1837]

You wanted to leave us. Neither the appeals to friendship nor the lure of a delightful country could keep you with us. How is it, then, that when you shook her hand you turned away so that she could not see your tears? How is it that when I pressed you to my breast I felt the repressed sobs that were about to burst forth from yours, despite yourself? Was it not you, and you alone, who wanted it this way? But who am I to ask why the brusque departure, why you left with apparently so little reason? You are at the difficult age when a young man shakes off affection like a shackle, when he hurriedly tries to appear insensitive in order to let it be known that he has become a man. The serenity of your life already tires you and the purity of your young face bores you; you wish that passions had ravaged the one and wrinkles had creased the other. You hear exotic voices in the distance exhorting you to live.

2. These pieces—*Le Lac de Wallenstadt, Vallée d'Obermann,* etc.—are part of Liszt's *Album d'un voyageur.* Ostensibly, they owe their inspiration to the tour of Switzerland in June-July 1835, but it is difficult to ascertain whether they were conceived at that time or at a later date (see Alexander Main, "Liszt and Lamartine," pp. 137–40).

3. The *Vingt-quatre* [sic] *grandes études* were a radical revision of the twelve studies Liszt first published in 1826. They, in turn, were also revised and republished in 1852 as the *Transcendental Etudes.*

1. *Gazette musicale,* 25 March 1838, pp. 125–29. Louis de Ronchaud (1816–1887) was a young writer and later an art historian whom Liszt and Marie d'Agoult had first met in Geneva and was one of their dearest friends. In later years, after the d'Agoult-Liszt affair had run its course, Ronchaud remained the countess's close devoted friend, advisor, and eventually her literary executor. He edited her posthumous *Mes Souvenirs 1806–1833* (Paris, 1877).

The demon curiosity goads you, and you are convinced that the noble poetic instinct stirring inside you like some anticipated remorse over inevitable mistakes can no longer be held in check. Go on, then, leave us. Scatter the treasures of your youth to the winds. Hurry and strip yourself of them. Abandon yourself to everything, since you want "to do something," as you say.

An artist's single-minded dedication and limited sphere of activity strike you as a symptom of weakness or inadequacy. You are almost reproachful when you see me plowing my narrow furrow, and my heaven appears very somber to you, as you find only one star there. Your restless spirit demands public controversies, the crowd's acclamations, the thrill of fame, and the excitement of fleeting love affairs all at once. You lay claim to the impossible with a simplicity that is charming. Nothing would seem more natural to you than the fulfillment of our most disorderly ambitions. Go ahead then, beautiful young poet. Soon, too soon, no doubt, you will return to us with your heart filled with disenchantment, or even disabused about the holy desire for the Good, and with your thirst for the Ideal sadly slaked by the bitter water of experience. May God keep you calm, as he does me, your elder by several weighty years, with my one furrow to plow on earth and one star to contemplate in the heavens!

The day after we parted I went up the Saône and arrived at Lamartine's home, finding there as you have often told me, the happy poet of the age. In an era of strife, instability, and fierce rivalries, his name suddenly appeared to us shining above the storms.[2] By revealing himself to everyone at the same time that he came to know himself, he experienced no lengthy period of waiting, no arrogant patronage, no cautionary advice from mediocre busybodies. He was not tormented by doubt, and even when he saw the crowd remain indifferent to his words, he never had to ask himself if the phantom he took to be his genius was not perhaps the gigantic spectre of his own conceit. The first song from his lyre reverberated in free, pure air. His breast swelled easily in an atmosphere that the breath of envy was unable to taint. From the moment he first appeared among us, the young man was greeted as the Annointed of the Lord, as one of those rulers of the mind whose very imperfections are holy, and on the day following his first moment of fame, his place in history was assured. There is no denying that there are many reasons for this exceptional destiny—for

2. Liszt is evidently referring to Lamartine's first published work, the *Méditations poétiques* (1820), which was a great and instant success.

this popularity so instantly attained and so constantly sustained—because a genius usually does not conquer in so peaceful a manner and must overcome a thousand obstacles to be recognized. He is misunderstood for a long time, violently attacked, and quite frequently repudiated for fully half of his century. But it was different with Lamartine; his poems were welcomed under the best circumstances possible.

Chateaubriand gloriously established a new literature in France. He made an unknown or, rather, a forgotten poetry burst forth from Christianity. By simultaneously striking those two chords, love and religion, that forever vibrate within humanity, he sounded celestial harmonies that held souls captive. But the arch-eccentricity of his style, the perhaps immoderate lavishness of his imagery, and the "romanticism" of his manner, to use an expression of the time, gave rise to much harsh criticism. Moreover, by creating such heroines as Atala, the free-spirited daughter of the Natchez Indians, or Velléda, the druidess crowned with mistletoe,[3] and by placing his lovers on the banks of the Meschacebé [Mississippi] river in the forests of America, he alienated a large group of readers whose minds are not very venturesome and who, as common sense dictates, prefer the known to the unknown, who want to enjoy themselves without effort and to recognize themselves clearly in the traits of the characters presented to them. A writer who innovates beyond a certain point does so at his peril. The poet, by the power of genius, may well entice readers a little beyond their accustomed limits, but if he rashly throws himself on unbeaten paths, across unknown distances, the reader is startled, becomes bored, and finally abandons him in the desert.[4]

Lamartine, however, had the gift of knowing just how far innovation could go. His Elvira[5] charms without surprising us, since there is hardly a man who did not believe in his youth that he would meet an Elvira, hardly anyone who has not sometimes fancied himself a dreamer "in the shade of an old oak tree" or "beneath the vaulted

3. Atala is the heroine, a chaste Christian convert, in the 1801 novel of that name. Vélleda, who appears in book 9 of *Les Martyrs* (1809), is a priestess in Gaul who urges her people to revolt against their Roman conquerors. Bellini's librettist, Felice Romani, used Chateaubriand's account of her as one of his sources for *Norma*.

4. In *Atala,* as in Abbé Prevost's *Manon Lescaut* (1731), the lands of Louisiana are described as a "desert," and both ill-starred heroines expire there.

5. Elvira is the idealized woman who figures in Lamartine's early poems. She is for the most part a poetic reflection of his deep love for a Madame Julie Charles, the invalid wife of an elderly Paris physician.

arches of a Gothic church." By not dramatizing his feelings and by contenting himself with a meditative lyricism, Lamartine also appeals to those basically subjective readers who love to find themselves reflected in everything and can thus easily inject their own stories into the harmonious framework of his divine poetry. But later, the characters created by his imitators cheapened the open-air reverie and vaporous passions to such an extent that if Lamartine himself returned after ten years, he would have had a difficult time forcing his way through the crowd of Elvira-lovers, the forest of old oak trees, and the flood of azure lakes. Still, when the hour for review and criticism first arrived, his name was sanctified and his fame was above question. The reviews were respectful and the criticism very deferential. And when his later works were attacked, his poet's crown of laurel was so laden with foliage and flowers that he could well afford to lose some of its lower branches.

Saint-Point is a delightful residence where Lamartine actively devotes himself to fulfilling those duties that our parliamentary practices have laid out for him in the Department's affairs.[6] It is a great source of wonderment to the populace, since they regard poets and artists as beings divorced from all reality, feeding on nothing but idle dreams, and slumbering like Brahma in a luminous mist. Lamartine the juror, Lamartine the member of the General Council, Lamartine the Deputy is for many people an anomaly, a problem; the good folks cannot reconcile themselves to it. They still do not perceive that the poets and artists of our modern civilizations are no longer glorious *pariahs* whose genius isolates them from the rest of humanity, but rather men who live a life common to all—loving, suffering, and working in communion with all those who live, suffer, and work—and that their behavior and domestic habits are no more outlandish than those of the most prosaic, middle-class citizens of Charpentras or Tarascon. How strange, you say, that despite experience and reason, popular prejudice presupposes that a man who is gifted with superior talents must for that very reason lack the simple good sense to manage civil and political affairs! Strange? No. Who doesn't know that prejudices that flatter mediocrity take hold with a marvelous ease in direct proportion to their absurdity? Who hasn't seen the incredible speed with which harebrained notions circulate? And aren't we aware that some errors are as endemic as those maladies which rule the atmosphere for a time, and that people adopt them as unthinkingly as the air they breathe?

6. Lamartine was elected to the Chamber of Deputies in 1833.

The *Grande Chartreuse!*[7] That mournfully mysterious name, doesn't it summarize all the hazy and indeterminate thinking about the world that Christian asceticism has given birth to for over ten centuries? The holy madness, the willing self-torture, the obscure martyrs, the stubborn self-denial, all the silent, somber protests against the rule of Satan, the mystical aversion to carnal pleasure—don't they seem to evoke the pale ghosts of those solitary men who, known only to God, went through life with their eyes fixed on the tomb, bending their will to an iron rule, and totally absorbed in the fierce and savage desire for an incomprehensible world?

It used to be that one could only reach Saint Bruno's retreat by a narrow, rocky path. The pilgrim's feet were lacerated by the stones as if to prepare his heart for the lacerations of penance. Today civilization, triumphing everywhere, has smoothed out the holy route; a road has replaced the steep path, and before the year is out one will be able to reach the *Grande Chartreuse* by carriage.

We climb a rather gentle slope beside a mountain stream and always in the shadow of fir, beech, and chestnut trees. The farther we go into the gorge, the narrower and darker it becomes. The murmur of the stream is replaced by silence. The vegetation of ever-increasing beauty seems to want to draw man to the Lord's peace and hold him there. I have made a great number of climbs in the Alps, but nowhere have I seen such continuity. The Alps are divided into three distinct and contrasting regions: the first consists of vegetation and farm lands, then comes the region of fir trees and pasture land, which gradually grows poorer and sparser until it reaches the region of cliffs and eternal snows. Here, though, there are no breaks, no divisions; a carpet of greenery is always under our feet, a dome of leaves over our heads, and everywhere a hidden voice that says: *Venite ad me omnes qui laboratis.*

It is the Feast of the Assumption.[8] After a four-hour climb, the bells tell us that we are approaching the monastery. I enter the chapel, where they are celebrating the triumph of the Mother of God. I take a seat beside the same pillar where I had heard the funereal chants of the Requiem Mass ten months before. For an instant I could well believe that I had never left my place, so little was the difference between the

7. The *Grande Chartreuse,* located between Grenoble and Chambéry, is the mother house of the Carthusian Order of monks. The order's founder, Saint Bruno, built the first "convent" on the site in the eleventh century. The present buildings date from the seventeenth century.

8. The 15th of August. The visit, to be precise, actually took place ten days earlier (d'Agoult, *Mémoires,* p. 103).

hymns of joy and the canticles of sorrow. Both were monotonous, un-accented psalmody; a cavernous murmur of voices broken by old age, destroyed by abstinence; more of a mysterious hum than music; sounds, like the breasts from which they issued, which had nothing of the living or the human left in them. I hurried to return to the open air and stood for a long time on the lawn stretching before the mon-astery, reflecting on a group of children playing knucklebones and two superb cows grazing nonchalantly and confidently on the scented greenery. Steep peaks covered with leafy trees rose all about me, and a bird, a single bird, filled the air with its repeated call.

What a contrast, my friend! What symbols of life! What an anachronism a monastery like the *Grande Chartreuse* is in the nine-teenth century! How is it that the papacy has not realized that the time has come to revivify an institution that no longer makes any sense, no longer stands for an idea, no longer fills a need and must necessarily crumble into dust? No doubt a pope of genius, a pope who under-stood his age as well as the Gregorys and Innocents had understood theirs, could have derived an enormous profit from the monasteries by converting them to intellectual enterprises or even to industrial use. He would thus have erased the stain of greed that has made monasti-cism so odious to the people. He would have added the religious ele-ment that is now missing from the speculation about industrial society which absorb every one today. Men of God, by sharing the labors of the working class, would have earned the right to preach Christian morality to them. Through this simple modification of monastic reg-ulations—with no change whatsoever in dogma—the papacy might have been able to reclaim a great number of people for Christianity and by thus working with the spirit of the times, it would have re-gained a portion of the influence that it had obtained by other means in the past.

The spirit of association[9] is spreading so among us that I would not be at all surprised to see the formation of a new sort of cloister before too long; that is, groups of artists, thinkers, and workers living together under an agreed-upon rule and sharing their investigations and discoveries in common. In this way, the egoism that isolates men from one another would be more assuredly overcome than by monas-tic isolation. There would be less time wasted on material concerns, not as many intelligent people would be smothered by poverty, and fewer errors and delusions would persist since the eye of all would play

9. The "spirit of association," that is, communal life and property, was one of the Saint-Simonians' major tenets.

over every individual. . . . But enough of suppositions and theories; I have many magnificent realities to tell you about.

A traveler's life abounds in contrasts. The ghost of Voltaire and the statue of Rousseau, those great destroyers of monasteries, awaited us on the shores of Lake Geneva. Farther on is the Castle of Ripaille, the retreat of that epicurian philosopher who rid his brow of the double burden of tiara and crown and wished to leave no souvenir of himself other than a popular saying that expresses joy and well-being in two languages.[10] Behold the Pissevache, that proud cascade, exposing its charms like a courtesan. And then the bashful nymph of Turtmann, hiding among the rocks and upon whom the waters fall soft and white, like the feathers of a young swan. We cross the rugged Simplon Pass whose angry chasms and marble blocks, entrenched since the beginning of the world, had forged a hero's will. We remain silent and lower our eyes because we feel very small wherever Napoleon has left his trace.[11]

When we arrived at Baveno on the shores of Lake Maggiore a boat took us to Isola Madre. Once an arid rock, the island is now filled with the most marvelous vegetation. Lemon and orange trees cover its walls with a perfumed tapestry. The sassafras, camphor, and magnolia trees create delightful bowers, and a Scotch pine lifts its stern head above them, like a disillusioned philosopher standing in the middle of a joyful, laughing crowd. The bronze-leaved aloe clings to a rock, spreading ardent stamens that flower only once in its life!—But night has come; the moonlight on the water plows a luminous furrow that trembles like the belief in divine matters in our doubting, hesitant souls. The holy bells from all the villages bordering the lake call and respond to each other. . . . Behold the stars as they too call across the heavens. . . . Tell me, what is this thing within us, worthless and miserable as we are, that puts us into communion with these infinite marvels?

10. The phrase is "faire ripaille"—or in Italian "andare a Ripaglia"—which means "to feast in convivial company." The epicurian who inspired it was Amadeus VIII (1383–1451), first Duke of Savoy. He renounced his crown when he abdicated in favor of his son in 1434. He then retired to the Castle of Ripaille with a select group of companions, the Knights of Saint Maurice, a semi-monastic order he had founded whose members divided their time between those days devoted to prayer and fasting and those given over to philosophical discussion and the good life. Amadeus was then elected anti-pope, Felix V, in 1439 at the Council of Basel, but he renounced his tiara when he also resigned that position a decade later.

11. Napoleon had crossed through the Simplon Pass early in 1796 on his way to take northern Italy from the Austrians.

At Sesto Calende an honorable police official detains me for three days over who knows what technicality about my passport.[12] They rummage through our trunks, but everything is in order. Decidedly, there is nothing less *pleasant* than an Austrian customs official standing in the shade of an olive tree, and Bernadin de Saint-Pierre himself would have had a very hard time discovering the *harmony* between these two providential creations.[13] It must be understood, though, that I am speaking from a purely picturesque point of view and do not mean to imply anything that would be contrary to the rights of His Majesty, the Emperor of Austria.

I think I would be lacking in gratitude if I did not mention the coachman who took us from Geneva to Milan, as it is difficult to imagine entering Italy under more pleasant auspices. Exquisitely civil toward "Your Excellencies," always laughing and singing, apostrophizing in turn "those damned flies" and the pretty girls, a matchless mimic, a consummate confidence man, Salvatore Bellatella is a paragon among coachmen. May heaven's dew descend on the hay he feeds his consumptive horses! May Lombardy long resound with the echoes of his song's gay refrain:

> Siamo vetturini, siamo, siamo,
> In ogni paës una ragazz'abbiam'abbiamo.[14]

MILAN.—I am here. Do you think I rush off to see the cathedral, the museum, the library? No, my God, no! Nothing like that. I do not read Valery's guidebook;[15] I have absolutely no idea how to travel profitably and go about ticking off one's admirations, classically and methodically. I have never known and will never know how to do things "by the book." Besides, I have a distinct dislike for the way tourists

12. The incident occurred on 18 August, but it was Madame d'Agoult's passport, not Liszt's, that was suspect. She finally had to bribe a porter to release the luggage (d'Agoult *Mémoires,* p. 108).

13. Jacques-Henri Bernadin de Saint-Pierre (1737–1814), a writer and ardent naturalist who maintained, more in sentimental than in scientific terms, that a providential order—"harmony"—was to be found throughout nature.

14. "We are coachmen, we are, we are; in every town a sweetheart we have, we have."

15. "Valery" was Antoine-Claude Pasquin (1789–1847), librarian at the Royal Library at Versailles. His informative, erudite, and thoroughly delightful guidebook, which Liszt facetiously denies reading, was *Voyages historiques et littéraires en Italie pendant les années 1826, 1827 et 1828, ou l'Indicateur italien,* 5 vols., 1830 and later editions. The citations here of the work follow the contemporary translation, *Historical, Literary, and Artistic Travels in Italy* (Paris, 1839).

look and behave. Thus I try to extricate myself from them as quickly and immediately as possible. What could be better, I ask you, for someone who is "exiled by his own decision, wandering on purpose, knowingly imprudent, everywhere a stranger and everywhere at home?"*

Here I am strolling the streets of Milan just as if I were sauntering along the boulevards of Paris, and soon, without knowing how, I find myself at the door of Casa Ricordi, right across from La Scala. You know—or perhaps you don't because, thank God, you have never written and sold sixteenth notes—that Ricordi[16] is the leading publisher in Italy and one of the most important publishers in Europe; now, mind you, a publisher is the musical republic's Resident Minister, the *salus infirmorum*, the *refugium peccatorum*, the Providence of a wandering musician like myself. So, I enter and promptly sit myself down at an open piano. I begin to improvise, which is my way of presenting my credentials. Ricordi is there. I do not know him, and he does not know me. He listens and grows excited, but, as he later confessed to me, he had not had lunch and was very hungry. The excitement whets his appetite. He thinks of the *risotto* that is waiting for him, so he rushes off during one of my cadenzas to revive his strength and returns in an even friendlier frame of mind than before. He still says nothing to me, but I overhear him tell his assistant: "This is Liszt or the Devil!" And so, finding myself challenged so openly, I go to him and identify myself. I do not know if I could recall what we said, but within five minutes Ricordi had given me the use of his country house in Brianza, his box at La Scala, his carriage and horses, and the fifteen hundred scores to which he owns the rights. In fact, except for the experiences of a friend who lived for a long time in Honolulu, capital of Tahiti [sic], I have never encountered such liberal and warm-hearted hospitality.[17]

That same night we went to La Scala together. The immense size

---

*"Durch eigenen Willen exilirt, mit Vorsatz irrend, zweckmässig unklug, überall fremd and überall zu Hause" (Goethe, *Letters from Italy*).

16. Giovanni Ricordi (1785–1853), the founder of the publishing firm.

17. Ricordi, on 3 September, also arranged an "accademia" at which Liszt played his Fantasy on "Frequenti palpiti" and the *Grand valse di bravura* with great success. Recording that event, Marie d'Agoult makes a comment that is to run like a refrain through a number of these articles: "The tour de force is the only thing that impresses them [the Italians]; the flattest melodies of Donizetti make them swoon, and any dramatic or poetic work would bore them terribly" (d'Agoult, *Mémoires*, p. 113).

of the theatre, its handsome lines, and the depth of the stage give it a rather imposing look. Yet the general appearance of its interior is monotonous and drab. The lack of light and the empty boxes* were surely two reasons that accounted for the cold and sad impression that struck us as we entered. But there are other reasons, more lasting and less easy to rectify. La Scala, unlike the Paris Opéra, does not have any diversity in its symmetry. In Paris, the orchestra floor rises like an amphitheater; the boxes of the first tier are above the dress circle and for the most part open at top; all of which, not to mention the magnificence of the red hangings and the gilded ornaments, obliges the women to wear opulent, formal gowns or, at the very least, to dress rather stylishly. In Milan the orchestra floor is flat, and the five tiers of boxes are completely uniform. Although the boxes themselves are deep and provide their owners with ample room, they are not designed to attract the eye. Their openings are quite small, and they are all hung with a deep blue silk which only drowns the already faint light given off by the oil lamps of the chandeliers. The gilding is massive and old fashioned. . . . But what about the productions, you say? The operas? The singers? . . . Alas, my friend, the productions can barely overcome the depressed feeling we got from the hall.

That evening they gave *Marin Faliero*[18] and, as is the custom here, presented it with very few rehearsals, since the production of an *opera seria* in this happy land is not a very serious matter, and two weeks of rehearsal usually suffice. The orchestra and singers, strangers to one another, do not get any encouragement from the audience, which is either gossiping or sleeping (the people on the fifth tier have supper and play cards), and so they—absent-minded, glutted, suffering from a head cold—come to the theater not as artists, but as people who are paid by the hour to make music. Thus, despite the exaggerated gestures and accents imposed by Italian taste, nothing is as chilling as these performances.[19] Nuances? None at all. Ensemble effects?

---

*"The season is very bad this year," is how the theater's impresario phrases it. Everyone complains about the directors, the singers, and the composers, and every one is right to do so.

18. An opera by Donizetti, first performed in Paris, Théâtre-Italien, in March 1835.

19. Berlioz had experienced much the same thing: "On arriving in Milan [in May 1832], out of a sense of duty I made myself go to hear the latest opera. Donizetti's *L'Elisir d'amore* was being given at the Cannobiana. I found the theater full of people talking in normal voices, with their backs to the stage. The singers, undeterred, gesticulated and yelled their lungs out in the strictest spirit of rivalry. At least I presumed

Never. Each of the singers thinks only of himself and does not bother about his neighbor. Besides, why bother to take pains for an audience that does not listen? Only the prima donna singing the currently popular cavatina has any chance of making an impression. The trios, quintets, choruses, and finales appear to be performed by sleepwalkers, and one can truly say that even though the performers all sing *at the same time*, they do not sing *together*.

Lest the audience's emotions, moreover, become too intense, and in order to allow those whose imaginations had become overheated by the dramatic action time to compose themselves, it is the custom here to give a ballet after the end of the first act and delay the opera's conclusion until after the pirouettes. The ballet I saw was *The Death of Virginia*.[20] Horsey movements, in the style of Franconi,[21] were meant to transport us in imagination to the consular galas; then a pantomime, dictated strictly by the rhythm of the music and full of square, precise, and angular gestures, apprised us of the rape of the young Roman girl; several admirable *entrechats* by the male dancer Brettin told us the rest—"And it was all over with a dagger's thrust," after which we went to Cava's Garden for some *sorbetti*.

I did not remain in Milan, as the heat there was still too oppressive. We went to find a cooler retreat on the shores of Lake Como. Only when I return will I tell you in detail about the state of the arts in Italy's musical capital. Many people in my place would not shy away from final judgments or definitive criticisms. As for myself, I do not make up my mind that quickly and feel the need to look and listen for some time yet before I give a judgment. I have given you my first impression, offering it as neither right nor wrong, but merely as my own. I will save the long discourse for another time. For today, however, a last friendly word and the most warm-hearted handshake you have ever received and that I have ever given.

---

they did, from their wide-open mouths; but the noise of the audience was such that no sound penetrated except the bass drum. People were gambling, eating supper in their boxes, et cetera, et cetera. Consequently, perceiving that it was useless to expect to hear anything of the score, which was then new to me, I left. It appears that the Italians do sometimes listen. I have been assured by several people that this is so. The fact remains that music to the Milanese, as to the Neapolitans, the Romans, the Florentines, and the Genoese, means arias, duets, trios, well sung; anything beyond that provokes only aversion and indifference" (*The Memoirs of Hector Berlioz*, p. 208).

20. A ballet by Giovanni Galzerani, first performed that August.

21. *Le Cirque Franconi* was a popular equestrian entertainment in Paris.

Lake Como
To Louis de Ronchaud[1]

Bellagio, 20 September [1837][2]

When you write the story of two happy lovers, place them on the shores of Lake Como. I do not know of any land so conspicuously blessed by heaven, and I have never seen a place where the enchanting life lovers lead seems more natural. The Alpine lands, so grand and majestic, are perhaps too imposing for our smallness. Their grandeur oppresses a man instead of elevating him. The glaciers' permanence makes him far too aware of his own instability. The immaculate purity of the eternal snows is a silent reproach to his lackluster conscience. The massive granite cliffs hovering overhead, the sinister fir trees, the harsh climate, the terrors of an avalanche, and the constant rumbling of a voice deep in the caverns are the stern symbols of a destiny that is being fulfilled in the ever-threatening shadow cast by an irrevocable fatality. But here, under a blue sky where the air is soft, the heart expands and our senses open to all the joys of life. The accessible mountains draw us upwards to their green peaks, rich farm lands flourish on their slopes, and the chestnut, mulberry, and olive trees, the corn, and the grape vines, all give promise of abundance. The cool waters temper the sun's heat. Splendid days are followed by voluptuous nights. Here a man can breathe freely, surrounded by friendly nature, and his harmonious relationship with it is not disturbed by gigantic masses. He can love, or he can empty his mind and relax, since all he seems to be doing is enjoying his share of the general bliss. Yes, my friend, if in your dreams you see the ideal form of a woman whose heaven-sent beauty is not a snare for the senses, but a revelation to the soul, and if a young man with an honest and sincere heart appears there beside her, write a moving love story about them and begin it with the words: "On the shores of Lake Como."

The delightful village of Bellagio rises on a sloping hill toward the middle of the lake at the place where it divides into two branches, one of which extends to Lecco while the other ends at Como. And notice right away the sweet sounds of those Greek names. In Paris when the Vigier baths open, when the first water carts appear on the

1. *Gazette musicale,* 22 July 1838, pp. 294–96.
2. As the places described and the events mentioned in the article refer to the entire stay through October at Lake Como—including the initial visit on 19–20 August (d'Agoult, *Mémoires,* p. 109)—the September date can be seen as the time when the writing was begun.

boulevards to let you know that spring has come, you hurry to enjoy its charms at Asnières, Patin, or Montmartre. Here we say: I am going to Lecco. I have come from Toreno. I am returning to Delfo. That difference in names, is it not enough to characterize the difference between your prosaic country and this poetic land?

At the place where I am staying I can hear the melancholy sigh of the waves breaking over the pebbles and see the last rays of the setting sun gild the mountain tops. If you only knew what magic colors it casts on the waves as it leaves them! Sometimes they are a transparent rose, much like a rather pale ruby, sometimes an intense reddish hue like the desert sands, and at other times a mixture of purple, violet, and orange, which produces a fantastic color that is impossible to describe.

I would be ashamed to tell you how many evenings I have passed oblivious to everything; just dreaming at first, then not even dreaming, but lost, sunk in inconceivable bliss, sensing that my soul was some-how *outside myself* and transported by one of those beams to the eternal spring of all Beauty! How many times did I feel that I was all set to smash the poor instrument which serves as my interpreter, losing all hope of ever being able to express even the tiniest part of what I experienced! How wretched, how truly wretched we artists are! We experience momentary flashes when we seem to have an intuitive grasp of the divine, when we can sense its presence within us, like a mystical insight, a supernatural understanding of the harmony of the universe; but as soon as we want to flesh out our sensations, to capture these evanescent flights of the soul, the vision vanishes, the god disappears, and a man is left alone with a lifeless work, one that the crowd's gaze will quickly strip of any last illusions it held for him. You wretched artists, satisfied with yourselves and your works, do you dare look at them in the resplendent light of the setting sun and still claim that they should be immortal!

During the hottest part of the day we often relax under the plane trees at the Villa Melzi and read the *Divine Comedy* sitting at the front of Comolli's marble statue of *Dante led by Beatrice*.[3] What a subject! And what a pity that the sculptor understood it so poorly! that he made Beatrice into a thickset, material woman and turned Dante into a rather shabby, insignificant person, a sheepish little man, not "The Lord of the most elevated song,"[4] as he himself had described Homer! But it took a Michelangelo to understand Dante!

Still, I must confess that I have always been terribly disturbed by

3. Giovanni Battista Comolli (1775–1830). The statue was done in 1810.
4. "Quel Signor de l'altissimo canto" ("Inferno," Canto IV).

one thing in that immense, incomparable poem, and that is the fact that the poet has conceived Beatrice, not as the ideal of love, but as the ideal of learning. I do not like to see a scholarly theologian's spirit inhabiting that beautiful, transfigured body, explaining dogma, refuting heresy, and expounding on the mysteries. It is certainly not because of her reasoning and her powers of demonstration that a woman reigns over a man's heart. It is certainly not for her to *prove* God to him, but to give him a sense of God through love and thus lead him to heavenly matters. It is in her emotions, not in her knowledge, that her power lies. A loving woman is sublime; she is man's true guardian angel. A pedantic woman is a contradiction in terms, a dissonance; she does not occupy her proper place in the hierarchy of beings.

Until now I had enjoyed being totally incognito in Bellagio, although I did bang mightily away on a Viennese piano bereft of almost all its strings. No one bothered to pay the slightest attention to it or to suspect that I was anything but an amateur endowed with a very strong wrist. But today when I returned to the inn, the Police Commissioner was there to greet me, my host solicitously inquired if I was satisfied with my dinner, and I noticed that when my barber Gerompino was shaving me he lathered the soap more officiously yet more deferentially than usual. I soon learned the answer to the mystery. Leafing through the *Gazzetta di Milano*, I saw that my friend Ricordi, eager to sell those compositions of mine that were cluttering up his shop window, had informed the lucky Italians, who could hardly doubt their good fortune, that in me they had the world's leading pianist and that I had absolutely no rivals "in the imaginative and inspired genre." Take careful note of this, my dear Louis, the "inspired genre," for I would especially commend "the inspired genre" to you for your next poem.

I have, moreover, acquired another sort of popularity in this area, one that you will find very amusing and which forces me to sharply curtail the number of walks I take in the countryside. Picture it, I cannot take a step without being surrounded, preceded, and followed by all the children in the district. You know that I love children, not that I really expect to see in them, as people typically do, angels of purity and innocence—I know that they have all our faults and vices in proportion to their age—but on their fresh faces the expression of even these faults and vices assumes an indefinable grace. The greedy look of a child to whom I gave a sugared almond charms me; later, however, the same expression on a man to whom I have tossed a penny arouses my pity, even if I succeed in suppressing my scorn. Finding myself, then, at a village festival recently, I amused myself by buying out a cart filled with cakes and fruits, which I handed over to be plundered by the little monkeys. I had a wonderful time watching them tumble all over each other, fighting with incredible energy over the dust-covered scraps of macaroons or the figs they had crushed between their dirty fingers. Judge for yourself the popularity such princely entertainment has brought me. Now when I am unlucky enough to come across a traveling peddler or some seller of spice cakes on one of my walks, I am, immediately and as if by magic, besieged by a crowd of urchins who look anxiously from me to the cart and from the cart back to me. There is nothing to be said; the game must be played out, and I must part with my last penny. The peddler takes me for a madman, the peasants for someone with money to burn, and the shrewdest among them for a bored Englishman.

Since leaving Bellagio, I have learned that my generosity has been far outstripped by one of those Englishmen who parade their spleen about the world and who are so serious about doing the most ridiculous things. This one decided to stand in the village square during the first snowfall when high mass was letting out and offer his big, wine-soaked nose as a target to my little cookie gobblers. Anyone who hit it with a snowball received five francs for his trouble. You can just imagine the joy, the laughter, the excited cries that broke out for every snowball that smashed against that stalwart nose—for every coin passed from *milord*'s silk-lined purse to the tattered pockets of one of these Italian scamps.

I have mentioned the village festivals to you. They generally take place on the Madonna's feast days and are announced on the eve by the continuous ringing of a clear little bell called the *campanella di festa,* whose rapid notes, sounded in a capricious and infinitely varied rhythm, fill the air with gaiety and high spirits. North of the Alps we know nothing of these playful bells, ours are so grave and serious. The bells are manifestations of the opposing spirits of the two Catholicisms; one bears the stamp of somber Scandinavian myths while the other has retained a scent of Greece, a recollection of paganism. How can we not be reminded of the ancient sacrifices to Venus when one sees young men and women at these festivals approach the altar with baskets decorated with flowers and filled with cakes, fruit, and even poultry, baskets that the priest blesses and which are then sold for the benefit of the church fund? The processions are grotesque affairs. Picture a long file of women, mainly old women, their heads hidden in a dirty shawl that serves as a veil, chanting litanies in a sour voice. They are followed by the male candle-bearers, all decked out in robes as tight as an umbrella's sheath. The robes were red at one time, but age and the inclement weather have now colored them with all the subtlety of autumn leaves. Then the grimacing and varicolored statue of the Madonna appears, carried on a makeshift platform. The whole procession looks more like a tawdry circus parade than a ceremony honoring the True God.

Despite the well-known reputation of Italian throats, I have yet to hear any proper singing in this land, except for three young girls whom we happened upon recently while they were singing ravishing melodies in parts and in their rather coarse dialect. As I wanted to take down some of them to send to you, we begged them to start over again. They hesitated a long time, looking at each other in a half confused, half mischievous way, until finally the youngest of them, not as timid as the others, or more partial to glory, summoned all her lung power and burst into the national song, "Barbarin, speranza d'oro," and her companions followed suit.

We could not take our eyes off these three beautiful girls with their pale coloring, large, widely spaced dark eyes, and ivory teeth— the true types that Luini painted.[5] The hair style that these peasant women have universally adopted could not be more picturesque: they gather their hair into tresses at the back of the head and then fasten them with long, fan-shaped silver hairpins. These hairpins sometimes cost as much as 50 or 60 francs and represent several years' savings. But the little flirts would consider it a disgrace to do without the ornament, which, incidentally, does wonders for their faces and deep brown hair.

We spend the better part of our days in a boat touring through the coves and enjoying the shifting, varied views that the mountains create by moving closer together or standing farther apart. A great number of villas are reflected in the waters. Across from us is the Villa Sommariva where there is a Mona Lisa, the third reputed original painting, and a magnificent bas-relief by Thorwaldsen depicting the *Triumph of Alexander*.[6] That bas-relief, which cost a great deal, is more notable for its detail than for its overall effect. One could, perhaps, criticize the artist for skimping on his work, since the number of figures in the various groups making up the procession is singularly limited; *one* fisherman holding his line begins the series of groups; next, *one* transport vessel and *three* figures to represent the people on the walls of Babylon; next come *two* musicians, and so forth. As I have

5. Bernardino Luini (ca. 1475-ca. 1532), a painter of the Lombardy school, known for his frescoes.

6. Bertel Thorwaldsen (1768–1844), Danish sculptor and a leader of the classical revival. The bas-relief Liszt saw was a marble copy of the *Triumphal Entry of Alexander into Babylon,* a work Napoleon had commissioned for the Quirinal Palace in Rome.

already had occasion to observe in several of his works, Thorwaldsen primarily excels in depicting figures in repose and the heads of old people. The nature of his talent is serene and noble. In this bas-relief the figure representing the Tigris River and the heads of the sages are extremely fine, but the more animated figures and, unfortunately, that of Alexander himself do not come up to the perfection of the others. But this great piece of classically styled sculpture, an Andromeda, and a few statues by Canova[7] amply compensate the enthusiastic traveler for the disappointment he experienced in the garden, where asparagus and turnips impudently display their utilitarian stalks in the privileged precincts where one had expected to breathe the perfume of tuberoses and water lilies. At the end of one of the lake's darkest coves stands the Villa Pliniana, where the famous intermittent spring that Pliny described flows impetuously and creates the most unusual cascades. The sight of that villa, with its back to the mountain, its open courts, and its watercourses cutting across the grounds in all directions, is unrivaled of its kind. Quite close to us, the Villa Serbelloni lifts the dark tops of its larch trees to the wind. Situated on a huge precipice, it commands the entire countryside. A considerable amount of construction is taking place there, and it should be an easy matter to make it into one of the most beautiful residences in Europe. Its three buildings, connected by the gardens, belong to Madame Pasta,[8] the middle one a small version of the Teatro alla Scala. The great singer had wanted the place where she sought repose to resemble the one where she had found fame.

Thus you see that our dear lake adds the indefinable charm of nostalgia to all its other seductions. Carried away by the enjoyment of the present, one loves to tell oneself that this is where the two Plinys may have written their finest pages; that, where Paolo Giovio lived out his epicurian life;[9] that, farther on beneath those trees, is where Volta's ashes rest.[10] Those old feudal towers standing up there are the Musso,

7. Antonio Canova (1757–1822), Italian sculptor, generally regarded as the founder of the modern classical style.

8. Giuditta Pasta (1797–1865), the dramatic soprano. She was a native of Como and had purchased the villa in 1829 against the time of her eventual retirement. Among the many roles that were written for her was Pacini's *Niobe,* the source of the cavatina "I tuoi frequenti palpiti" on which Liszt wrote his much-performed fantasy.

9. Paolo Giovio (1483–1552), humanist writer and historian who had maintained a luxurious villa, Gallia, at Vico.

10. Count Alessandro Volta (1745–1827), native of Como, physicist and pioneer in electricity.

the refuge of Gian Giacomo Trivulzio;[11] there is Castle Baradello, where the natives of Como fought so often against those renowned bandits, the Viscontis and the Sforzas. And if we move closer to modern times, we have the Villa d'Este, where the dear memory of the Princess of Wales is preserved,[12] and the palace [La Rotonda] that was home to Napoleon Bonaparte, that pale, frail young man who came to this country to win Charlemagne's crown with Caesar's sword.

At night we have an enjoyable time fishing by torchlight. Armed with a long harpoon, a veritable Neptunian trident, we glide over the water watching for the fish that are slumbering or stunned by the light of the torch burning at the front of our boat. All about us we hear the sound of the little bells that fishermen attach to their nets at night so they can retrieve them more easily in case they drift with the current. That sound, which always makes us think of herds, gives us a peculiar feeling coming as it does from the middle of the lake. One might even expect the underwater herds of Glaucus to appear, and a vision of that sort would surely not astonish anyone in a land where the imagination is so naturally overheated.

But adieu, my friend. For over five minutes now I have had no idea of what I was writing because I am listening to some delightful music under my windows—three fine unaccompanied voices singing the trio from *William Tell*. I ask who these three great artists are and am told that they are the Counts Belgiojoso, who, knowing that I am in Bellagio, have come to serenade me. I must hurry to thank them and ask them above all to continue singing. I have never heard anything to compare with those voices floating over the water, rising and fading in the starry night.

11. Trivulzio (1440?-1518), marshal of France and governor of Milan under Louis XII. Cristina Belgiojoso was born a Trivulzio.

12. Valery writes: "I went down to the Villa d'Este, which was inhabited for three years by the Princess of Wales [Caroline of Brunswick]. Her cipher may still be seen in the drawing-room and the theater she built there" (*Travels in Italy*, pp. 84–85).

6

MILAN

CHRONICLE

Mid-November 1837. Liszt begins to frequent Milan, just thirty-five
miles south of Como. He has pianist friends from Paris—Peter
Pixis, Ferdinand Hiller (1811–1885), and Louis Mortier de la
Fontaine (1816–1883)—who are staying in the city. He is, moreover, especially pleased to learn that Gioacchino Rossini also
plans to spend the winter season there.[1] He becomes a frequent
guest and performer at the musicales Rossini gives every Friday.
3 December. Liszt plays at a concert given by Mortier.
10 December. Liszt gives a concert at La Scala, performing in the
main hall.
24 December. Marie d'Agoult gives birth in Como to their second
child: another daughter, baptized Francesca Gaetana Cosima.
Like Blandine, she is quickly put in the care of a foster family.
26 December. Liszt performs at a benefit concert in Como.
11 January 1838. Liszt returns to Milan, where he meets Nourrit. The
following evening they entertain most successfully at Rossini's.
29 January. Marie, having recovered from giving birth, which was always difficult for her, arrives back in Milan.
18 February. Liszt gives a concert in the *ridotto* (reception hall) of La
Scala.

---

1. Rossini had recently obtained a legal separation from his wife and decided to
enjoy his dismarital freedom by spending a few months in Milan with his friend and
future wife Olympe Pélissier. As he had not spent any appreciable time in the city for
some years, his unwonted presence was sure to give a fillip to its musical season. "I
am here in Milan," he wrote a friend, "enjoying a rather brilliant life. I have musicales
or musical gatherings at my home each Friday. I have a handsome apartment, and
everyone wants to attend these reunions" (to Carlo Severini, 28 November 1837; in
Herbert Weinstock, *Rossini,* p. 199).

12 March. La Scala produces a gala concert featuring Pixis. Liszt performs as an assisting artist.

15 March. Liszt gives a farewell concert in the *ridotto*. The following day he and Marie depart for Venice.

Liszt devoted two of his travel articles to Milan. The first is his essay on La Scala, the "long discourse" he had promised in his earlier Letter to Ronchaud. The second is the Letter to Massart, or, more precisely, the first half of it, which is the portion devoted to his personal experiences as a concert artist in the Lombardian capital. (The second half, a long postscript discussing Vienna, appears in the next chapter.)

La Scala | To Maurice Schlesinger][1]

Milan, 10 March [1838][2]

The Teatro alla Scala, which opened in 1778, was built according to plans drawn by Piermarini[3] and on the site of the old church Santa Maria alla Scala, as if the ancient serpent, the Prince of Demons, had wanted to confound prophecy by boldly placing his fine foot on the woman's shattered head.[4] In an earlier Letter I mentioned that the hall is divided into five tiers of boxes, not counting the top gallery, called the *loggione*. There are 800 seats set out in twenty rows on the orchestra floor, and the theater can accommodate a total of 3,600 people. The interiors are due to be completely renovated for the coronation of His Majesty the Emperor of Austria.[5] The expense involved has become

1. *Gazette musicale,* 27 May 1838, pp. 217–22. Maurice Schlesinger (1797–1871), editor-proprietor of the *Gazette musicale* and an important publisher whose firm also issued a number of Liszt's compositions.

2. This Letter was actually completed in April, sometime between the 7th and the 20th. See note 27 below.

3. Giuseppe Piermarini (1734–1808), an architect active in northern Italy and a leading exponent of the neoclassic style.

4. Possibly an allusion to Genesis 3:15, which states that Eve's descendants shall bruise the serpent's head, or possibly to the "miraculous" medal which depicts the Virgin, the Christian Eve, standing on a serpent. The medal, the design for which had appeared in a vision to a Sister of Charity in Paris, Catherine Labouré, in November 1830, was a current topic in the French press; an immensely popular book about it had appeared in 1834, and in 1836 ecclesiastical authorities launched an investigation into the miraculous origin from which the medal takes its name.

5. Ferdinand I, who was to be crowned late the coming summer as King of Lombardy.

necessary; I do not know of anything that is dirtier, darker, and more malodorous than the staircases and corridors of La Scala, which is, and moreover desires to be, the world's leading theater.

In Milan, a person is known to be a stranger when he asks the simple question: "Are you going to La Scala this evening?", an unnecessary, idle, useless question which the Milanese never ask each other. For them there is never any doubt—it is rather like asking someone if he is still alive. There is no salvation, except for La Scala. It is the unrivaled meeting place, the great home, the true center of gravity for Milanese society. When La Scala closes, society disappears. One could say that society here depends on the theater's smoky atmosphere for its very existence, and that the sound of instruments is indispensible if it is to divest itself of its own emptiness. Every evening the elegant, the less elegant, and the inelegant gather in this immense cavern and, having divided themselves into tiers of boxes, observe each other across the dusky intervening space. Most of the boxes are privately owned. They are purchased like a house, and the price usually varies between 20,000 and 50,000 francs. Some of them are even hung, furnished, and lighted inside like little salons. Each woman presides alone over her box, and all during the performance she receives a string of visitors, to whom her husband is obliged to relinquish the better seats one by one, until the visits and pleasantries reach the point that he finds himself politely crowded out of the box.

Accordingly, some husbands, those who value their comfort, have a box of their own, where, freed from the prescribed rituals of the conjugal box, they can watch the performance in peace and enjoy the more self-centered pleasures of bachelorhood.

Since it is understood that the number and status of the visitors depend upon how *fashionable* a box is, every woman considers it a matter of pride to see that hers is always well filled, and the tacit rivalries that develop as a result have their more piquant aspects for the social observer. In Paris, people frequenting one salon can only depend on hearsay to learn what is happening in another, and only after a considerable time does a woman establish the enviable reputation of being the gracious mistress of the house, but here, all it takes is a glance. Every evening two thousand persons, without leaving their seats, can observe the various degrees of elegance flowing through the boxes and point out the different social constellations governing them. The women here thus lead a kind of public life which would seem quite odd to Parisian women, who are accustomed to being a little mysterious about the relationships that are constantly forming and dissolving about them—those tenuous, frail threads which, by crossing and recrossing in a thousand different ways, weave the wonderfully subtle web of their private lives. In Milan no mysteries are possible. A sympathetic understanding no sooner develops between two people than the public is aware of it. Everyone has foreseen it, everyone has guessed it, and nothing about a heart's growing interest escapes them—nothing, not even those imperceptible nuances that distinguish yesterday's admirer from tomorrow's happy lover. Is this bad? Is this good? You are a wise man, decide for yourself. I must confess, however, that the custom results in a sincerity of moral behavior which strikes me as preferable in every way to the prudery of the French. In Milan there is no need for a knowing smile or a hypocritical circumlocution to say that a woman has taken a lover. It is simply acknowledged, without malice and without that feigned expression of pitying surprise or virtuous indignation required in France. With us the virtue of a woman of the world is a flagpole on which to unfurl her vanity; in Italy respectable women would not think of making a special point of it. The do not shut themselves up in the ring bristling with barbs that protects the chastity of French women, and they certainly do not look down on their fellow humans from a lofty, arrogantly virtuous point of view. While it is *possible* that this attitude could be quite *moral,* it is certain that it is infinitely more amiable.

People generally lament the fact that the custom of attending the opera has destroyed the art of conversation in Milan. Without question, the startling bursts from the brasses, that desperate "anything goes" from composers on their last legs, are not very conducive to the attention required for sustained conversation. There is also no doubt that the perpetual comings and goings in the boxes and the ever-repeated "And how are you?" which constantly interrupts the talk, rather like a hornet demolishes a spider's web, render all serious discussion impossible. I believe, however, that one should look elsewhere for the main reason behind the dearth of conversation, which even the Milanese themselves deplore. To make a partridge pâté, the most logical mind of our times has said, first get yourself a partridge. Thus, to hold a conversation, first get yourself subjects for conversation; but where are they to be found in a country that has no political, literary, and artistic movements? In Paris, if we were suddenly to cut off all the parliamentary debates, the publication of new books, periodicals, and newspapers, to close all the theaters except the Opéra, and to suppose for the moment that all our great artists stopped producing, don't you think that the much-vaunted conversation of the Parisian salons would receive a death blow? Shouldn't the lack of conversation be attributed to the lack of interesting things to talk about? Shouldn't the constant theater going be considered more of a result than a cause, more of a mysterious necessity than a tiresome choice? And instead of criticizing the Milanese, shouldn't we admire the instincts of a people who throng to the only remaining focal point for their activity, the only circle where they can air their views with total freedom?

All classes of society take an interest in what happens at La Scala. From the great lord who is going to yawn magnificently in the best box, down to the humblest grocery clerk who from time to time pays his 75 centimes and insinuates himself into the top gallery, everyone takes a stand for or against the prima donna, the tenor, the bass, or the maestro. It is tantamount to a matter of national concern that occupies everyone's mind and keeps everyone's imagination in suspense. The young waiter who stirs your chocolate at the café tells you that Francilla Pixis sang the rondo in *La Cenerentola* very nicely.[6] The man who polishes your boots is not pleased with the scenery in *Il Giuramento*. . . . This year there was a general *outcry* against the *impresario*[7] because he failed to live up to his contract and did not give the public the two new operas to which they were entitled. A cut in yearly income would have no greater an effect upon a middle-class Parisian than a reduction in opera has upon the Milanese. It is all very simple: *panem et circenses!* That is still the cry of the Italians.

Opening nights are always extremely lively. Except for those times when a composer has given away a lot of free tickets and has a "risotto" success, since it is assumed that he has invited his partisans to a huge risotto dinner, the public at La Scala expresses its feelings freely, without regard for big reputations. It applauded and booed Madame Malibran[8] in the same aria; it does not care whether the maestro is named Rossini or Mr. X.; and it does not bow blindly to critical judgments that were made elsewhere. What pleases it is good, what does not is bad. That is all well and good, you will say, as long as its instincts are right and its judgments are fair! Frankly speaking, I have found Milan to be like most other cities in this respect. It is not the beautiful that first impresses the crowd, the sublime even less, and the ugly not at all. I would say that they respond to the best of the mediocre. In the arts, as you know, we are primarily moved by the secret correlation

6. See note 17 below.

7. Bartolomeo Merelli (1794–1879), impresario at La Scala from 1836 to 1850.

8. Maria Malibran (1808–1836), contralto, a member of the Garcia family of singers and one of the most celebrated singing actresses of all time. Liszt had been acquainted with her in Paris.

that is established between the artist's thoughts and our own, by the hidden magnetism that attracts like objects; and since the crowd's thoughts and feelings are mediocre, they are usually moved by the mediocre. Still, as even the most uncultivated minds have a need for some measure of the ideal, they do exercise a choice among the mediocre works, and that choice is right because it does not exceed the limits of their faculties. Hence, during all the performances given in the season that has just ended, I have always seen the public single out the most tolerable pieces from intolerable operas for their applause. I have also seen them distribute their bravos quite fairly to the singers. But, despite this, I am still convinced that a type of beauty exists which is almost completely foreign to Italian feelings, a depth of thought, a sober truth that they do not seek. They shy away from everything that demands the slightest attention, the least mental effort. Music for them must be as beautiful and open as the fields of Lombardy itself—glistening prairies laughing in the sunshine, not craggy mountains nor steep precipices—the song of the lark, not the cry of an eagle—the murmur of a zephyr wafting through the corn fields, not a blast of wind in the virgin forest. Everything in the sphere of art corresponding to the feelings immortally exemplified by Hamlet, Faust, Childe Harold, René, Obermann, and Lélia is for the Italians a foreign, barbaric tongue that they reject in horror. Beethoven, Weber, and I would even say Mozart, are familiar to them. . . . but in name only. Rossini, that great master who possessed a fully strung lyre, scarcely sounded anything but the melodic string for them. He treated them like spoiled children, entertaining them as they wanted to be entertained. And who is to do what Rossini did not attempt?

You already know how quickly operas destined for the Italian stage are written. One might say that it is a manufacturing operation where everything is known in advance and nothing is required but the actual time needed to put the notes on paper. So little inspiration and thought seem to go into the composition of an opera that recently, when a certain composer fell behind in his work, the proprietor of La Scala had him confined to his room and kept out of sight until he finished it. You can well imagine what spirit, what truth, and what grace are to be found in such pieces, composed on command and with recourse to the police commissioner.

The business arrangements between impresario and composer are not the same as they are for us in France; the composer here receives a fixed sum proportionate to his fame, and once the money is received, he no longer has any rights to the score or to the work's performances. The work's success or failure affects only his self-esteem, not his purse. He takes no risk, as he does in France, of receiving nothing for his work. It is only the impresario who risks the work's success or failure. And it may well be that the composer's lack of direct interest in the opera's success has some influence on the careless and nonchalant attitude he takes toward his work. Mercadante,[9] however, must be exempted from this criticism, which can properly be leveled against the mass of composers on this side of the Alps. He composes with wise deliberation and reviews his compositions carefully; thus his operas are, beyond question, the most correct and best orchestrated of all those I have heard in Italy.

During an opera's first three performances, it is the custom here for the composer to stand at a specially designated place in the orchestra. He is obliged to attend the fateful trial in person. He must confront the jeers and whistles impassively, or thank the crowd for the approval he received with a respectful nod. There is something rather tactless and uncivilized about this custom that would surely offend the delicate feelings we have in France for certain social proprieties, but here in Italy no one is shocked by it, and it seems to be a necessary consequence of the artist's relationship with the public. When an opera creates a *furore*, the composer is noisily called to the stage. At the end of each act the cries of "fuori, fuori" resound throughout the entire hall.[10] People clap their hands, stamp their feet, and cry and scream until the unlucky conqueror shows himself before the curtain and, with eyes lowered, his hand to his heart, goes through a ridiculous pantomime to express an even more ridiculous sense of humility. After he has first appeared alone, he usually returns with the prima donna in hand, and then for a third time with all the singers, at which point the applause, clamors, and hurrahs redouble. The composer no longer knows what bearing to adopt. Three-quarters of the time dancing lessons were not part of his education, and so his deep bows are awkward, his gait unsteady, and his gestures silly. More often than not he looks like a busboy in a lemonade shop apologizing for having broken a glass rather than a proud conqueror who has just been crowned. We in France have no idea of the Italian public's mania for calling artists to the stage. When we call them back for one bow, that is that. But in Italy a beloved artist is usually called back ten or twelve times during the evening. Malibran took thirty-six curtain calls for her performance

9. Saverio Mercadante (1795–1870), Neapolitan-trained composer of some sixty operas, plus much chamber and church music.
10. "Come out, come out!": the Italian equivalent of "Author! Author!"

in *La Sonnambula*. When the performers are mediocre the ritual is patently ludicrous; but when, on the other hand, they have stirred us powerfully and emotions have run deep, so that art has triumphed and we have been transported beyond reality to the realm of illusion, it becomes reprehensible—a glass of ice water dashed in the face of a feverish man.

These customs also give us an idea of what dramatic music means to the Italians and how they listen to it. For them an opera is little more than a concert in costume. The rapport between the plot and the music does not concern them. The philosophical aspects of a musical work count for next to nothing in the pleasure they derive from it. As long as a piece delights the ear and a melody is sweetly gentle and melancholy, they do not ask how the composer introduced it into the opera, nor how it suits the character's role. They enjoy the music and the performance, giving no thought to its poetic presentation. They never confuse the singer with the role he is playing. They always know perfectly well that they are dealing with Madame Schoberlechner and not Semiramide, with Pedrazzi and not Otello. The Italians consequently find it quite easy to honor a singer after he has just been stabbed or during the most crucial points of the drama, and they do not realize that the practice is a shock to our sensibility, since such feelings are scarcely known to them.

When I have given you the names of the operas performed at La Scala this winter, I will have said almost everything that I could say about them. Except for Mercadante's *I Briganti* and *Il Giuramento*,[11] they have all vanished without a trace. *Gli Arragonesi* by Conti[12] disappeared on its first night in a terrible storm of disapproval. *Le Nozze di Figaro*—yes my friend, *Le Nozze di Figaro* as "redone" by Ricci[13]—and *La Solitaria* by Coccia[14] had a very difficult time completing their announced runs. Then, *La Cenerentola* and *Semiramide* were revived at the season's close for Francilla Pixis's debut with the company. Only two operas by Rossini? Alas, that is true. The great composer's works are no longer the foundation of the repertory in Milan; the impresario

---

11. *I Briganti,* first performed in Paris, Théâtre-Italien, March 1836. *Il Giuramento,* the composer's most enduring work, first given Milan, La Scala, March 1837.

12. Carlo Conti (1796–1868), composer and notable professor of counterpoint at the Naples Conservatory.

13. Luigi Ricci (1805–1859). His opera was not, as Liszt implies, a reworking of Mozart, but a revision of his own *Il nuovo Figaro,* first given in Parma in 1832.

14. Carlo Coccia (1782–1873), a Neapolitan composer of thirty-seven operas. Also active as a conductor.

holds them in reserve "just in case," as they say, since these masterpieces were so overplayed in the past. More than anything, the Italians today are very eager for something new, and even though they are often quite frustrated in their expectations, they still love to see a new name on the posters, hoping constantly that some young composer will strike the rock and bring forth a gushing, miraculous spring of musical pleasure. But the branches of great trees crowd out the sun; their shade is deadly and creates an arid space around them. One might say that no musician could grow in the shade of Rossini's genius.

The prima donna Madame Schoberlechner[15] is well liked by the public, which is pleased with the zealous way she has almost single-handedly borne the burden of all these mediocre operas. Gifted with an imperturbable memory, strong lungs, and an equally strong will, she is always ready for everything. Never does a cold, a headache, or anything else interfere with her keeping her engagements. Unlike many others who hold back during the ensemble pieces so as to appear to better advantage in the duets and solos, she gives, lavishing her voice whenever it is needed: quartets, quintets, and choruses, she enlivens them all. Her voice is the keystone of the musical edifice. Thus it was that she finished the season exhausted, short of breath, and asking for a respite because her chest no longer sufficed to fill the immense hall, which like a veritable minotaur seems destined to devour two or three sopranos every year. Madame Schoberlechner is a serviceable singer rather than a great one. Although her voice is strong and has considerable range, it lacks style and her handling of recitative is monotonous. Her predilection for certain exaggerated effects, dictated possibly by the public's taste and the immense size of the hall, causes her to neglect subtle details, the delicacy of shading, that final polish which, although frequently lost on the crowd, nevertheless establishes a great artist's reputation in the long run. All Madame Schoberlechner's characterizations are *pedestrian,* so to speak. The divine secrets by which Mesdames Malibran and Pasta gave an irresistible lift to a single note or the most banal phrase are unknown to her. In her acting and singing you never encounter that gripping sense of the unexpected, that emotional abandon which is so artfully managed that it transcends art. In Schoberlechner's roles everything is planned before-

15. Sophie Dall'Oca Schoberlechner (1807–1863), soprano, wife of the Austrian pianist-composer Franz Schoberlechner (1797–1843). Though born and raised in St. Petersburg, she was of Italian descent, the daughter of a well-known vocal teacher Filippo Dall'Oca.

hand, well thought out, nothing is created spontaneously. They are always adequate, but never exceptional. One can almost always say that her performances are good, but one rarely feels that they are beautiful.

Madame Brambilla,[16] who sings the contralto roles, is a delightful person. Her voice possesses some fine, sinister notes, which she frequently spoils by forcing. Her method, or rather her manner, is hesitant and uncertain—she is not the mistress of her art. She does not lack for tenderness or pathos, but she usually seems to be perplexed by her gifts. Someone has remarked that she is always on the verge of possessing great talent; and that, in effect, sums up the impression of being unfinished and tentative that she conveys to the public.

Since you know that Pixis is an old and good friend of mine, do not expect me to give you an *impartial* opinion of his adopted daughter's talents.[17] A witty woman, speaking about one of our most clever critics, once remarked that she could find no fault in him, except that he was "too impartial about his friends." I, on the other hand, am full, crammed, and overflowing with faults, but I do not have that one, no doubt precisely because it has the surface respectability and flattering sheen of a virtue. I think that all my friends are delightful, perfect, more than perfect—almost adorable, and, above all, inimitable. That said, you have the right to challenge my personal opinion of Francilla, and so I will limit myself to repeating what appears to be the public's view. Francilla Pixis is basically German at heart. She is full of soul and feeling but still lacks a sense of liveliness, an ability to open up fully. Her talent is too delicate, too intimate for the big theaters. One senses that it has not been gilded yet by the southern sun. It is too reserved for a public that always wants to be swept away. It must have more freedom, greater abandon. In this connection more engagements with the various theaters in Italy can only be helpful to her, because she, without sacrificing her innate qualities of purity and truth, would then acquire the warmth and the Italian *brio* that are still lacking.

Madame [Desiderata] Dérancourt, whose huge success in Lyons made her decide to approach La Scala, has not enjoyed a comparable success here. Her totally French method of singing did not please the

16. Marietta Brambilla (1807–1875), a very popular performer. Among her many roles she sang Maffio Orsini at the premiere of Donizetti's *Lucrezia Borgia* (1833) and created the title role in his *Linda di Chamounix* (1842).

17. Francilla Pixis, born 1816 as Franzilla Göhringer, mezzo-soprano. She made her debut at La Scala 16 January 1838 in Rossini's *La Cenerentola*. Later, Pacini wrote *Saffò* (1840) for her. In 1845 she married an Italian nobleman and retired from the stage.

Milanese, and, unhappily for her, she was also involved in the horrible *fiasco* of *Gli Arragonesi* that I mentioned.

Pedrazzi and Badiali, the first tenor and the baritone, are service-able singers,[18] but neither one nor the other has ever known what it is to study, to declaim, or, as we quite justifiably say in France, to *create* a role, especially when we consider our peerless Nourrit.

Lucio Pappone is one of those Neapolitan buffos who have an unsurpassed natural flair for comedy. He is an instinctive comic, with nothing of the intellectual or philosophic about him. But he makes you laugh continuously, openly, stupidly, and, consequently, in the most wholesome way possible. A foreigner would never be able to imitate the flood of words, the lively gestures, or the comic stance of the Italians, nor would he ever approach that incredible jumble of comic faces—it is enough to drive the most obedient jaw and the supplest joints to despair. If I did not think that you would chide me for being too gastronomic in my allusions, I would paraphrase that well-known adage and say that in Italy "one is born a buffoon," while in France one "becomes a comic actor."

You can see from all this how poorly the Milanese belief in their right to have consistently first-class opera works out in practice, and they should hardly have any illusions about remedying the situation in the coming years. Here, as everywhere else, it is simply a matter of money. The Italians want very much to amuse themselves, but they have the very bad habit of wanting to be entertained at very little cost. They would not hear of paying more than the modest sum of 2 francs 60 centimes to go to La Scala, and for that they usually insist on an opera and two ballets. You can decide for yourself if the impresario is amply supplied with money and able to compete with his counterparts in Paris and London for the leading performers! He is, therefore, reduced to relying on young talents who offer nothing but promise or old talents who offer nothing but regrets.

I have already mentioned the ballets. All the past winter Ali-Pasha regularly blew up the fortress of Janina in a pantomime that lasted an hour and a half and was as boring as it was absurd. Only the delightful dance by Mademoiselles Varin and Elssler[19] managed to break the ghastly monotony of this "riddle of gestures." Of the two, Mademo-

---

18. Francesco Pedrazzi, known for his singing of Rossini and Donizetti, and Cesare Badiali (ca. 1810–65) a renowned *basso-cantante*.

19. It is difficult to ascertain whom Liszt has in mind, since the renowned Fanny and her sister Thérèse were appearing in Paris at this time.

iselle Varin, with her modest grace and nobility of style, reminded one at times of the sylph Taglioni.[20] The stage settings, so acclaimed when Sanquirico[21] was the designer, have really become second-rate. As for the stage machinery and the use of perspective in the scenery, the theater in Milan can hardly compare to the Paris Opéra.

In summary, now that you have read the record, you would conclude, and rightly so, that La Scala has fallen into a bad state. There is no way of knowing how long it will last. Yet hardly more than a month ago you could have seen two men in a stage box who, if they agreed to it, could return the theater to the splendor and brilliance of its great days . . . for Rossini and Nourrit[22] still enjoy the vigor of their maturity. Let a new masterpiece leap fully armed from the Olympian brow of the former and the latter would be there to seize it and transmit it to the crowd, thus adding art to art, light to light, flame to flame. The priest is waiting for the god to speak. But isn't that an unfathomable smile on the god's lips? And that smile, doesn't it indicate the most amiable contempt for fame that is bought with fatigue, as well as a philosophical appreciation of what the crowd's caresses are worth? Doesn't the conquering brow seem to be weary of mental effort? Those eyes where flashes of genius sparkle so on occasion, don't they most often demand the easygoing tranquility of a thoroughly enjoyable good life?

Rossini has returned to Milan, the city of his youth,[23] a youth so exuberant, so filled with love, and so addicted to every crazy caprice. Rossini, now that he has become rich, idle and illustrious, has opened his house to his countrymen, and all winter long his rooms have been filled with people eager to come and pay homage to one of Italy's greatest glories.[24] Surrounded by a swarm of young dilettantes, the maestro has delighted in making them study his most beautiful com-

20. Maria Taglioni (1804–1884), acknowledged the greatest of the Romantic ballerinas, famed for her role in *La Sylphide* (1832).

21. Alessandro Sanquirico (1777–1849), scenic designer at La Scala from 1807 to 1832 and responsible for some 350 productions.

22. Nourrit was then traveling through Italy looking for a suitable opera engagement. He was in Milan for about ten days in mid-January 1838. See Louis-Marie Quicherat, *Adolphe Nourrit* 3: 82–97.

23. Liszt is mistaken here: young Rossini had no special ties to Milan. He was born in Pesaro in the Italian Marches, grew up and studied in Bologna, and enjoyed virtually all of his early success in Venice.

24. About this time Liszt paid his own homage to Rossini by transcribing the Overture to *William Tell* for piano solo, a work that created a sensation at his later concerts. He had already, in 1837, transcribed Rossini's delightful collection of songs

positions; amateurs and artists alike have considered it an honor to be admitted to his concerts.[25] There, next to Madame Pasta, you could have seen the two Branca sisters, whose voices are as fresh as their faces. Standing beside Nourrit was Count Pompéo Belgiojoso and his cousin Tonino, of whom Tamburini and Ivanoff[26] might well be jealous. One evening our friend Hiller arranged a performance of his choral setting of the psalm "The Lord is my shepherd," and even though that fine piece was restrained and a bit German in its harmony, it aroused a lot of enthusiasm. On another occasion[27] the very talented Madame Cambiaggio played a duo for two pianos with a wretched artist who, I swear to you, played more wrong notes in one half hour than he ever did in his entire life, so distracted was he by that lovely face set between two masses of brown curls. In this regard you should know that there are few cities in Europe where music making is cultivated to the extent that it is by Milanese society. Rossini has justly remarked that all we other artists would be soundly beaten in the competition here.

---

and duets, *Soirées musicales,* and prior to that had composed two fantasies on songs from the same collection soon after it appeared in Paris in 1835.

25. Clearly Rossini was having a wonderful time for himself. In December 1837 he wrote a friend: "My musical evenings make something of a sensation . . . . Dilettantes, singers, *maestri,* all sing in the choruses; I have about forty choral voices, not counting all the solo parts. Madame Pasta will sing next Friday. As you can imagine, this will be counted an extraordinary novelty, as she doesn't want to sing in any other home. I have all the artists from the theaters, who compete to sing and feel driven to struggle all day long to prevent the admission of any new satellites. The most distinguished people are admitted to my soirées; Olympe does the honors successfully, and we carry things off well" (Weinstock, *Rossini,* p. 200).

26. Antonio Tamburini (1800–1876), baritone at the Théâtre-Italien, part of the famous "quartet" there that also included soprano Giulia Grisi, tenor Giovanni-Battista Rubini, and bass Luigi Lablache. Nicholas Ivanoff (1810–1880) was a lyric tenor.

27.The passage that follows was written by Marie d'Agoult. In a letter from Venice, 20 April [1838], she told Hiller: "When leaving here [for Vienna, Franz] left me a letter about La Scala and the general musical facade of Milan to finish. And so I went about it wholeheartedly. I had him be almost in love with Madame Cambiaggio, an admirer of the Marchesina's *polished* talent, enraptured by Countess Somaglia's voice like the scent of a violet. I expect [*espère*] that this letter will raise a great oh-oh when it reaches the Lombardian capital" (in Chantavoine, "La Comtesse d'Agoult," pp. 578–79). Some writers have cited this passage as evidence that d'Agoult wrote the *entire* article on La Scala, but that claim hardly seems justified in light of the limited scope of her remarks. Furthermore, in describing what took place at Rossini's Fridays, she can only be reporting or embellishing on what Liszt had told her, since she, being at Como when they were held, never attended any of the gatherings.

To all the names that I have already mentioned, I would like to add those of the Marchesina Medici, whose talent is so polished; Madame Vanotti, who makes the solitude of Varese resound with her poetic harmonies; the two young R——sisters, who play the piano and harp with a superiority that they alone undervalue; Countess Somaglia, whose voice is as sweet and penetrating as the scent of a May violet . . . and many others whom you will hear when you come to Milan, and who will lull you with sweet melodies and keep you here for an entire winter, as they did me, without your giving further thought to the fact that you should not have stayed for more than a day, that you are just starting out on your journey, that there are other cities in Italy and that these cities are called Venice, Florence, Rome, and Naples.

To Lambert Massart[1]
[Part I, Milan]

[Venice-Lugano, March-July 1838][2]

Truly speaking, my friend, there is nothing quite as ludicrous as the traveling musician. I do not know of anyone who cuts a more pitiable figure or wears a more disagreeable expression as he journeys from land to land, city to city, town to town; an itinerant marvel among nature's immutable marvels, a temporary wonder passing through the shadows of the great names that have spanned the centuries; a useless clown, an ill-fated troubadour who mixes the sound of his guitar with the din of civil strife, with the echoes of the struggles and upheavals that torment the world.

1. *Gazette musicale,* 2 September 1838, pp. 345–52. Lambert Massart (1811–1892), a violinist who was born in Liège and, like Liszt, was refused admission to the Paris Conservatory because of his foreign birth. He studied instead with Rudolph Kreutzer (1766–1831), the dedicatee of Beethoven's Violin Sonata, Op. 47. Unsuited by temperament for a virtuoso's career, Massart became a teacher, and as professor at the conservatory from 1843 to 1890 he trained a long, distinguished line of violinists, including Henri Wieniawski. A dear friend, he also acted as Liszt's publishing agent in Paris during this period. Later, in 1844, when the relations between Liszt and Marie d'Agoult became so strained that they would only communicate through an intermediary, it was the steady, reliable Massart to whom Liszt turned.

2. This letter was completed about the end of July 1838, at which time Liszt wrote his mother: "Tell Massart that I have written a letter addressed to him for the *Gazette musicale.* He will have it very soon" (Liszt, *Briefe an seine Mutter,* pp. 48–49).

The traveling painter does not get involved with such shocking contrasts. He exists independently and alone. The nature he loves and admires is at once both the object of his worship and the direct aim of his art. He has nothing to ask of the crowd. He can give himself whole-heartedly to earnest contemplation, sink and lose himself in a feeling for infinite beauty, for the more he comprehends it, fathoms it, under-stands it, the more fertile, free, and plastic does his work become. When a sculptor travels through Greece and Italy—those countries where the human form received its perfection from God's hands and the dream of art was realized in all its splendor—his eye grasps the contours, while his intellect studies the relationships among them. He then reproduces or creates them in his quiet studio according to the dictates of his talent or his genius. Neither one nor the other hinders his flight, neither one nor the other puts him at odds with the harmo-nious development of his powers, neither one nor the other forces him to submit to the debasing encounters and petty annoyances that result from direct and daily contact with the public.

By contrast, the musician—and I mean the performing musician, the concert giver, be he a pianist, harpist, violinist, horn player, accor-dionist, jew's harp player or clarinetist—has nothing to do with nature or the masterpieces of art. Contemplation and dreaming are a waste of time for him. Let him arrive in Venice, Florence, or Rome, and he can barely give a passing glance to the ducal palace, the Apollo, or the Colosseum; he must hurry to appear, to display his virtuosity; he must organize a concert. But in order to launch that amphibious vocal and instrumental creature, that motley, red-eyed, green-tailed, blue-nosed monster, that dreaded bugbear of a pleasant sojourn, he must secure the cooperation of a host of individuals, each of whom holds one of the strings that set the misshapen machine into motion. To begin, he must beg an audience with His Highness the *Impresario,* who will open the negotiations by refusing him the services of all the opera singers, but who will finally succumb to the artist's repeated pleas by allowing him the use of the theater's reception hall for about five or six times the price any honorable man would ask for it. Then he must present himself to the police commissioner in order to get permission to ex-hibit his modest talents. After that he must negotiate with the gentle-man who distributes the posters, so that the notices can be prepared in a new and striking manner. He must also inquire after some errant soprano, who never fails to be as ugly as a lichen and to assume the airs of an unrecognized Malibran. He must also provide for the ser-vices of an available baritone—the dual-purpose singer who can fill either the tenor or bass roles as needed. If, by some unlucky chance, the concert giver wishes to undertake a concerted piece or one that calls for orchestral accompaniment, then alas! his trials and tribulations never cease. He spends days and nights climbing staircases that reach as far as the eye can see, scaling boundless heights step by step.

The rehearsals, those ever-necessary but ever-impossible sessions, drive him to his wit's end. After all this, behold the pretentious counselor, the knowing friend who plagues him with weighty advice about the poor weather (it is always too hot or too cold, too dry or too damp to give a concert) and about his choice of a program (quite respectable, of course, but not quite suitable perhaps for local tastes). The friend bitterly deplores the anti-musical temperament of the town. He recalls an appearance by Paganini that attracted only a small, select audience or a concert by Mademoiselle B. that did not make expenses, and he breathlessly recounts a hundred other sorry tales which can only strike fear and discouragement into the poor artist's heart. Then there is the question of ticket prices. If they were set on the basis of the artist's merit, they could surely never be too high, but one has to accommodate oneself to the circumstances; the bourgeoisie is thrifty, the nobility is stingy, and the collections that were taken for the fire and flood victims have emptied all the purses. As each new "but" is mentioned, the artist reduces his expectations by one franc per ticket. He ends up giving a concert at discount prices, because, as his friend's soothing words continue, he sees his prospects melt like winter snow in a soft April breeze. He is then presented with the list of all the local people who from time immemorial have claimed the right to a *free* ticket. There are so many of them that they will fill half the hall. True, the custom is rather disagreeable, but it does give the concert a surer guarantee of success, because a *free* ticket buys enthusiasm, which is a recognized fact in every country of the civilized world. But even then, do you think the artist's troubles are over? You forget the wrangles with the man who lights the hall, the negotiations with the lady who rents the chairs, the conferences with the administrator of the charities, etc., etc.

This tiring and ridiculous effort must begin all over again everywhere an artist wants to establish a reputation or wherever he has a pressing need for money. What a contrast between these mean and merciless necessities and the needs of his nature! How these endless altercations make him writhe, sapping all his strength! What abstruse wrangling confines him to the meanest levels of society while his soul is powerfully drawn to the elevated spheres of art and ideas! One day, perhaps, when I am old enough to look back kindly on my youth, even with its disappointments and miseries, when I have positively developed a philosophical attitude toward life, I will write the true story of it for my octogenarian friends—a book of recollections whose title might well be *Of the Great Tribulations Involved in Making a Small Reputation,* or better yet, *A Musician's Life: A Long Dissonance with no Final Resolution.* In the meantime I continue on my way, carrying my annoyances like so much necessary baggage and very cleverly steering a course between the Ideal and the Real, without allowing myself to be overly seduced by the former, nor ever to be crushed by the latter.

The first concert I gave in Milan was at the Teatro alla Scala, which, as you know, is one of the largest in the world, so big that it seems to have been built to challenge Lablache's voice[3] and the powerful sounds of the Paris Conservatory orchestra. Quite honestly, I must have cut a strange figure there—me, so thin, so emaciated, all alone with my faithful Erard piano, face to face with an audience that is accustomed to lavish, spectacular productions and the most overpowering musical effects. If, in addition to the setting, you also consider the fact that the Italians generally regard instrumental music as a secondary matter that does not compare with vocal music, you will have an idea of the foolhardiness of my undertaking.[4]

Very few great pianists are known in Italy. Field, I believe, is the last (if not the only one) to be heard here.[5] Neither Hummel, Moscheles, Kalkbrenner, nor Chopin has appeared on this side of the Alps.

The gilded magnet that attracts talent lies to the north these days. The Medicis, Gonzagas, and d'Estes sleep on their marble pillows. The illustrious *Maecenases* no longer summon illustrious artists to their palaces. For a musician to visit Italy these days he must be, as I am, more eager for sunshine than for fame, more desirous of rest than of money,

---

3. Luigi Lablache (1794–1858), bass, part of the "quartet" at the Théâtre-Italien, and also active in Italy and England.

4. Liszt gave his concert on 10 December 1837. The idea of presenting it in the theater instead of the reception hall (*ridotto*) originated with La Scala's impresario Merelli. Liszt, somewhat apprehensive about it, wrote Marie d'Agoult early that month: "My business is getting settled, the concert will take place sometime from the 7th to the 10th. Merelli is to choose the date. The conditions are neither good nor bad. It is something to try. Two hundred francs in preliminary expenses, and we share the receipts. He is providing the singers, the hall, the orchestra, and even a quartet of dancers. They claim that that will attract everyone. So be it. . . . I am, moreover, not unhappy about playing in La Scala for my debut [here]; it is more grandiose" (*Corres. Liszt-d'Agoult* 1: 206; the date [1838] given there is not correct). Liszt need not have been concerned; the concert drew a capacity audience.

5. John Field (1782–1837). He had appeared at two concerts in Italy (in Milan only) in November and December 1833. They were not successful, as his physical condition was then deteriorating rapidly.

in love with painting and sculpture because he understands nothing about them, and very tired of music because he does understand something about that. It was, therefore, for a public that was largely unprepared for certain old ideas of composition and performance—ideas that have made the pedantic critics wince at times, but which I cling to stubbornly despite the critics' infallibility—it was to an audience whose taste had been *reduced* almost entirely to music reduced from opera that I ventured to present two or three fantasies in my own style—not very restrained or very learned, to be sure, but which, for all that, certainly did not fall back on the usual stereotypes. They were applauded; thanks, perhaps, to some octave passages played with quite laudable dexterity and to several cadenzas, spun out over the melody, that might have issued from the throat of the most determined nightingale around. Encouraged by the flattering approval and feeling sure of my ground, I became even more foolhardy and nearly compromised my modest success by offering the public one of my favorite newborn children, a prelude-etude [*studio*], which in my opinion is a very fine piece. But the word "study" immediately alarmed everyone; "I come to the theater to be entertained, not to study," cried a man from his seat on the main floor, thereby expressing the feelings of a frightening majority of the audience. And, indeed, I did not succeed in persuading the public to like the odd idea I had had of performing, anywhere but in my own room, an *étude* whose apparent purpose was to make my joints limber and my ten fingers supple. Thus, I regarded the audience's patience in hearing me through as a special mark of their favor.[6]

On another occasion I performed Hummel's Septet in the theater's reception hall.[7] The straightforward course of that piece, the majesty of its style, and the clarity and prominence with which its ideas are presented make it an easy work to understand. Besides, the passages that close each movement never fail in their effect, and as a result, the masterpiece was greeted quite warmly.—I would have loved not to stop there but, continuing, to have given the Milanese an opportunity

6. Liszt performed three of his works at the concert: the Fantasy on Pacini's "Frequenti palpiti," an unidentified etude, and *La Serenata et l'Orgia*, Grand Fantasy on themes from [Rossini's] *Soirées musicales*. The etude was poorly received, but the two fantasies were very successful, the latter one encored. To complete the program, Merelli, as agreed, furnished the orchestra, a half-dozen soloists (Schoberlechner, Dérancourt, Pedrazzi, etc.) and, if not a quartet of dancers, the La Scala chorus (program in *Gazzetta privilegiata di Milano,* 9 December 1837).

7. 18 February 1838. Other works on the program included Liszt's performance of the *Hexameron* and a twelve-hand, three-piano version of the Overture to *The Magic Flute.* The complete program is given in Julius Kapp, *Franz Liszt,* p. 101.

to hear Beethoven's trios, some works by Moscheles and Weber, etc. But in addition to the lack of time, it would have been very unwise, perhaps, to offer their wild, northern beauties to ears that have been lulled by the sensual sounds of a Bellini, a Donizetti, or a Mercadante. The Austrians may well have given their laws to Lombardy, but many years will pass before their music is accepted here. Bayonets can impose laws; they cannot impose taste.

As my concerts have always been criticized for being too serious, I hit upon the idea of adding a little life to them by improvising on themes proposed by the dilettantes and chosen by acclamation.[8] This style of improvisation establishes a closer contact between the public and the artist. Those who propose the themes realize that their self-esteem is involved to some extent, and thus the use or rejection of a given melody becomes a triumph for one, a defeat for another, and a source of interest for all. Everyone is anxious to hear what the musician will do with the idea that has been imposed upon him. Every time he presents it in a novel way, the person who proposed it takes pleasure in the fine effect it produces, as it is something to which he has contributed. The improvisation becomes a joint effort, a matter of the artist's polishing the jewels that have been given him.

At my last concert,[9] a lovely silver cup of exquisite workmanship, attributed to one of Cellini's most gifted pupils, was placed at the door to receive the thematic ballots. When I proceeded to decipher them I found, as I had expected, a goodly number of themes by Bellini and Donizetti. But then, to the audience's great amusement, I read a carefully folded, unsigned note from a person who had not a moment's doubt about the towering superiority of his suggestion, "The Cathedral of Milan." Ah! I said, now here is someone who profits from his reading. This gentleman remembers Madame de Staël's definition that "music is the architecture of sounds." He is interested in ascertaining its validity by comparing the two architectures; the debased Gothic of the cathedral's facade and the Ostrogothic of my musical edifice. I would have loved to have given him this esoteric satisfaction, allowing him to confirm or deny the renowned writer's assertion for himself, but as the public did not show the slightest interest in watching me erect steeples of thirty-second notes, galleries of scales, or spires of

8. This may have been a novelty for Milan, but in cities like Vienna and Paris it was, as Liszt well knew, standard procedure for a pianist to improvise on themes proposed by members of the audience.

9. 15 March 1838. Before improvising, Liszt had performed Pixis's Grand Duo from Meyerbeer's *Les Huguenots* (with Pixis), and his own Fantasy on *I Puritani*.

tenths, I moved on to the other suggestions, which became better and better, cleverer and cleverer. One respectable citizen, preoccupied with the progress of industrialization and struck by the benefits of being able to travel from Milan to Venice in six hours, gave me "The Railroad" as a theme. The only thought I had for conveying that idea was an uninterrupted series of glissandos ranging from the top to the bottom of the keyboard, but as I feared that I might break my wrists in trying to rival the speed of the railroad cars, I hastened on to open the last note. What do you think I read this time? One of life's most important concerns, and I was supposed to settle it in arpeggios! It was a subject which, if treated broadly, would call everything into question; religion as well as physiology, philosophy as well as political economy—namely, "Is it better to marry or to remain single?" Not being able to answer that question with anything but an infinitely long sigh, I preferred to remind my audience of what a wise man once said: "No matter what decision a person makes, whether to get married or to remain single, he is always bound to regret it."

As you can see, my friend, I found an excellent way to add some life to an concert, that entertainment so tiresome that it seems like a duty. Besides, in this land of improvisation and improvisors, why shouldn't I say, "Me too"?

I would be ungrateful if I did not say here that the kind reception the Milanese gave me greatly exceeded my expectations and that the acclaim they lavished upon me was enough to satisfy a far more exacting ego than my own. You know what I think about success in general and mine in particular. I will not deny that there is an indescribably powerful enchantment, a proud yet loving delight, in exercising a faculty that draws the thoughts and hearts of others to us, that causes other people's souls to break into the fiery sparks that consume our own and to shine with that mutual enthusiasm that sweeps them irresistibly along with us toward the realm of the beautiful and the ideal— toward God. Sometimes an artist imagines that the effect he has had on some individuals reaches to the entire audience, and he feels like the king of all minds; he senses an infinitely small particle of creative force inside him because he has created emotions, feelings, and ideas with his sounds.

It is a dream that ennobles his existence. It was mine during my young, passionate years, when I sensed a tremendous vitality stirring within me that I felt had to be shared and communicated. Back then, I confess, I frequently regarded the cheap triumphs of vanity with pity; I railed against the rapture with which I saw that compositions having neither integrity nor significance were greeted; I wept over what oth-

ers termed my "success," as it was perfectly clear to me that the crowd
chased after an artist to demand some fleeting entertainment from him,
not some serious instruction in heightened sensibility. Thus I refused
to recognize such frivolous judges, since both their praise and their
criticism were almost equally offensive to me, and I would repeat the
poet's words: "I want *neither* the impertinence of their jeers, nor the
arrogance of their applause. I will remain calm and stoic when faced
with success or failure, defying the former and indifferent to the latter.
It is within myself alone that I will find the support I need. My conscience will be my only judge." A most arrogant attitude, certainly, but
be assured that the unruly arrogance of youth does not last very long;
it diminishes and abates year by year; experience trims and pares it
down until it reaches a more acceptable level of egotism. There are
very few people indeed who have gone through life and to the grave
with all the arrogance of their youthful ideas, their early desires, and
their virgin ambitions intact. All others submit to time's effects. Their
hearts and spirits strike a balance with each other, settling for a reasonable mediocrity within that wretched wisdom which guides men's actions.

A little more time and the process will be completed in me, as in
so many others; a little more time and I will have become what people
call a "sensible man," which means . . . but Lord preserve me from
definitions!

It would take too long to give you the particulars of all the musical soirées and concerts I attended either actively or passively during
my stay in Milan. I will only tell you about one, the one sponsored by
the Countess Samoyloff, that young and beautiful foreigner who has
made Milan her home and who, with the help of her immense fortune
and lavish magnificence, has conquered a small social kingdom there.[10]
The ordinary people love and swear by her because her charity and
generosity are limitless. The middle classes keep an eye on her because
there is an element of strangeness in her tastes and something rather
grand about her person. Her peers envy her greatly because her home
is a center for delights and amusements that eclipse all others. When
you arrive in Milan, the first name you hear is that of the Countess.
Wherever your business or daily routine takes you, the Duchess of

10. Julia Pahlen-Samoyloff (1803–1875), a Russian noblewoman, known for her
beauty and her unconventional lifestyle. Marie d'Agoult disapproved of her, noting
her "uninterrupted succession of mediocre lovers, almost all musicians" (d'Agoult,
Mémoires, p. 126). Liszt, for his part, apparently joined the parade for a short time
during later visits to Milan and Vienna. He also dedicated the Ricordi edition of his
transcription of the [Rossini] *Soirées musicales* to her.

Litta's salon or the bootmaker's shop, people talk to you about the Countess. Go to the perfumer's and he will offer you the essence preferred by the Countess; enter the stationer's store and he will try to sell you the paper that the Countess uses; glance at a New Year's album and it is dedicated to the Countess. Is there a crowd in the street? That is because the people have formed a circle around the Russian carriage and the English hounds belonging to Madame the Countess. In fact, when the Countess sneezes all Milan says "God bless you!"

People had waited impatiently for the soirée that the Countess had long since promised to give. They were to hear a great singer, Madame Pasta, who had retired from the stage but was in no sense replaced on it. Many people wanted to indulge in the melancholy pleasure of comparing their current impressions with their past feelings, of noting the differences between the woman of forty and the one of twenty-five and saying to themselves, "This is what she is, that is what she had been." The younger people, never having heard her, wanted to take the measure of her fame. Such overwhelming fame, such a heavy a burden for an artist to bear, now that the years have left her perhaps with all her powers to feel but diminished her ability to express those feelings, now that her talent has kept all of its clarity but lost its splendor, and now that younger and more vigorous talents have been able, simply by their youth, to arouse a warmer response than her lifeless perfection.

Oh! that is true death for an artist a slow, perfidious death which, drop by drop, dries up the poetic spring from which he draws the renewed strength of his existence! How people mourn those who, having provided such wonderful enjoyment, have died prematurely. But the artist is almost envious of the fate that befell Malibran, who carried her beauty, glory, and genius to the tomb before the years had stripped her of them and before the acclamations of the crowd had subsided into indifferent silence.[11] The artist is not frightened by the blow that struck Bellini at a time when the dawn of his talent was promising such a radiant day and when his contemporaries, by applauding his works, welcomed them as the brilliant guarantee of an even more glorious future. Indeed, isn't the unfulfilled promise he left behind more valuable than the reality? Man's imagination takes its greatest pleasure in magnifying and embellishing what "might have been." The criticism that assails the present can have no quarrel with

---

11. Malibran was twenty-eight years old when she died, as the result of injuries sustained in a horse-riding accident. Bellini, mentioned next, was thirty-three when he succumbed, apparently of cholera.

the future, and those whom death has spared their declining years have no reason to complain. Happy is the bard who dies while striking the most powerful chord of his lyre! But as for those who are still gathering life's freshest flowers in the sunshine of their youth, we wish them neither long and colorless days, nor resignation, that pale, scentless bloom that only grows in the arid desert of old age.

At the concert, Madame Pasta was what she has always been and will always be—great, noble, and majestic. Poggi[12] captivated us with the touching purity of his voice and his finely wrought sensibility. He is one of the best, if not the best, of Italian tenors today. The finale of *Lucia di Lammermoor,* admirably performed by Madame Pasta, Poggi, and Count Belgiojoso, made a tremendous impression, as usual. Even though there were over ten selections on the program, the concert seemed short. Then, while the guests strolled through the apartments, where Gothic and Rococo styles competed for attention and the paintings of Hayez and Liparini faced Marchesi's sculptures across a perfumed space,[13] the music room was quickly converted into a lovely ballroom. A bevy of pretty young women flocked to it, eager to show off the style and richness of their finery to better advantage. Diamonds and flowers, gauzes and satins floated, fluttered, and swirled to the captivating strains of a Strauss waltz.[14] It was a dazzling fairyland.

I tried for a moment to join the others in the happy swirl, to open my senses to the party's enchantment, to enjoy my rightful share of the noisy amusements. I wished that I was young in the same way that the others were young and that I could let myself experience the frivolity of pleasure in the same way that I had frequently experienced the sting of suffering. But no.—The music had produced its usual effect on me; it had isolated me in the midst of a crowd; it had wrenched me from the external world only to plunge me into the depths of an interior one. As the memories of my recent busy and solitary life also succeeded in making me indifferent to worldly pleasures, I asked myself what I was doing in the midst of this elegant gathering, why I found myself mixed up in the worldly tumult, and what had led me into the company of these rich possessors of the earth. These questions

12. Antonio Poggi (1808–1875), a tenor remembered for his singing of Rossini and his later roles in several of Verdi's early operas.
13. Francesco Hayez (1791–1882), Venetian born, northern Italian painter, known for his historical frescoes and his portraits (including one of Countess Samoyloff). Lodovico Liparini (1800–1856). Pompéo Marchesi (1789–1858), Roman-trained sculptor, professor at Milan Academy. His portrait busts include those of Malibran and Pasta at La Scala.
14. The elder Johann Strauss (1804–1849) is meant.

and the many others that I silently asked myself soon led to an unbearable feeling of uneasiness. I felt so out of place, so dejected, so embarrassed at my uselessness that I left the ballroom and went in search of a secluded, unoccupied corner where I could be alone. I crossed through several rooms where people were chatting. The noise of the ball faded little by little as I moved farther and farther away and then ceased entirely when I entered an isolated boudoir. It was furnished in Gothic style and dimly lit by an alabaster lamp that shed its rays on dark clusters of tropical plants—strange flowers, pale, beautiful, with drooping heads, flowers that seemed saddened by their sumptuous exile. Some of them had woven graceful spirals around delicate, ebony trellises, and upon reaching the tops had let themselves fall dejectedly, as if they were discouraged by not being able to reach the sky's air and light.

I sat down in a huge armchair whose black carvings and Gothic forms carried my imagination to a past age, while the scent of the exotic flowers conjured up visions of distant climes. I do not know if I dozed off in that poetic silence far from the activity and noise. I do not know if my imagination, excited by the music, or my nerves, agitated by green tea and the phantasmagoria of the gala, caused me to see a startling, supernatural apparition. All I know for certain is that I very quickly lost all sense of reality, all feeling for time and place, and that I suddenly found myself wandering all alone in an unknown land on a deserted beach beside a stormy sea.[15] Then, as I vainly tried to recall how and by what path I got there, I noticed the tall, serious, and pensive figure of a man walking along the sand a few steps away from me. He was still young, although his face was pale, his look intense, and his cheeks haggard. He stared at the horizon with an indescribable expression of anxiety and hope. A magnetic force drew me after him. He did not seem to notice that someone was following him and continued to walk without stopping. Although his pace was slow and measured, he, by some terrifying magic, covered immeasurable distances, leaving plains, mountains, forests, and valleys behind him. Overtaking him was impossible, yet I persisted in following him. The farther I went, the more it seemed to me that my existence was linked to his, that his breath animated my life, that he held the secret of my destiny, and that we, he and I, had to merge with and transform each other.

The sky, which had been clear and bright when we began our journey, soon became overcast. The vegetation gradually grew sparser.

15. A dream sequence prompted by Heine's dream? It would seem so (see app. B).

We found ourselves on an arid plain, where there were no trees to punctuate its vast expanse, no breeze to refresh it. It simply lay there bearing the weight of a dull, scorching day. Nature, I noticed, took on a dismal air. A bird with dark plumage and a hideous head was flying about and uttered a high-pitched cry as it brushed against my face. It was a mocking, cursing cry. Overwhelming terror gripped me. I collapsed on the dry earth and thought I was going to die. Making one last effort, I called out—but to whom? To him whom I did not know. I called to him, but I cannot recollect his name. He turned briefly and from a distance looked at me with compassion. He then continued on his way without a word. Thus abandoned, I screamed in desperation and rage. My foot had struck a reaper's sickle. I clutched it and was about to stab myself when the unknown man stopped again. This time, I thought, I am saved. Now, I thought, he would be moved by my pleas and fervent prayers. "Oh, whoever you are," I cried, "incomprehensible being who has fascinated and taken complete possession of me, tell me, tell me, who are you? Where do you come from? Where are you going? What is the reason for your journey? What are you seeking? Where do you rest? . . . Are you a condemned man under an irrevocable sentence? Are you a pilgrim filled with hope eagerly traveling to a peaceful, holy place?"

The traveler stood there and made a sign that he was about to speak. I noticed that he was holding an oddly shaped musical instrument whose bright, metallic finish shone like a mirror in the rays of the setting sun. An evening breeze rose, carrying with it the notes of the mysterious lyre: broken notes, unconnected chords, vague and indefinite sounds, suggesting at times the crashing of waves over a reef, the murmur of pines defying a tempest, or the confused buzzing of a beehive or large crowds of people. From time to time the music would stop and I heard the following clear words:

"Do not trouble to follow me; the hope you attach to my steps is deceptive. Do not ask me what I do not know; the mystery you want to fathom has not been revealed to me.

"I come from a distant land that I can no longer remember. For a long, long time I descended the slopes of a high mountain. I have crossed the celebrated valleys; I have heard the roar of the waves; I have gazed at the lightning that split the clouds while the centuries-old oak fell at my feet; I have seen the terrifying avalanche crush the shepherd's stronghold and the dove's nest; I have bathed my tired limbs in the angry torrent that had just broken its embankment and flooded the ripening crops; I have heard infants wail, women groan, and men blaspheme.

"In the desert I have faced the jackal, the vulture, the hyena, and the crocodile—in human society, the tyrant, the slave, the hangman, and the parricide."

. . . .

"In time, I was disgusted by an earth so empty of blessings, so full of tears. I quickened my steps. I walked, walked ceaselessly, looking toward the distant horizon for my unknown homeland.

"So far, it has all been in vain. I yearn, I sense the future, but nothing is apparent yet. I do not know if after all this time I am coming to the end of my journey. The force that drives me is silent; it tells me nothing of my path.

"At times the breeze coming over the water carries ineffable harmonies to me; I listen to them rapturously, but as soon as I think they are coming nearer, they are smothered by the discordant din of human strife.

"At times, too, in the dying flickers of the day, the white clouds hovering around the mountain tops take on pure, transparent colors. Their subtle tints change continually as they merge and produce an indescribable, shifting array of color and light, as though thousands of souls had been transfigured and were ascending to the heavens. But the sun, sinking behind the mountains, reclaims its magnificent rays; the clouds become thick, heavy, and dull again . . . and I resume my desolate and uncertain way.

"If it is a malevolent force that harasses and torments me, why these divine dreams, these inexpressible, voluptuous floods of desire? If it is a beneficent power that is drawing me to it, why does it leave me in the anguish of doubt, with the pangs of a hope that is always alive yet always thwarted?

"Adieu.—Do not look for *knowledge;* your fate is ignorance. Do not look for *ability;* your fate is impotence. Do not look for *enjoyment;* your fate is abstinence."

. . . .

A jolt, like an electric shock, restored me to my senses. I descended the steps of the Samoyloff mansion. The party was over, and some of the more intrepid dancers were hurrying off to their carriages.

"Well now, Liszt," said the young Marquise of G—— as she passed close to me, "Why are you looking at us that way? Aren't you going to say goodnight to us?" "Let him be," said the Duke of C ——, who was with her. "You can see he doesn't recognize us. That demon inspiration has him, and he looks at the moment like he is composing a Requiem, which will surely be thoroughly enjoyable. I wager that he will arrive at Como this morning firmly convinced that he has been on his way to the 'Bella Venezia'[16] all the while."

Once back in my room, I sat down to the piano. "The Wanderer" came to mind, and that song, so sad and so poetic, affected me more than it ever had before. I seemed to sense a tenuous and secret analogy between Schubert's music and the music I had heard in my dream.

What would you have said if you had seen me a few days later, standing at a window on the *Corso* ludicrously armed with a long pewter spoon and digging relentlessly into a cloth sack for *curiandoli,** which I then threw into the face of similarly armed people with truly ferocious force? Had I lost my mind? Had I gone totally mad? Well, yes, if you grant that the entire city was also gripped by the same madness, because on the day I am talking about, the last day of Carnival, there is not a single person—rich or poor, great lord or peasant—who does not take part in the unique frolic. Imagine, if you can, all the windows, all the balconies, all the rooftops along a broad street filled with men and women covered with plaster dust and throwing *curiandoli* at the passersby for hours on end. Just imagine the carriages disappearing into that artificial hail storm; the unbelievable crowd both defying and provoking it; a war being fought at all the crossroads and street corners; an unspoken pact against all clean suits and new hats; an epidemic of folly, mischievous will, wicked pleasure, and the sense of pride that is involved in throwing and receiving as much of this harlequin confetti as possible. And that is how they celebrate the last days of Carnival in Milan.

If you had a bird's-eye view of it, you might observe primly, "What a stupid pastime!" But be part of it and the fever grips you; you no longer look for philosophy and logic where there is nothing but action and noise. You spend several hours outside yourself, and that is not a bad thing for many people.

Adieu, my friend. The lamp is going out, day is approaching. I have allowed myself to chatter on, just as we used to do in my garret on Rue de Provence. Poor little garret! You haven't forgotten it, have you? Do you remember those dozen square feet always flooded with sunshine and cluttered with those indispensable knicknacks, against which my good mother's sense of neatness and order waged such an unpitying war? Do you remember the big folio volume of Plutarch that we alternately used as a music stand and a judge's bench? Do you remember our loud, senseless laughter, our innumerable jokes, or

* Plaster pellets shaped like anise seeds.

16. Liszt's hotel in Milan.

some critical essay or other that took me seriously to task, while teaching us the aesthetic principles of beauty? Do you remember all this as vividly as I do? Do your thoughts sometimes reach out to your absent friend, inviting him to sit beside you, share your activities, applaud your successes, and smile at your joys? Oh! Tell me that it is so. Tell me that nothing has changed. Tell me that when I return I will still have my place at your fireside, a refuge in your heart. Tell me, too, that I will hear those energetic and vibrant chords again, those most tender and melancholy songs that I have never been able to listen to without being moved, and which are for me the ideal expression of your warm and faithful friendship. [The text of this Letter continues in the following chapter, p. 138.]

7

VENICE AND VIENNA

CHRONICLE

ca. 22 March 1838. Liszt and Madame d'Agoult arrive in Venice and, like most tourists, immediately set out to visit the famed places of interest: Piazza San Marco, La Fenice, the art galleries, the Doge's Palace, and the like.

28 March. Liszt performs ("Frequenti palpiti") at a concert of the Apollo Society. Three days later, 1 April, he gives a concert of his own at the Teatro San Benedetto.

ca. 1 April. Liszt learns that a disastrous flood has swept through Hungary, and he promptly decides to go to Vienna to give a benefit concert for the flood victims. Marie, who does not like the prospect of being left alone in Venice, objects, but Liszt persists. (Vienna was not just any city, it was the Austro-Hungarian capital he had left fifteen years before as an acclaimed prodigy.) At this point a young Venetian, Count Emilio Malazonni, steps in, offering to look after Marie while Liszt is away.

7 April. Liszt leaves for Vienna, fully intending to give only two concerts—one for flood relief and the other to pay his expenses—and return by the end of the month.

18 April–25 May. Liszt's two concerts grow to ten, plus any number of private soirées. Vienna goes crazy over Liszt. The demand to hear him is insatiable; it becomes virtually impossible for him to leave. In Venice, meanwhile, Marie falls ill and pleads with him to return.

ca. 1 June. Liszt finally arrives back in Venice.

The three articles pertaining to these two months are a miscellaneous lot. The first, addressed to Heine, is not really a travel article, but a highly personal response to an article that the poet had published earlier in the year (see app. B). The second, "Venice," is by far the longest and in some ways the most ambitious of the travel articles. Music plays a secondary role in it, as Liszt and his collaborator, delving into Venice's history, customs, art, and architecture, present their idiosyncratic view of the complex city. The last—the second half of the Letter to Massart—is Liszt's account of his experiences in Vienna.

To Heinrich Heine[1]

Venice, 15 April [1838][2]

I stood in Venice, on the Bridge of Sighs.[3]

Ah! my God, yes, just like Byron and just like the thousands of imbeciles who came after him, following his footsteps in order to glean some scraps of poetry, which their rough hands immediately transformed into appalling commonplaces. In any event, I was in Venice when an old friend, a great lover of art, arrived from Paris carrying a tasty spring morsel, the issue of the *Revue musicale* that contains the

---

1. *Gazette musicale*, 8 July 1838, pp. 279–81.

2. This date presents a problem, whether it is taken as the date of the Letter or as the day on which Heine's article reached Venice, as the first paragraph states. To interpret it literally would mean that Heine's article arrived while Liszt was in Vienna and, by implication, that Marie d'Agoult was solely responsible for the reply. A literal reading is not justified, however, in view of the bantering style of the opening portion and several important logistical points that also should be taken into account. First, it is very difficult to believe that the issue of the *Gazette* (4 February 1838) containing Heine's article took nine weeks to reach Italy, when the mails between Paris and Milan generally took only four to six days. Second, four days after the article had appeared Berlioz wrote Liszt, informing him: "Our friend Heine has recently spoken about the two of us in the *Gazette musicale* with as much style as irreverence, but without being malicious in any way. As for Chopin, on the other hand, he wove the splendid laurel crown that Chopin has deserved for a long time" (Berlioz, *Correspondance générale* 2: no. 538). As this letter reached Liszt, via Ricordi, in Milan in mid-February, he would certainly have made every effort to secure the article as quickly as possible. Third, the route given in the opening paragraph that the "old friend" took in delivering Heine's article from Milan to Venice is the same route that Liszt and Marie d'Agoult had traveled the month before. It is thus reasonable to assume that Liszt read Heine's article in Milan and, upon arriving in Venice, wrote a reply which he left with Marie d'Agoult to polish, along with the article "La Scala," while he went to Vienna. Liszt may not have actually seen the final text she sent to Paris, but he surely drafted the substance of the reply to Heine.

3. Byron, *Childe Harold's Pilgrimage*, canto 4, line 1. Quoted in English.

second of your Confidential Letters. That friend came here directly—the passport he held proved that—but his "direct route" took him to Milan and the frescoes of Luini, to Brescia and the paintings of Moretto, to Verona and the tombs of the Scaligeri, to Vicenza and the villas of Palladio, to Padua and the bas-reliefs of Donatello. Undoubtedly he must have lingered for weeks at a time in ecstasy before these masterpieces, for it was only today, the 15th of April, that he, with most laudable dispatch, brought me your letter of 4 February. Through another friend who is returning to France this very moment I send you my thanks for all the flattering things you have said about me. But Heavens! the man is a raving naturalist. God knows how many anemones and saxifrages he will analyze while he recrosses the Alps! Who can tell for how many days, months, or years a lichen, a moss, or a cricket will keep him on the slopes of Stelvio or on the ridge of Saint Gotthard? By that time—"The king, the ass, or I might well be dead."[4]

No matter. Let us talk as if there were neither time nor space between us. Let us talk through the medium of sylphs, gnomes, water sprites, hobgoblins, your first cousins,[5] and a few of my relations too, if I am not mistaken. By the time my letter arrives, if it ever does arrive, they will have long since whispered its contents to you, and more besides.

For a start, you will hardly be surprised to learn that your letter remained in my hands for no more than a quarter of an hour. It got away without my noticing it, and before the day was over everyone in Venice had read those amusing lines in which my friend Chopin figures so clearly, my friend Berlioz so irreverently, Messers Kalkbrenner and Thalberg so judiciously, and I, your most humble servant, so fantastically. Then just imagine, if you can, my great astonishment and the deeply embarrassed look on my face when all my Venetian friends suddenly began to arrive one after the other. They have taken your postprandial fantasies seriously and are here, asking me for an account of the various political and philosophical phases it amused you to have me go through. One begs me to please show him my Saint-Simonian outfit;[6] another to play the last fugue that I composed on themes from *Palingenesis;* a third is vainly taxing his wits trying to reconcile my

4. " [Avant l'affair] le roi, l'âne ou moi, nous mourrons" (La Fontaine, "The Charlatan," book 6, fable 19, line 35).

5. "Cousin" was a friendly pet name for Heine that Liszt, George Sand, and others bandied about.

6. Saint-Simonian adepts at Menilmontant wore a symbolic costume that consisted of white trousers (symbolizing love), a red waistcoat (work) and a blue-violet

devilishly handsome way of life with the Catholic austerity you have me raving about; a fourth considers my piano an infernal machine pure and simple. . . . In short, I do not know to whom I should listen; it is a regular cross-examination, and I feel as though I were back in the Inquisition. . . .

Fortunately, a boat is passing beneath my windows just now. It carries musicians, and a man's beautiful voice, accompanied by a chorus, is singing "La notte è bella."[7] . . . They are going to the Lido; I shout that we must follow them; we leap into my gondola; no one bothers about me or my beliefs, and I am saved for the night. . . . But no; because when I returned, I thought I had better reread your letter, and I find who knows what sober purpose, what sense of conviction cutting through its many charming pleasantries, and it moves me, against my will, to reply seriously.

Publishing the feelings and thoughts of someone's private life in the press is one of the evils of our time. We artists do each other a great injustice when we judge one another not just by our works but also in personal terms, and when we, as a result, mutually hold up to public scrutiny—often quite brutally and almost always inaccurately—a part of our lives that should at least wait until we are no longer alive to be investigated. This manner of gratifying the public's curiosity or an individual's vanity, of giving a course in psychological anatomy, has become habitual with us. No one no longer has a right to complain about it, because no one has spared others. Besides, if the truth be told, most artists are not overly offended by the publicity, favorable or not, since it puts their names in circulation for a few days at least. Let me assure you, though, that I am certainly not one of them. When criticism is directed towards me as an artist, I accept it or reject it; in either case, it does not harm me. But when it seeks to judge the man, then it arouses a fierce sensitivity in me that balks at the slightest reproach. That, you see, is because I am still so young; my heartbeats are too strong for me to be patient and tolerate anyone's placing a hand on my heart and doing an accounting of them. The things that I admire, that I hate, and that I hope for have sunk their roots too deeply into my soul for anyone to expose them that easily. People have very often done

---

tunic (faith). The waistcoat was also a symbol of cooperation, the spirit of association, since it laced up the back and could not be donned without help.

7. A song by Giovanni Battista Perucchini (1784–1870), an amateur composer of charming and popular Venetian songs. The *Gondoliera* in Liszt's little collection *Venezia e Napoli* is based on Perucchini's song "La Biondina in Gondoletta."

it with hostile intentions, and I have responded with silence. But you have now done it with the hand of a friend, and it is to the friend that I wish to reply.

You accuse me of having an "unsettled"[8] character, and to prove it you enumerate the many causes that I have, as you say, eagerly embraced, those "philosophical stables" from which I selected one "hobbyhorse" after another. But tell me, shouldn't the accusation you level at me alone be leveled, in all fairness, at our entire generation? Am I the only one who is unsettled these days? Or rather, aren't we all, despite our fine Gothic armchairs and Voltaire-styled cushions, very unsettled, existing between a past we no longer want and a future we have yet to know? Even you, my friend, who seem to be taking your share of the world's miseries so lightly at the moment, have you always been so well settled? Not long ago, when your country was closed to you and you arrived in our midst,[9] welcomed on all sides as a powerful new force, did you suddenly become and remain forever settled? On the contrary, haven't there been many hours and days when you felt unsettled about your beliefs? You, with your noble calling as a thinker and poet, have you always seen the light of your own star that clearly?

If I am not mistaken, during the time when I was quietly attending the Saint-Simonian lectures—along with many others who drew more than I did from that gushing spring of ideas, and who are now very well settled in the armchairs of Louis-Philippe's respectable society—I saw you from a distance, you the illustrious poet, being inducted into the sanctuary itself, and you had no qualms about owning up to this fact later by dedicating a fine book to Père Enfantin, one in which you asked him to allow you to "commune with him across time and space."[10] Still later, the kindness accorded me by Ballanche permitted me, together with you, to meet with him and to echo humbly, on occasion, those words of admiration which, in your mouth, could have been flattery. We, you and I, were still very unsettled in our seats then because, to tell the truth, the great philosopher scarcely had any time to think about renovating his furniture.

It is true that you have always managed to dispense with the Cross of Golgotha better than I have. Moreover, you have energeti-

---

8. *Mal assis,* which literally means "poorly seated," hence Liszt's references to arm chairs, cushions, and the like.

9. Heine had arrived in Paris in May 1831. His choice to remain there as an expatriate was a voluntary one.

10. Heine's *De l'Allemagne* (1835) is the work dedicated to Enfantin. It is a French version of his *The Romantic School* and *Salon II.*

cally rejected the accusation that you belong with those who erected it for the Savior of the World.[11] . . . And the "Jacobin cap," what do you say about that? Isn't it just possible that someone searching carefully could find it in your own wardrobe? A bit faded, a little threadbare perhaps, and rather embarrassed, above all, at being found there between an old-fashioned dressing gown and an old pair of slippers? Believe me, oh my friend, no accusations of instability, no recriminations: our times are sick, we are all sick along with them. But mind you, a poor musician should not be held overly accountable for that, because he who does not hold a pen or wield a sword can, without too much compunction, give himself over to his intellectual curiosity and turn whichever way he thinks he sees the light.

He is often unsettled sitting on the stool that serves as his judging bench, but he does not envy those who are well settled in their self-interest and who, disregarding their heart and mind, apparently live only for their mouth and stomach. Oh, my friend, we are not like that, are we? We are not like that, and we will never be.

But putting aside this solemn tone which almost sounds as if I were reproaching you when I really owe you my warmest thanks, do you know what my favorite hobbyhorses are at the moment? Oh, this time I am sure that you will find no fault with them; they are the ancient bronze horses, those sad voyagers who have seen so many lands, so many things, and who have witnessed the fall of four empires! They are those favorites of the great men, which Constantine did not want to leave behind, he who left Rome behind! which Dandolo[12] did not refuse, he who refused Constantinople! which Napoleon wanted to possess, he who possessed the world! So here they are, back at their old resting place, and the doors of St. Mark's once more open beneath their hooves.[13] What strange change took place during their short absence? Where is the doge? Where are the patricians who followed in his train? Who are those people walking sullen

11. Heine, like a number of Jews during this period, found it socially prudent to "convert" to Christianity. He was baptized in 1825, just prior to receiving a doctor of laws degree.

12. Enrico Dandolo (died 1205), doge and leader of the Fourth Crusade, which captured Constantinople in 1204.

13. Originally the four gilt-bronze horses probably adorned Nero's triumphal arch and afterwards that of Trajan in Rome. Constantine then sent them to embellish the imperial hippodrome in Constantinople, whence Doge Dandolo took them to Venice in 1204 as spoils of war. In 1797 Napoleon removed them to Paris, but in 1815 they were restored to their former position at Saint Mark's by order of Emperor Franz of Austria.

and silent under the marble colonnade, under the mosaic cupolas? The palace is deserted, the piazza is mute; no more cries of victory, no more joys. Grandeur, iniquity, terror, and glory all have fallen into the abyss of history. Faliero's black sail is spread over the entire republic,[14] an unknown language fills the air, and the noble coursers no longer recognize familiar voices. All they see is their old bronze comrade, the winged lion of Saint Mark, still atop his African column and still gazing toward the sea.

But I am mistaken; some of their other friends are still here. Behold the gentle birds, those trusting pigeons who flutter fearlessly about them, swooping down on their motionless manes as they did in the past. The winged republic, which owed its origin to the symbolic games of Catholicism, continues to exist, young and vibrant, long after the other has ceased to be. The state that provided so carefully for their feeding is no more, but the people, in the midst of their greatest disasters, did not forget their beloved birds. Everyone, rich or poor, contributed his share, so that the birds would not be aware of the evil times and would continue to soar over the dying city, like the memory of a happy boyhood does around the bald pate of a drowsy old man.

Have you ever been to Venice? Have you ever glided on the sleepy waters in a black gondola down the length of the Grand Canal or along the banks of the Giudecca? Have you felt the weight of centuries crushing down on your helpless thoughts? Have you breathed that turgid, heavy air that oppresses you and thrusts you down into inconceivable languor? Have you seen the moon cast its pale rays on the leaden domes of old Saint Mark's? Did your ear, uneasy about the deathly silence, ever seek out some sound, just as the eye seeks out light in the darkness of the dungeon? Yes, no doubt about it. Then you are familiar perhaps with the most poetic desolation in the world.

But I think I am succumbing to the effusions of a sentimental tourist, which is not really to your taste, nor to mine. Besides, the bell of the Capuchins is tolling the midnight Office. It is the hour for me to go and smoke my sea-cane pipe on the *Riva degli Schiavoni,* asking myself at times what secret power has brought us together—the pipe, that humble cane from the Adriatic marshes, and I, a child of the Danube—in order for us to be broken: the pipe by my hand tonight after

14. Marino Faliero (ca. 1278–1355), commander of Venetian forces; elected doge in 1354, he was soon convicted of conspiring to murder patricians and have himself proclaimed prince. He is the subject of tragedies by Byron and Casimir Delavigne, a tale by E. T. A. Hoffman, and an opera by Donizetti (1835).

it will have served my empty dreams for an hour, and I by an unknown hand tomorrow, after having served—what? I do not know.

Venice[1]

[March–November 1838][2]

"Well, this is the third time I have been to Venice," said the colonel,[3] who was having a difficult time trying vainly to squeeze his lanky form sideways through the gondola cabin's narrow door, "and I still haven't been able to figure out how to board these damned gondolas in a proper way."

"'Proper' is the most arbitrary word in the language," said Arabella with a slight smile that tweaked our friend's foul humor and desperate efforts. "What is proper in a salon is not proper in a church. What is proper during a coach ride certainly does not apply to a trip in a gondola. Come now, colonel, don't be shy. Board the gondola the same way King Louis XVIII used to leave his carriage and come, sit beside me." Emilio was already growing impatient; we were wasting precious time on senseless formalities, he cried. He could not imagine that anyone would have the slightest hesitation about entering a gondola the Venetian way, even in the presence of a foreigner.

"You must admit, however," answered the colonel, dropping heavily beside poor Arabella and half crushing her in the process, "that this is an indecent way to present oneself to a lady."

"To be honest," she said, "I am still not completely convinced of the ineffable delights of a gondola, and so I find myself quarreling with Emilio every time we touch upon that delicate point. He absolutely insists that I admire this species of black-draped coffin, which is so

1. L'Artiste, 16 June–11 August 1839, in 5 installments: pp. 91–93, 132–34, 220–23, 237–39, and 255–57.

2. Although the narrative in this article ends with the departure from Venice in June 1838, the writing of it was not finished until November. It was then that Liszt sent it to Schlesinger (Liszt, Briefe 8: no. 22), fully realizing that he would probably reject it as unsuitable for the Gazette, which he did. The manuscript was then turned over to Jules Janin for eventual publication in L'Artiste.

3. The colonel is not identified, nor is the abbé Z. who appears later. Both may be fictional creations. Arabella, on the other hand, is Marie d'Agoult, Emilio is Count Emilio Malazonni, and Cornelio is the gondolier whom Liszt had hired for the entire stay in Venice.

narrow and so low that you can neither enter nor leave it without hitting your head or, what is worse for us women, without disturbing your hat, your dress, or your shawl. To say nothing of the pleasure of getting your feet wet on the steps of all the houses or having your hair mussed by the rude gust of wind that seems to be standing sentry at every door. . . ."

"You are talking like a Parisian," said Emilio, who was sitting on the little side bench facing me. "You don't understand the charm of our floating retreats, which the Greeks said were invented by a jealous god who was in love with a mortal woman. If they are narrow, people will tell you that it is so they won't obstruct our canals. But I say that it is to bring lovers closer together. If they are low, people will tell you that it is so they can pass under the bridges that link our houses together, even during the highest tides. But I swear to you that it was done on purpose so that the only way a woman can sit in one is to recline in a most voluptuous position. To experience the poetry of a gondola you have to have jealously hidden your beloved away in one; you have to have skimmed over the waves with her, as if you were riding a seabird's wings, gliding furtively in the shadows of the Moorish palaces or along the wall where the seaweed weep; you have to have traveled all through this populous city in the way that lovers would like to travel through life, alone, absolutely alone between the sea and sky, free from all prying eyes, defying everyone's narrow minds, and stealing away to do whatever you wish. What other sort of tryst could possibly be as charming and enchanting! The cabin, you say, resembles a coffin, but what of it? Isn't the thought of death always present in the heart of a man who loves ardently? Isn't death the only thing that he could or would want to have end his happiness? Aren't lovers dead to everything except their passion? Oh! Who can possibly describe the languor of the starry night, when the soft murmurs of the waves mix with the sighs and declarations of love; when the breeze coming through the black jalousie carries with it the perfume of flower-filled balconies and a caged nightingale's song that plays among the masses of long ringlets that grace your darling's brow; when two ivory arms sink their erotic contours into the downy cushions, and the gentle rocking of the waves numbs the mind and plunges the senses into indescribable rapture! . . . And so, you see, he who has not loved in Venice has missed all the poetry of love, and he who has lived in Venice without being in love has missed all the poetry of Venice!"

While Emilio was talking, the colonel more or less managed to get settled; he moved to his side as best he could, tucking his long legs beneath him, legs worthy of the Russian ballet.

"In your dithyrambic enthusiasm you have overlooked the most important thing," said Arabella. "What about the songs of Tasso?[4] And those melodious voices calling and answering each other as they celebrate the charms of pale Hermione or haughty Clorinda?"

At that moment the guttural voice of our gondolier Cornelio gave a screeching cry. We were at a turning in the canal, and the cry was a precaution to prevent the collision of two gondolas that unexpectedly met without seeing each other.

"I am hesitant to talk to you about things that no longer exist," replied Emilio. "But that startling, raucous cry also has its poetry, for no other reason than it stirs your imagination to yearn for melodies to which you ascribe a charm that they perhaps never possessed. The contrast between our sorry condition today and the ideal grace with which you cloak the past is the source of the sad, bitter poetry that envelops my dear home like a mourner's veil. What does it matter how our emotions are stirred? Besides, is reality ever poetic, except for the feelings and regrets it awakens within us?"

"That's all quite true!" Arabella replied. "I do admit, however, that my first impression of Venice was a great disappointment. I don't like your dirty canals, reeking of death. I am irritated by the endless silence, broken only by the monotonous tolling of bells and the slapping of oars in the water. My ears are eager to hear noise, in the way that eyes in a dungeon yearn for light. I am looking for a tree, a shrub, a grassy knoll. I would love to see a bird that was not in a cage, a plant that was not in a pot, a gondola that was not black, and, above all, a runaway horse. My God, what a beautiful thing a runaway horse is! How is it possible to live in a place where one does not run the risk of being trampled by a horse! . . ."

The colonel smiled approvingly at Arabella's witticism and asked me if my first impression was different from hers.

"You are going to have a poor opinion of my artistic faculties," I replied, "when I tell you that I hardly know what a first impression is. It is very rare for me to experience any emotion when I first arrive at my planned destination. It almost always takes some time for things to have an effect on me, and I might say that I am penetrated by them rather than struck by them. Besides, when you travel in any way but on foot with a pack on your back, the first moments after you arrive anywhere are taken up by certain types of people, certain business mat-

---

4. Torquato Tasso (1544–1595), the Italian epic poet. Liszt, while in Venice, heard a gondolier sing some of Tasso's verses and used the melody as the main theme of his later symphonic poem *Tasso, Lamento e trionfo* (1849).

ters that leave very little time for excitement. Paying the coachman, clearing customs, and negotiating with the hotel keeper are not the sort of mental operations that prepare the mind for rapturous flights. Personally, I would say that whether you arrive in Venice, Vienna, London, or St. Petersburg, it is all the same; some differences in temperature, a few more police formalities, a few less, and that's all the difference you find."

Chatting this way, we arrived at the ferry landing for the piazza and disembarked between two columns, one of which supports the winged lion of Saint Mark, while the other holds Saint Theodore, the city's now-abandoned patron to whom Venice, like a true courtesan, left some vestige of her favors after she had given herself to his more powerful rival.

"It is here, between these two columns," Emilio remarked, "that state criminals used to be put to death. It was here in the sixteenth century that a young nobleman, Alviso Sanuto, chose to die rather than defile the name of the woman he loved by uttering it to his judges. At that time, the uneasy and terribly suspicious Senate had passed a law that condemned to death any patrician who was convicted of having any dealings with a foreign ambassador. Sanuto had seen the French ambassador's daughter, the lovely Amélie, at a number of ceremonial functions. Almost immediately her wonderful face, the grace of her carriage, and something both coquettish and dreamy about her inflamed him. He conceived one of those imperious passions that demand to be satisfied, even if the whole world should fall apart. His diligence in stationing himself along the noble foreigner's path caused her to notice him. He was handsome, with a proud yet modest bearing, and she was sixteen years old. Their glances met. A few mad words of love were exchanged in the dark shadows of Saint Mark's pillars, and they once clasped each other's hand. That night Sanuto bribed one of the embassy servants; the chambermaid became a part of the amorous plot; a plank was thrown across the canal, a window left open. . . . The young lovers were in each other's arms. But a state spy—they had them then in all the houses, in all the families—had seen Sanuto and denounced him. At the moment when the first light of dawn wrested him from the arms of the trembling virgin, at the moment when he, still ecstatic from one last embrace, put his foot on the threshold of the house, he felt the hand of the Tribunal's agent on him. He knew he was lost. Without saying a word, he entered the ominous gondola that was waiting to take him before the inquisitors. But neither prayers, threats, nor pain broke his spirit, which harbored more happiness than the inquisitors had torments. He allowed himself to be accused of conspiracy against the state, condemned to death, and led to the scaffold, reverently protecting in the depths of his heart the name that could have saved him, but which he wanted to carry, pure and undefiled, to the realm of eternal love!"

"And the lovely Amélie?" asked Arabella.

"The chronicles tell us that on the following day while standing on her balcony she saw a convoy of patricians on the Grand Canal, and that, already troubled and agitated by presentiments and dreams, she asked for whom the funeral chants, lugubrious torches, and trappings of grief were. The name she heard struck like a thunderbolt. She fell onto the marble pavement, and her skull was broken. Our chronicles are full of such incidents."

"I know of nothing more dramatic than the history of Venice," I said to Emilio. "The mystery with which your government cloaked its actions, the arrogant injustice of its judgments, the harshness of its sentences, and the brilliance with which incomparable artists depicted everything stagger and shock the imagination. Look there, close to us, those gigantic symbols of the republic. See those three buildings crowded so close together which represent the concentration of power in Venice—the palace, the basilica, and the prison! The palace, whose imposing structure is ornamented by arabesques, trefoils, and a thousand delicate and finely wrought carvings, stands for mighty and impenetrable power and seems to embody everything that the most ostentatious luxury could provide in order to divert the populace with celebrations and solemnities. The basilica, which was only the doge's chapel attached to the palace, is an excellent symbol of a clergy that, here more than anywhere else, was subservient to the wishes of the chiefs of state. And the prison, joined to the doge's palace by a covered passageway, does it not proclaim that swift, vindictive punishment was the first law of that ferocious State?"

"I don't know why they call Venice the Rome of the Adriatic," the colonel remarked. "They ought to call it the Carthage of the Adriatic. Venice in modern times is what Carthage was in ancient times: a merchant power, extremely eager to make money, jealous of its industry, thankless and treacherous toward its great men, and fighting, for the most part, only with mercenary troops."

"Yes, but it was far more artistic than its rival," added Arabella. "It wanted its story to be written by the hand of genius in marble, in bronze, and on canvas. It summoned Donatello, Michelangelo, Titian, Veronese, Sansovino, and heaped glory on them!"

"Don't talk to me about Sansovino,"[5] I replied. "I cannot forgive him for wanting to raze that oriental marvel, that fantastic Arabian dream, the doge's palace, and replace it with one of those cold symmetrical edifices, so typical of the Renaissance. It was colossal vanity on his part to think that proper, straight lines could outshine the palace's inimitable caprice, the immense charms of its curved vaults, the interlacing of its arches, and the thousand lovely details of its rose-windows and spires."

"That was more a fault of the times than of Sansovino," said Emilio. "You can read the contemporary authors and see how scornfully men of taste regarded the Gothic or *Tudor* style. They preferred the most wretched imitations of Greek art to the most poetic conceptions of vaulted architecture. But enough of talk," he continued, raising the purple curtain that covered the entry to Saint Mark's, "this is the time when the sun is directly over the cupolas. Its light floods the floors. The mosaics shine splendidly, and the haloes of the saints and their blessed company beam brilliantly. It is the best time of day to contemplate the riches of the Christian mosque."

We were awestruck upon entering the church, so extraordinary in its general effect and its details, so unlike anything we had seen before. Despite the incredible profusion, the prodigious diversity of colors and forms that went into its construction, it was easy to take in the unity of its design in a single glance. The grand lines, the majestic sense of order, appeal immediately to the eye, which is not to be distracted nor turned aside by secondary elements. The light pours harmoniously through the openings in the five domes and spreads softly through the three naves, separated from each other by massive pilasters and columns with gilded capitals. The walls are entirely faced in fine marbles, and the columns by mosaics. The earliest mosaics date from the time of the Greek masters, while the most accomplished were done during that prosperous period when the Bianchinis and Zuccatis worked from the cartoons of Palma Vecchio, Padovanino, Titian, and Tintoretto; thus these decorations present an interesting, uninterrupted series of steps in the progress of art.*

The choir is separated from the nave by eight columns that sup-

* One of the mosaics that impressed me most was the Blessed Virgin's family tree. The artist has created a tree with all its branches, limbs, flowers, and fruit. The branches are arranged in such a way as to show the succession of generations, and one of Mary's ancestors perches in an odd stance on each branch.

5. Jacopo Sansovino (1486–1570), sculptor and architect. He was appointed Venice's state architect in 1529.

port an epistyle, upon which stand the statues of Our Lady, Saint Mark, and the twelve apostles. From two sides of that baluster, there rise two pulpits, both of which are supported by priceless columns. The main altar stands under a baldachin of *verd antique*. The celebrated *Pala d'oro* that decorates it on solemn occasions is a magnificent piece of enameling done on sheets of gold and silver surrounded by pearls and precious stones; it is divided into twenty-seven sections depicting scenes from the Old and New Testaments. They say that this exquisitely chased work was begun in Constantinople by order of the Doge Saint Peter Orseolo [928–987] and was enlarged, embellished, and completed in Venice about the year 1345. But the true marvels of the church are the four columns of oriental alabaster that support the [baldachin of the] altar of the Blessed Sacrament. They are spiral in form; two of them are translucent and perfect in their whiteness. There is nothing like them in all Europe.

The church's floor is done in mosaics, in what was formerly called the vermiculated style. Unfortunately, a large portion of the symbolic designs set into the floor is seriously damaged. The floor has borne the weight of centuries and bent beneath human misery. The knees that have fallen there have worn down the resistance of the stone, and the penitents' tears have dimmed the brilliance of the glass. What a long series of sorrows the church has seen! What ostentatious suffering and what obscure griefs have come to kneel before these altars! From the Doge Foscari—that proud old man who outlived the sight of his only son being tortured, and who died in despair upon hearing the bells celebrate the accession of his successor[6]—to the humble wife of Chioggiote, a fisherman who had been surprised by a storm! How many sighs have been lost in the depths of these vaults! How many unknown penitents! How many broken hearts! How much despair! . . . Their names are forgotten, their destinies unknown; the individual does not count in the march of humanity. It took many generations for the floor to sink imperceptibly, and just as many were needed to gild the cupolas, sculpt the capitals, and assemble the bits of glass that outline the glories of Paradise on the walls. But then, when all the work is done, when the last hand has completed its task, when one could only embellish perfection, so that the edifice finally seems worthy of the powers that are offered to the Creator of All Power, what happens to it? A conqueror comes along; the republic is an inconvenience to him

---

6. Francesco Foscari (ca. 1372–1457). His son Giacopo, an incorrigible political plotter, was the bane of his old age and the cause of his downfall. Father and son are the subject of Byron's tragedy, *The Two Foscari*, the source for Verdi's opera.

and so he overthrows it. Henceforth there will be no Doge, no inquisitors, no senate here. Saint Mark's opens its doors to barbarians, and
the state that owed its origins to the terror that spread before the name
Attila owes its demise to the fear inspired by the name Napoleon.[7]

Emilio is brokenhearted about the misery of his land. Greek on
his mother's side and Venetian on his father's, he bears his double
heritage of grandeur and misfortune with dignity. On his sad, pale face
one can see the mark of noble but repressed thoughts, energy that
gnaws on itself, suffering that will not be distracted. His large and
slightly veiled dark eyes light up his face in a truly divine way; his long
hair, ash blond, silky and fine, falls in graceful waves on either side of
his forehead, softening its severity. Emilio speaks little. Each of his
words is like an involuntary, fortuitous expression of a deeply personal
and uninterrupted meditation. He has read a great deal, but surpris-
ingly, his reading has had no influence upon him. His native sadness
separated him from other men early in life. Their judgments, opinions,
and prejudices really do not exist for him. He is not one to adopt other
people's views through weakness, or to banter them about to please
his vanity. Taking error and malevolence as an inevitable necessity
forced on mankind, his spirit remains calm, fair, firm, and forgiving.

The simplicity of his language and the perfect cadence of his
speech surprised me greatly, I who am so inured to today's extravagant
phraseology; I who hardly know of a college student who does not
think he has to play a role—what am I saying, a role?—a reformer's
mission! That, as you know, is because every scholar fresh from school
in Paris today not only has some *neo-* system about some *neo-*matter in
his portfolio, but also one or two volumes of intimate poetry which
are destined to inform the world about the great struggles, the bitter
disappointments of this beardless missionary, who unfailingly has
plumbed the depths of learning like Faust, turned his back on worldly
joys like Childe Harold, and dreamed of an impossible love like Réne
or Lélia. You know this sickness of our time; it disturbs even the finest
minds and damages even the best natures. It is a kind of solemn, moral
vanity, a religion of the self that fills the hearts of these poor children
with a host of silly ideas and foolish desires. They intoxicate themselves
with these notions, sometimes even to the point of death when the
realization of their own uselessness, which they disguise as the injustice

7. Venice was governed by a doge and a republican council until the French
occupation of 1797, at which time its territory was divided between Napoleon's Cisal-
pine Republic and the Austrian Empire. In 1806 it was incorporated into the Kingdom of Italy (with Napoleon as king), but then returned to Austrian rule in 1815.

of fate, succeeds in becoming the mistress of their misguided imagination. How many people have I known who felt that the world was too small to contain the immensity of their ideas, human life too short to demonstrate the full power of their thinking! . . .

I had become so accustomed to these inflated personalities that Emilio was a new experience for me. A warm, lively feeling drew us to one another, and as I could remain in Venice only for a short time, he never wished to leave me. He most graciously took it upon himself to show us his native city and spare us the bother of a tiresome *cicerone*.

We spent two hours going all through the church, pausing for a long while to examine the delightful mosaics in the sacristy, that exquisite tableau which might perhaps have been more suitable for a reception room in a Moorish bathhouse than for a vestry for Catholic priests.

A strange spectacle awaited us as we left Saint Mark's. Clouds of pigeons were coming from everywhere in the piazza—from the clock tower, the galleries of the church, the balconies of the doge's palace, the *Loggetta* of the campanile—and flying toward one of the Old Law Courts [*procuratie vecchie*]. I cannot tell you how delightful it was to watch the flocks of similarly tinted rose-gray birds make the air vibrate with the beating of their wings and fly in ever narrowing circles until they were exhausted enough to alight for an instant on the pavement or a windowsill, only to fly right off again and resume their aerial tactics.

"When you see the pigeons of Saint Mark's descend on the piazza you know that it is nearly two o'clock," said Emilio smiling. "They are never wrong. I have often set my pocket watch by them. It is dinner time in the pigeon republic. At this time every day the Countess Polcastro distributes grain for them. See how they fly about her windows, how they hurry to the banquet, and how excitedly they call to the tardy housekeeper who is to provide their meal! Look, she is opening the window."

"For shame!" cried the colonel. "It is an old toothless servant. Her cap is filthy, and her hands are calloused. She is throwing barley and hemp seed to the lovable doves as if she were throwing acorns to filthy swine. I was expecting to see a damask curtain part and a lovely young patrician girl call to the dear birds in her sweet voice as they came and perched familiarly on her shoulders and golden blond hair."

"Some Princess Nausicaä, no doubt," replied Arabella laughing. "I am quite amused to see, colonel, that your mind sometimes takes as strange a turn as mine does. You are beginning to complain about the way things are, which is a good sign. As we continue with our walks, you will see how many disappointments of this sort await us. I can tell you that during the few years I have been traveling in search of the beautiful and picturesque, I have yet to come across anything that has given me complete satisfaction. Something untoward always spoils the effect created by the finest things; some unforeseen, trying circumstance always interferes with the enjoyment. If you go to look at a beautiful picture, it is badly lighted or poorly restored. If you want to contemplate an extraordinary place, you wear yourself out just getting there. If you go to hear a great soprano, the music she sings is detestable. If you attend an imposing ceremony, your feet get cold or you find that you are hungry. Either the things themselves lack something for us, or it is we who lack something with respect to them. I have never understood how the idea of perfection was able to secure a place in the human mind."

"That idea," said Emilio, "is similar to those of the infinite and the immutable; we can scarcely account for them, except by some vague recollection of an earlier state of being. . . ."

"It is too hot to discuss metaphysics," Arabella asserted. "Let us each hurry back to where we are staying. . . . Until this evening, then, in the piazza?"

Saint Mark's Square is where the Venetians gather every evening. Prince Eugene[8] may well have done a fine thing for them by planting a garden where they could go and enjoy the cool evening shadows, scented flowering shrubs, and a walk along the sandy paths with a fine view of the lagoon and the islands. But to be a Venetian is to prefer marble to foliage, a palace to a garden. The garden has been forsaken in favor of the piazza, a huge, open-air salon where all classes of society gather to rest from their toil or to relax after the idleness of the day. The three ranks of buildings forming the sides of that huge space give it a certain likeness to the Palais-Royal. The piazza, however, is not adorned with lavish little shops that are splendidly lighted when night falls; it does not have a lovely, murmuring fountain to mark its center; and the fact that it narrows perceptably even gives it a rather awkward and unpleasant configuration. The Old Law Courts are heavy and commonplace; the modern structure that connects them to the New Law Courts bears no relation to either group. The look of Saint Mark's Square, however, is striking. The sight of it creates a most memorable

8. Eugene de Beauharnais (1781–1824). He had been adopted by Napoleon as his son and ruled as his viceroy in Italy from 1805 to 1815.

impression. And what better background for that picture than the basilica and the Campanile, that superb tower that was built nine centuries ago on marshy soil and still has not shifted an inch! What grandeur these immobile, strong masses impart to the common little drama that takes place at their feet!

Awnings of every color have been raised over all the spaces in front of the arcades. The well-bred people take their sherbet at certain of them, while the common people patronize others. Six or eight Greeks can regularly be seen on the piazza nonchalantly smoking their long, cherry-wood pipes. Crowds of strolling musicians approach different groups of people one after the other, pestering them by singing mutilated versions of opera tunes. A dealer in Maltese oranges, a candied-fruit peddler, a match seller, all have designs on your purse and deafen you with panegyrics about their merchandise. The vice-reine, who has the good taste to be the grandest and most majestic woman of the kingdom, promenades in the midst of the crowd. An improvisor recounts his fabulous adventures to a dumbfounded audience, while the pert flower-seller—all decked out in a modest bodice, a short skirt, and a hat decorated with plumes—wanders back and forth with an engaging air, offering her friends, the young gentlemen, a fresh rosebud, a scented jonquil, a sweet mignonette, and her smiles!

The people of Venice are chatterboxes. They have a way of speaking that is both mocking and affectionate. Their dialect is marvelously suited to their bantering disposition. Abounding in double-meaning epithets, in flattering phrases that can turn ironic with a simple change in inflection, the dialect has all the grace and treachery of a cat who scratches with velvet paws. Nothing amused us more than listening to Emilio talk with the little flower sellers and strolling peddlers. We made a flock of ridiculous purchases just so we could enjoy the onslaught of the bittersweet words, the witty remarks, and the picturesque turns of phrase.

Quite often Arabella would lead us to one of those delightful displays of fruits and vegetables that can only be seen in Venice and point out the sylvan elegance with which the baskets of strawberries, almonds, and pine nuts, the strings of cherries, the appetizing heaps of truffles, and the rosy pyramids of tomatoes were arranged on a bed of leaves intermixed with flowers. A little later, we saw the sturdy mineral-water carrier, barefoot, wearing a beaver hat and bent under the weight of his water buckets; the old oyster dealer; the lemonade maker; and, above all, a baked-apple hawker, whose street cry never failed to make us laugh heartily:

Peri cotti, pomi cotti
Pettorali per il petto
Che regn' avan sti raffreddori![9]

We also stopped many times to listen to the gondoliers quarrel. Asleep in the shade during the hottest part of the day, they rarely interrupted their naps except to exchange insults and hurl harmless curses at each other in the most frightful language. At any moment one might have thought that these men would attack each other, that a drawn knife or, at the very least, a good fist fight would reduce one or the other to silence, but it was not at all like that: the Venetian is prudent by nature, and he does not relish jeopardizing his life. Fights are extremely rare in Venice, even though the people quarrel about everything.

· ·

We devoted an entire week to visiting the picture galleries at the Academy of Fine Arts, the Barbarigo and Manfrini palaces, etc., etc.[10] Little Abbé Z. had joined our party. He was the sort of abbé that one often encounters in Italy: a man who places little faith in the Mass beyond the two Austrian dollars saying it will fetch him; has a passion for the arts and women; sings the love songs of Bellini with gestures; sculpts little figures of Venus, which he calls "Eve" in order to avoid being reprimanded by his bishop; and writes opera librettos for third-rate composers when he should be reading his breviary. Besides that, he was a nice fellow, a warmhearted and lively man. As for the colonel, he accompanied us only to be polite; he had no liking for painting, except for those lively, laughing images of pagan times. The gloomy paintings of the old masters, the martyrdom of the saints, and the emaciated madonnas were distasteful to him, and he expressed his opinions in a sincere and very original manner:[11] "What a pity," he told me, "that so many skilled artists have wasted their time painting such subjects. What pleasure would you have me feel when I look at a man's body pierced with arrows, or another who is leaving his tomb, livid and fleshless, or a third who has been tortured with hot pincers? What insipid monotony pervades those virgins of the beatified smile, forever seated between two nude, grinning infants! What a lack of ideas! What

9. "Baked pears, baked apples, Protection for the chest, To keep you from catching cold!"
10. The last week in March (d'Agoult, *Mémoires,* p. 134); that is, before Liszt left for Vienna.
11. The discussion of Christian and pagan art (this paragraph and the next two) follows the d'Agoult, *Mémoires* (pp. 120–24) and dates from the stay at Lake Como.

a dearth of life and interest! Don't talk to me about 'Christian art'; that phrase is self-contradictory. How is it possible for a religion that anathemizes the world as the realm of Satan, that advises its followers to mortify the flesh, and that forbids love as if it were a shameful weakness to foster the cultivation of art at the same time? Art elevates the material, it exalts beauty, and because of its perfection of form, it opens a man's heart to all the seductions to which Christianity enjoins him to close his senses."

"Consequently," added the abbé, "during the era when the faith was pure, in the first centuries after Christ's preaching, we see that the Christians who were more consistent in their thinking were very eager to burn, smash, and destroy the works of antiquity, and thus they contrived, just as the barbarians did, to delay the Renaissance, even though one would like to attribute all the honors of that period to them. A very important sect, which was at the point of seeing its views prevail, absolutely forbade the worship of images because of the old and the new [biblical] laws, and since then almost all the reformers whose aim was to restore Christianity to its original purity have barred painting and sculpture from their churches. True beauty remains embodied in Greek art. Apollo, Venus, Jupiter, and Hercules will always endure as symbols of nobility, sensuality, majesty, and strength. Has Christianity any martyrs to compare with Laocoön and Niobe? Or virgins more poetic than Arethusa and Daphne?"

"In order to conclude this discussion on a proper level of appreciation," I said to the abbé, who was always carried away by his enthusiasm, "let us say that Christian ideas did not of themselves create an art, but that they were manifested through art, in the same way that all the ideas and beliefs that have dominated different parts of the globe at various times have been. Let us say that legend provided the subjects for the plastic arts, just as fable and history have done. But let us not be quick to shout, 'Art is here, art is there!' Art exists eternally through its own inherent power. It does not wait to be summoned by a Pericles, an Augustus, the Medicis, or a Louis XIV. It exists in humanity, just as it does in the Word, because art is the supreme expression of society; it is the voice of genius, of those men who exist, so to speak, in the confines of two different worlds, and who contemplate the things of the one as illuminated by the divine light of the other."

The *Mary Magdalene* by Titian at the Barbarigo gallery pleased the colonel. He was not disturbed that the artist had conceived and painted her as a figure of repentance and atonement, since he was frankly taken with the wonderful lines of her face, her misty eyes, and the way her abundant hair fell in marvelous disarray over her palpitating breast. Noticing the colonel's unfeigned ecstasy, the proprietor of the gallery mistakenly assumed that he was the one true connoisseur in our group and made every effort to lure him into a learned discussion of the most urgent questions of art. Repeated signs from Arabella kept the colonel from ending the conversation with the simple, frank admission that he knew nothing about art. He saw that he was amusing us and goodnaturedly continued the delightful deception. The proprietor, moreover, was doing almost all the talking and was satisfied with the assenting nods and penetrating gaze of his partner. Bit by bit, theory by theory, he reached the point, however, of asking the colonel which school of painting he had studied most particularly. It was not an easy question to answer, because any response whatsoever would undoubtedly have led to a serious discussion, so you can well imagine what a fix our poor friend was in! But a heaven-sent inspiration saved the day: "Above all others," said the colonel with disdainful aplomb, "I prefer the Spanish school." The proprietor was flabbergasted. Never having seen anything but a few apocryphal canvases attributed to Murillo or Velasquez and not having any Spanish works in his collection, he now felt intimidated by a man who ranked the Italians below the Spaniards, and not caring to prolong a discussion that had taken such a disconcerting turn, he bowed deeply and departed, leaving the colonel the master of the field.

"*Te Deum laudamus!*" cried Arabella with a burst of laughter. "Victory is ours! Now that is what I call having sport with people. Colonel, you are indeed a clever man. You have a look that would intimidate Titian himself, if he ever returned to earth."

"Ouff!" said the colonel. "I can breathe now! You got me into a fine mess, and without that lucky remark about the Spanish school I would have made a fool of myself. But the devil with it. Had it not been for Marshal Soult,[12] whom I went to see when I was in Paris, I wouldn't have known that there was such a thing as a Spanish school!"

· ·

Titian, Tintoretto, and Paolo Veronese—behold the great men of the Venetian school.[13] Giorgione, Pordenone, Paris Bordone, Bonifaccio, Bassano, and the like rank below them. (Giorgione not because he was not as gifted as the three leaders—Titian envied him!—but because he died so young and left so few works, the most important of

12. Nicholas Jean de Dieu Soult (1769–1851), a lawyer's son who rose to become one of the most distinguished marshals of France.

13. Titian, or Tiziano Vecellio (1477–1576); Tintoretto, or Jacopo Rubusti (1518–1594); Paolo Veronese, or Paolo Caliari (1528–1588).

which, the fresco *Fondaco dei Tedeschi,* was destroyed by the salty mists of the canals.)

If I had to characterize the talent of the three great Venetians in a few words, I would say that Titian's is the fullness of life, quiet strength, and the nobility of truth; Tintoretto's is the passion of nature, animation, and a tremendous feeling for fantasy; Paolo's is transparency, harmony, and splendor. Titian, in my opinion, has no fault, except for his nearly total misconception of what we understand to be the Christian ideal and what we today call the philosophy of art. It is a fault he shares with the entire school,* which copied the most perfect aspects of nature, but did not really create ideal types. It did not bother about historical fidelity, nor about local color. It clothed Jews and Romans in Venetian style; it placed popes, doges, and German emperors in the Holy Virgin's company. Titian's Mary Magdalene looks just like his Venus, and when the wife of Saint Marcellus accompanies her husband to his martyrdom, she is dressed like a lady of a sixteenth-century court. All the angels and the putti have the same fat cheeks, the same chubby smiles; and paganism, it must be said, predominates in all of this.

Three principal works, three compositions based on the story of Christ, stand out in Venice's rich treasure of paintings and attest gloriously to the power of the three painters. They are *The Assumption* by Titian, *The Supper at Levi's* by Paolo (both at the Academy of Fine Arts), and Tintoretto's *Crucifixion* (at the San Rocco school). As the first of these paintings is familiar to you through many engravings, there is little purpose in telling you about Mary's beautiful and radiant face, the striking groups of angels that support and contemplate her, and the astonishing vigor to be found in the virile, harmonious, and bold placement of the apostles. As to its coloring, it is Titian's greatest work and, consequently, a masterpiece of painting. It is too bad, however, that the artist decided to place a white-bearded half-figure among the clouds to represent the Eternal Father. However fine it may be, the figure does not convey the idea of an infinite and universal God, and it seemed to me that the Virgin Mary, floating on the blue ether of the sky, would have been sufficiently beatified without two arms of flesh extended to receive her. It is true, though, that Titian in this respect was only conforming to the spirit of his times. Society then had virtually no understanding of the spiritual aspects of Catholicism. Popular tradition and simple beliefs drawn from earlier times still dominated art and poetry. Dante created a totally material Hell and placed cloven-

---

* It is understood that I am not talking about Giambellino, Palma Vecchio, or earlier painters.

hoofed demons, dragons, centaurs, and who knows what else in it. It is not surprising, therefore, that Titian and Tintoretto did not hesitate to portray God Himself as a majestic old man, a stern yet serene and smiling Father.

When *The Assumption,* which had been commissioned by the brothers at the convent Dei Frari, was delivered to them, it did not meet with the good friars' approval. It was not finished or polished enough to suit them, and so they returned it to Titian with the request that he retouch it, making it worthier of its setting. But the indignant painter, well aware that he had created a masterpiece, took up his paintbrush and scribbled a second *fecit* below his signature. Thus, it reads: *Tiziano Vecellio fecit, fecit.*[14] The friars, as you might imagine, were not really satisfied with this but they did not dare to insist further. It was not long, however, before the growing fame of *The Assumption* and the generous offers they received for it reassured them that their money had been well spent.

What do you say about that *fecit, fecit?* Isn't it the most forceful expression of fully justified pride that ever was? Isn't it the only worthy response a noble artist could make to unjust criticism? *Tiziano Vecellio fecit, fecit.* What a great man it takes to nurture such a heartfelt feeling for his own personality! This awareness of self gives him an anchor of fortitude that the waves of human injustice can never snap. When he is hurt or outraged he turns inward for support, saying "I am Titian!" and lets the clamor of the anonymous crowd fade in the distance— they cannot disturb his noble serenity.

The Crucifixion by Tintoretto is a much larger canvas and depicts a huge, restless mass of people. In the foreground Christ, already raised onto the cross, is mourned by Saint John and two female saints. On His right, one thief is being raised on a cross, while on His left, but farther back, the other thief has already been nailed to his. Those carrying out the execution and the people attending it form the secondary groups. The painting's principal virtue, in my opinion, is its realism. It has such animation, such a feeling for life, that the viewer is drawn into the midst of the figures. The artist has captured their evident confusion with such skill that the eye grasps it easily, even though it always returns to the central group, which stands out from the others because of the immutable feeling of death and despair it conveys. Tintoretto's shortcoming is his abuse of his talents. There is no lack of his paintings in Venice; entire churches are decorated with them. It is impossible to conceive how one man could have produced so many paint-

14. "Done by, done by Tiziano Vecellio."

ings in a single lifetime. It is not surprising, therefore, that many of his canvases are little more than hasty, impassioned sketches, improvisations that betray a powerful genius straining the limits of his ability. Tintoretto is too partial to foreshortened figures and tormented stances. His works are the best possible proof of the profound truth in Larochefoucauld's maxim: "It is not enough to possess great qualities; one must also be economical with them."

Having perused the first gallery at the Academy of Fine Arts and suddenly found ourselves at the doorway leading to the second, we could not help experiencing a momentary feeling of dizziness at the sight of the Veronese canvas that occupies all of its far wall. We were not sure of what we were looking at. The columns in the painting are so forceful and realistic that they seemed to be a continuation of the two marble columns separating the two rooms. The sky is so transparent, the perspective so clever, that we thought we had come upon an open terrace. But while the immobility of the people on the terrace, the dinner setting, and the figure of Christ destroyed the illusion for us, they led us to admire one of the most astonishing works ever created by the hand of man. The table is set under a large portico. Two wide staircases lead to it; servants ascend and descend the steps, and there is even a Negro among them; Paolo's favorite greyhound feeds on scraps from the feast. Christ is seated in the midst of His companions. The joy and life the Dear One imparts to them show on all their faces; only Christ Himself is serious and calm. Daylight floods the scene, the costumes are splendid, and the many figures that fill the vast frame are admirably placed in relation to the two beautiful columns, which serve to diversify the groupings in the most artistic way possible, imbuing the whole composition with inconceivable majesty.

Veronese's most remarkable distinguishing trait is his somber use of shadow and *black*. He does not rely on contrasting colors to produce his effects. Only a very practiced eye can perceive the technique he uses to highlight certain sections of the painting, since light seems to be spread evenly throughout it. This manner of painting produces a marvelously unified effect, but there is often something rather cold and monotonous about it. The types of people in his paintings are also less diversified than those of Titian and Tintoretto. One finds the same woman in all his works, and no matter whether she is called Saint Catherine, Europa, Suzanna, or Sophronia, she always has the same pale shoulders, the same bright eyes and blond hair. His male figures are, for the most part, noble enough, but not very lively.

Once again, these are the three great names of the Venetian school. But would you believe that there is not a single monument to any of them in the city they embellished? We looked in vain for Tintoretto's tomb. Titian is buried in the Dei Frari church, since an exception was made for him alone regarding an ordinance that forbade the burial of the plague's wretched victims within church walls. A simple stone in a dark corner marks the final resting place of the great Vecellio's remains. Paolo is interred in the Church of Saint Sebastian, whose choir, ceiling, organ, and sacristy are decorated with his work. The story has it that a quarrel forced him to seek refuge in the convent attached to the church and that in gratitude for the hospitality shown him by the superior and the affection he received from the brothers, he left them this magnificent memento of his stay there. Artists in those days were not nearly as docile, well-behaved, and conciliatory as they are today. Just as these men possessed great talent, they also had great passions. Their friendships were animated, their hatreds violent, and their jealousies shameless. They held a paint brush in one hand and a dagger in the other, always ready to mete out their own justice on every occasion, because these spoiled darlings of the princes knew that the law would wink at their infractions and that some house of peace and charity would shelter and welcome them, even if they were still breathless from a duel or bloodied from a godless brawl. Paolo's refuge proved a fertile one. While he was there he painted an *Assumption,* his two versions of the *Martyrdom of Saint Sebastian, Esther before Ahasuerus,* and several other very beautiful canvases. When he died his body was carried into the church. Afterward a bust (which is completely defaced today) and a stone bearing the arms of the Caliari family were placed there, thanks to his brother's efforts. Of all the sepulchers I have visited, all the famous tombs before which I have bent a knee, none has moved me as deeply as Paolo's. What, in effect, could be more touching than to see an artist lying like this at the foot of his works, placing both them and himself in the Lord's protection, finding his repose in the very place where he worked—buried, as it were, in his own triumphs?

"We are going to the Lido," said Emilio, who planned our excursions and regulated our time as he saw fit. "The moon will be rising, the weather is fair, and nothing will keep us from spending the whole night there if we have a mind to." We heartily approved of the idea and got into the gondola. To everyone's delight and the colonel's special satisfaction, Cornelio had removed the cabin, and we all had to agree that nothing could compare with a gondola unencumbered by its doleful trappings. It barely touches the water, playing lightly and nimbly over the surface of the waves and slitting through them with its iron prow. Its elongated shape makes it supple and docile under the hand of the gondolier, who, standing at his hazardous post, propels it through the labyrinth of canals with incredible speed and daring. A second gondolier usually stands on the prow, but we preferred to trust ourselves entirely to Cornelio, who stood behind us and led the way without our ever seeing him and often without our hearing the slightest sound from his oar. Nothing, therefore, interfered with our view of the vast horizon. Our little craft seemed to skim over the waves like a nautilus, as if it had a life and will of its own.

We left the viceroy's palace, the Zecca, and the Riva degli Schiavoni behind us, and when we skirted the public garden, the coquettish clusters of acacia blossoms, delicately poised on the night breeze and exhaling their perfume, showered Arabella's black shawl with white petals.

"Those are enticements of the dryads," said the abbé, ever ready to revert to paganism. "We can greet them when we return. Down there, to the right, do you see that reddish brown building standing in the grove of fig trees, grape vines, and oleanders? It is the Armenian convent. That is where the cloistered monks dedicate themselves to the education of their young countrymen. They work constantly on Armenian manuscripts and translations of our literature, which they print themselves and send to Armenia. If you would like to visit the place, Father Pasquale is a friend of mine and would be delighted to show you his island."

"How is it, abbé, that an orthodox man like you is a friend of a schismatic?"[15]

"Egoists are the only schismatics I know," replied the abbé. "They are the ones who really cause a schism in humanity. I consider any man who serves mankind orthodox, even if he was marked ten times over by the claws of the Inquisition, or even if he is an Arab, a Turk, a Jew, a Greenlander, or a Peruvian."

"With such fine beliefs, my poor abbé," said the colonel, "you run the great risk of never administering the sacrament of confirmation. You will surely never wear red stockings, and we will never address you as 'Monsignore,' unless, of course, they give you a bishopric on an island like that." He pointed to San Servilio, where they imprison the insane.

"No, I have no favors to ask of Rome," replied the abbé. "I have

---

15. Despite the point Liszt wishes to make, the monks were not schismatics. They were Mekhitarists: an order of the Armenian Rite which professed the Rule of St. Benedict and was recognized by Rome.

renounced all ambition. As long as they let me earn enough money to support my aged mother, I ask for nothing more. . . . At one time, however, I did dream of another future," he added, striking his forehead. "I, whom you see casually molding little terra cotta figurines and humming Perruchini's tunes with my terrible voice, I thought for a time that I did have a mission in life. I believed that my life would be valuable, that I could dedicate and consecrate it to the betterment of my fellow man. . . . In a word," he added with a melancholy smile, "I believed that it was my vocation to become a schismatic."

Then, as he saw that we were silently waiting for an explanation of these extraordinary words, he continued: "Once there was a man[16] who had risen within the bosom of the Catholic Church, a man with a big heart and a marvelous mind. He was thoroughly familiar with the evil and corruption of those who call themselves the Servants of God. He knew that the Bride of Christ had prostituted herself to earthly powers and that 'the corruption was in her bones.'[17] He had seen the people suffer under the domination of their godless pastors. Realizing that a new era of enlightenment was approaching, and sensing a fiery influx of limitless charity within him, he prophesied a future of more liberal rights and brotherhood to the world. Filled with the zeal that possesses such souls, he did not shrink from the accusations with which the mob enjoyed assailing the consciences of men of genius. He dared to part company with his former self. As the scriptures say, he truly stripped off the old self and put his past errors aside, just as one would discard an old coat. He disassociated himself nobly from the camp of the oppressors, who, not understanding his words, would have liked to keep him among the oppressed. Even though he had already reached middle age, that time when a man thinks only of peacefully enjoying the reputation or the power he has acquired, he had the strength to break with the brilliant past that had placed him among the great men of this earth, and, by dint of his own will, to fashion a new youth for himself. He transformed, revived, and retempered his energy in the bitter waters of calumny that the world poured over him. If he had wanted to go a step further and break with Rome and found a new church, all the young clergy, let me tell you, would have flocked to him. All the priests who had not been totally smothered or cor-

16. Lamennais. The parallels between the story the abbé tells and Liszt's relations with Lamennais are far too striking for it to be otherwise.

17. Possibly a reference to Lamennais's *Paroles d'un croyant,* chapter 14, an apocalyptic passage in which seven evil and divisive spirits, plainly symbolizing the Church, chant a litany: "We have sown corruption, and it has germinated in us and devoured our bones. . . . Christ has conquered, cursed be He!"

rupted by the trappings of power and wealth would have joined him. We would have followed the prophet, and his voice would have worked miracles.

"Oh," added the abbé, carried away by excitement, "how profoundly happy I would have been to sacrifice my life if only he had summoned us! How I would have believed in his words! How I would have prostrated myself at the feet of that thrice-venerable old man who had erred because he was a man, but who had realized his error and purged himself of it because he was so much more than a man. Oh, if only he had deigned to say to me, 'Come, be as strict with yourself as I am, be abstinent and do penance, because you will then be less unworthy of heaven's inspiration, and the Divine Word will appear in your liberated mind with all its brilliant clarity,' how I would have silenced my passions! How I would have tamed those pangs of the flesh, which I certainly do not want to subject to the hypocritical torments of sterile devotion! Oh, who has not wanted that," continued the abbé, wiping two big shining tears from the corners of his eyes. "Why didn't he send us to the ends of the earth to preach his word, teach his precepts, and distribute his heavenly manna to all those who hunger and thirst for justice? Then the people would have realized that if we priests are sluggish and indifferent today, it is not because we are afraid of struggle or martyrdom. It is because we are oppressed by lies, and we keep all the power of our souls to ourselves for fear that we will defile it by using it to spread error and superstition."

The abbé fell silent. His emotional words had touched us, and no one broke the silence until we reached the Island of San Lazzaro.

Apprised of our arrival, Father Pasquale soon joined us in the cloister where we were waiting for him and welcomed us very cordially. Father Pasquale is a little old man with dark, piercing eyes, a white beard, a lively step, and an intelligent smile. He speaks all languages and carried on a most lively conversation with us in French, German, Polish, English, Italian, and Latin. He showed us the printing press, a few bad paintings that he considered very fine, a number of beautiful Arabian manuscripts, and the armchair in which Byron sat during that impetuous, hotly passionate period when he bound himself to the study of Armenian, hoping that the dry labor would occupy that part of his personality which was always breaking loose and throwing him wholeheartedly into a world of fantasy and frenetic activity.[18] Then

18. Byron, writing to Thomas Moore 5 December 1816, said: "By way of divertisement, I am studying daily, at an Armenian Monastery, the Armenian language. I found that my mind wanted something craggy to break upon; and this—as the most

Father Pasquale, learning that I had come from Paris, asked me a number of questions about our contemporary celebrities. As you might imagine, he was not very current about the religious, political, and literary disputes that are stirring in France, and he was oddly confused about names and other matters. No doubt I would have found him better informed if we had been talking about the court of King Cyrus, the campaigns of Sesostris, or the conditions that led to the fall of the first Assyrian Empire. After I rectified several of his notions about our current political situation, he asked me if, by some chance, I knew a very attractive young woman who had visited the convent some years before and had written, or so he was told, a long conversation in which he was a participant. I told him that that young woman had now become the most renowned author in Europe.[19]

"I wouldn't doubt it," said the priest. He had given us a tour of his garden as we were talking and now picked a half-opened bud from a bush of deep red roses, which he offered to my companion after carefully removing the thorns. "I wouldn't doubt it. I have a feeling for faces and their expressions. . . ." So saying, he directed his lynx-like eyes toward Arabella, who, without waiting for another compliment from the good monk, leaped like a gazelle into the gondola. We exchanged our wishes for peace, health, and happiness with Father Pasquale and followed her. Cornelio took to his oar with a vengeance, and soon we were at the Lido.

The name Lido, I am sure, stirs your imagination to picture bright, laughing groves and lush, green retreats and to think of a place where nature has put her most enchanting, seductive charms on display. The Venetians' liking for it and the smug pens of some travelers have, however, given it a highly inflated reputation. The Lido is a long, narrow strip of land that protects one side of Venice from the incursions of the Adriatic. Most of the island consists of a sandy beach that has been driven and shaped by the whims of the sea winds. The vegetation is sparse: parched, scraggly grass, which barely survives the avid teeth of grazing sheep, covers the ground from place to place. Toward

---

difficult thing I could discover here for amusement—I have chosen to torture me into attention" (Leslie A. Marchand, *Byron* 2: 673–74).

19. George Sand. Her conversation with Father Pasquale (Paschal Aucher), whom she calls Father Hieronymus, is reported in her *Lettre d'un voyageur*, no. 3, which was dated Venice, July 1834, and published two months later. Their conversation dealt with Lamennais and the controversy caused by his *Paroles d'un croyant*. One might assume, therefore, that Liszt's visit to San Lazzaro was not quite as impromptu as the Letter makes it out to be.

one end of the island you can find the place that has been allotted to the Jews and Protestants for burying their brothers' bones. The area is not protected by walls as our cemeteries are, and there is not a single cypress, poplar, or willow—any of the trees associated with the dead— to shed its shade over the tombstones that lie scattered here and there in no particular order and without the Church's blessing.

"Nothing I know is sadder than our tombs," said the abbé. "Those bodies that we put underground to rot so that they can provide sustenance for filthy animals leave the mourners with nothing but the most vile memories, and this feeling of revulsion inevitably spoils all thoughts of grief. Less than two years ago I buried my only sister, a girl of sixteen, taken without warning in her mother's arms like an April flower destroyed by Alpine winds. And would you believe that I was tortured by a single thought for a long time: it was not the moral sorrow of having lost someone, of no longer being with that good angel whose smile embodied heaven, who graced our home and dignified even the most mundane behavior of my coarse life; it was not our mother's silent despair; it was not the horrible certainty of eternal separation. No, it was a far more realistic image that obsessed me every moment of the day and night, and nothing could rid me of it: I constantly heard the dismal sound of a spade striking against the coffin, and I was appalled to see the first worm engendered by the forces of corruption feeding on the young virgin's immaculate body. That hideous image filled my senses and numbed my mind. I could not summon the courage to return to the cemetery, and yet it seemed to me that my whole universe was centered on that little patch of ground where, together with my sister, I had buried the better part of myself— the sweet memories, the glad heart, the holy tears—all the good that her simple presence had awakened and sustained in me—that idealism, in effect, that she possessed and that was her only reality. . . . How I have berated myself for not having acted on an idea that passed timidly through my mind at times, for not having dared to violate church regulations, for not having followed the example of the ancients, our great teachers in matters of life and death, and built a funeral pyre for that noble young woman! Once I had piously collected the ashes in a holy urn, they would never have left me, no feelings of revulsion would have tainted her memory, and her ever-present remains would have protected me from the evil temptations, the guilty desires, and rebellious feelings that have taken over my life since she last placed her angelic hand on my weary brow and her virgin's breath last purified the air I breathe."

"Dear abbé," said Arabella who had been listening to him, deeply moved. "No doubt there is something in our funeral customs that is repulsive to some people with sensitive imaginations. I can tell you, however, that I am not at all repelled by the thought that the material part of my being will return to the earth whence it came, that Nature, beautiful and strong, will take me to her breast, and if one day the elements of my body return to life as a bit of moss or the tiniest blade of grass, that is good enough for the wretched clay from which we are made. Look here," she added, reaching into the shadow of a large tombstone and plucking a stunted daisy that the infertile soil had not allowed to develop. "Look, this neglected little product of nature has an indefinable and melancholy charm that I find attractive. Even this frightfully desolate cemetery holds no terrors for me, for I tell myself that the pale moonlight gliding over these gray, lichen-covered stones might carry some mysterious hope to the dust of the dead, and that they can perhaps hear Jehovah's name amid the dull rumbling of the waves."

"Death is nothing but a transformation of life," observed Emilio. "And as our spirit does not cease to exist during that transformation, it would be a sign of weakness—as indeed it is, in my opinion—to surround a man's last moments with all the trappings of grief."

"In effect," I added, "we rejoice wildly at the birth of a child whom we surely know is condemned to struggle and suffer in a world where, as Saint Augustine says, 'things are full of misery, and hope is devoid of joy,' while we despair and become inconsolable at the very moment when the soul, according to all our fine beliefs and lofty instincts, is about to enjoy a better existence or eternal peace."

Our discussion of the somber subject continued for a little while. Then, as each of us gradually became absorbed with the memory of a loved one's death, we silently returned to the gondola, where Cornelio was waiting for us, deep in the sleep of the just.

The following day Arabella went to visit the studios of Venice's most renowned painters. Emilio, blinded by his national pride, believed firmly in modern Italian painting. He was infuriated when I told him that the present French school was far superior. "One would look in vain among the Italians," I would sometimes tell him, "for artists who are on a par with Ingres, Scheffer, Delacroix, Delaroche, Decamps, or with men of even lesser standing. Mannerism and chicanery dominate the work of your most famous painters. Even at first glance, one can tell that their works betray a total lack of study, either of nature or of antiquity. Your painters are neither idealistic nor realistic, and they have blundered into a convention of insipid sentimentality and grimacing grace, the grace Vasari called 'a most disgraceful grace.' They paint pink flesh without bone or muscles, architecture that is all pale lilac or pearl gray, non-existent landscapes, melodrama rendered as heroism—the emotion of shop girls. They have no freshness, learning, boldness, or simplicity, and they even lack the "pretty" style that flourished in Louis XV's day. It is difficult to understand how the constant presence of masterpieces by Raphael, Leonardo, Correggio, and others did not prevent them from falling into such complete decadence, because if the sight of beauty was not enough to foster genius, it should at least have encouraged good taste and protected it against some of these aberrations."

As these and some other remarks led to my being declared totally incapable of appreciating modern painting, I was barred from the tour of the studios, although the colonel gladly went along, anxious to see some fresh and pleasing colors at long last. The abbé generously offered to console me in my exile, and I asked him to take me to the Pisani Palace, to the studio where the ill-fated Robert had ended his days.[20] The abbé had known Léopold Robert rather well; that is, he saw him often, because the painter was difficult to really know. Habitually taciturn, Robert almost never spoke freely except about matters of art, which he discussed eagerly and warmly. He lived a secluded life, devoting himself to his endless work. Before starting his painting *The Fishermen*, he settled in Chióggia in order to study the features, movements, and gestures of the townspeople, since he intended to use them as models for his figures. His idealism, however, carried him beyond a sense of realism, and he painted fishermen who were doubtless more heroic than any who will ever be seen on Chioggia's banks.

It was not without a great feeling of apprehension that I found myself beneath the dark portals of the Pisani Palace, inside a building with which one of the republic's greatest and purest names is associated and to which the gifted artist's distressing death added a new and sad dimension. An old serving woman came and showed us the studio where Robert had worked and which is used today by an Italian artist who seems destined to spend a good long time in the bosom of a happy family. The servant had been Robert's housekeeper, and she gratefully recalled his goodness and generosity. With tears in her eyes

---

20. Léopold Robert (1794–1835), a Swiss-born painter noted for his scenes of Italian life. The painting *The Fisherman* that Liszt mentions was on exhibit in Lyons for the benefit of oppressed workers there (d'Agoult, *Mémoires,* p. 98).

she gave us the details of the fateful morning when Robert put an end to his life, which, however short, will be remembered in the history of art. Her simple way of telling the story touched me far more than any eloquent paean to his genius could have done. Then, as I was pensively looking at the spot where his desperate brother had found him bathed in his own blood, the abbé said: "We tried very hard to discover the cause of his suicide, and a number of possible reasons were advanced. Many people attributed it to an unhappy love affair, while others said it was because he was despondent over the unjust criticism he had received."

"I don't think that either of those reasons explains everything," I replied. "From what I know of him and his talent, he strikes me as one of those beings who are sadly fated to commit suicide and who could only have been prevented from doing so by extraordinary circumstances. He was one of those artists whom Jean-Paul[21] so ingeniously called the *Grenzegenies*, the border geniuses. He was one of those men whose creative gifts are not in balance, men who can conceive more than they can actually accomplish and who, after exhausting themselves in the pursuit of an ideal that always seems to elude them, develop a disgust for the world, fall prey to self-pity, and look to death for a refuge. The sickness that gnaws at them is holy; it is surely not the misery of life that overcomes them, nor the disappointments to their worldly ambition that crushes them. They remind me of the legend of Milo of Crotona: their eyes take in the whole of creation, while their hands are violently crushed by the tree of fate."[22]

The same decree that had barred me from the studios nearly kept me from attending the opera, since my inability to enjoy the music of the *maestri* "creating a *furore* and a *fanatismo*" was even more evident that my incapacity for experiencing the beauties of modern painting. Nevertheless, I claimed my personal rights, and as I had been in exile all day, the abbé interceded for me. After a few objections, they finally consented to allow me to accompany them to the opera house that night. It was, moreover, the last night that our party would spend together. Immediately after the performance, we were to go to Jasina, where our carriage was awaiting us, and our friends had promised to accompany us as far as Padua.

21. Jean-Paul Richter (1763–1825), writer known mostly for sentimental fiction, but also the author of a *Vorschule der Aesthetik* (1804).

22. Milo of Crotona was a Greek olympic wrestling champion. Walking in a forest one day in his old age, so the legend goes, he happened upon a tree that had been partially split by woodsmen. He decided to finish the job, but got his hand caught in the tree, and thus encumbered, he was devoured by wolves.

Liszt. Lithograph portrait by Achille Deveria, Paris 1832.

Liszt's travels with Mme d'Agoult, 1835–1839.

Countess Marie d'Agoult. Painting by Henri Lehmann, Rome 1839.

Geneva. After the drawing by W. H. Bartlett, pub. London 1836.

George Sand's manor house Nohant. Watercolor by Maurice Sand.

Mont Blanc and Chamonix. After the drawing by W. H. Bartlett, pub. London 1836.

Sigismund Thalberg. After a
lithograph by Josef Kriehuber,
Vienna 1838.

Liszt and George Sand: "Mama is astonished listening to Liszt."
Watercolor by Maurice Sand, ca. 1837.

View of Lake Como. After the drawing by Samuel Prout, pub. London 1830. (General Research Division, New York Public Library; Astor, Lenox and Tilden Foundations)

Dante led by Beatrice. Statuary group by Giovanni-Battista Comolli, 1810.

Caroline Ungher. Lithograph by Josef Kriehuber, Vienna 1839. (Music Division, New York Public Library; Astor, Lenox and Tilden Foundations)

Teatro alla Scala, Milan. Casa Ricordi was directly across the street. After the drawing by Philippe Benoist, ca. 1840. (Museo teatrale alla Scala)

Teatro alla Scala. Engraving by Citteric, Milan, early nineteenth century. (Theatre Museum, Victoria and Albert Museum)

Venice. After the drawing by Adolphe Rouargue, pub. Paris 1856.

Teatro La Fenice, Venice. Engraving by Cagnoni, ca. 1836.

Notice of Liszt's first concert in Vienna 1838, "for the benefit of the flood victims in Pest and Ofen [Buda]."

Mittwoch den 18. April 1838,
um die Mittagsstunde,
wird

FRANZ LISZT
zum Besten der in Pesth und Ofen
durch Ueberschwemmung Verunglückten,
im Saale der Gesellschaft der Musikfreunde,
ein

CONCERT
zu geben die Ehre haben.

Vorkommende Stücke:

1. Ouverture zur Oper: Die Tage der Gefahr, von Cherubini.
2. Concertstück für Fortepiano mit Orchesterbegleitung, componirt von C. M. v. Weber, gespielt von LISZT.
3. Declamation von Madame Rettich, k. k. Hofschauspielerin.
4. Reminiscences des Puritains, große Fantasie für das Fortepiano, componirt und vorgetragen von LISZT.
5. Adelaide, von Beethoven, gesungen von Herrn Benedict Groß, auf dem Claviere begleitet von LISZT.
6. Valse de bravour et grande etude, componirt und vorgetragen von LISZT.

Zur Beförderung dieses menschenfreundlichen Zweckes haben Madame Rettich und Herr Groß ihre Leistungen, so wie Herr Carl Holz die Leitung des Orchesters mit größter Bereitwilligkeit übernommen. Auch hat die löbl. Gesellschaft der Musikfreunde ihren Saal dem Concertgeber unentgeltlich zu diesem Zwecke überlassen.

Sperrsitze zu 3 fl. C. M. und Eintrittskarten zu 1 fl. 20 kr. C. M. sind in der k. k. Hof-Musikalienhandlung des Herrn Toh. Haslinger am Graben, und am Tage des Concertes an der Casse zu haben.

Der Anfang ist um halb 1 Uhr.

Gedruckt bey J. B. Wallishausser.

Florence; view from the Boboli Gardens. After the drawing by Corrodi, ca. 1843.

Lorenzo Bartolini.
Engraved portrait by
Paolo Toschi,
ca. 1836.

Liszt. Marble
bust by Bartolini,
Florence 1838.

Benvenuto Cellini, *Perseus with the Head of Medusa*. (Giraudon/Art Resource, New York)

Raphael Sanzio, *Saint Cecilia*. (Alinari/Art Resource, New York)

Nonnenwerth and the ruins of Rolandseck. After the drawing by L. Lange, ca. 1840.

La Fenice is one of the most attractive theaters in the world. Destroyed twice by fire, it has, like the bird whose name it bears, risen twice from the ashes.

Although the hall is not as big as La Scala (it only accommodates about three thousand people), its proportions are better, and its decoration is more restrained and in better taste. The pale blue hangings in the boxes create an excellent effect. The custom of visiting boxes and conversing is the same as in Milan,* with the difference, however, that the opera house is not the only place in Venice where people gather. Several very pleasant houses are customarily open to foreigners. But, to tell the truth, one longs for those fine days when *conversazioni* were held at the Benzoni, Albrizzi, and Cicognara residences.[23] Those choice gatherings, each centered around an exceptional woman, no longer take place. Gracious women can still be found in Venice, as elsewhere, but they no longer know how or no longer want to play the central role. People visit their homes but they do not gather there. *Soirées* are given, but the *salon* no longer exists.

That evening they gave *Lucrezia Borgia* at the opera.[24] The author of the libretto follows Victor Hugo's drama step by step. The only place he departs from it is in the supper scene, where, in place of the terrifying effect created by the waiting coffins and the sacred chants resounding in the midst of a festive banquet, he has substituted a kind of police patrol that arrives on the scene to *arrest* the guilty parties in true middle-class fashion. I suppose the change was made, not with an

---

* I have just heard a very amusing story along these lines: A young Frenchman, unfamiliar with Italian customs, was attending a performance at La Pergola [in Florence] and was very put out by his neighbors' chatter, since it kept him from following the music. He began to "shush" those about him; naturally, no one paid any attention to him. He began to "shush" again louder and louder until, pushed to his limit, he shouted that all those who continued to talk were rude and ill-mannered. His nearest neighbor then felt obliged to respond that those who wanted other people to keep quiet were impertinent boors. Calling cards were exchanged. The following day when the young Frenchman heard a knock on his door he had no doubt that it was the Florentine, accompanied by one or two seconds for a duel. Just imagine his astonishment when he saw that it was a police official, followed by two gendarmes who had strict orders to keep a close watch on him for as long as he remained in Florence.

23. Monthly literary gatherings which Byron had attended.

24. Opera by Donizetti, first performed at La Scala in December 1833. The opera was not given in Venice until the fall season of 1838, which opened on 4 October (Giovanni Salvioli, *La Fenice*, p. 24). The following passage, in other words, postdates the period that Liszt and Marie were in Venice. Yet it is quite possible that he paid a quick return visit to the city sometime between his stay early that October, without Marie, at Cattajo (the Duke of Modena's castle near Padua) and his continued journey on to Bologna the same month.

eye to *revising* Hugo, but simply to keep within the limits of daring permitted by the censors.[25]

The action of the drama moves quickly, the plot develops steadily in an interesting way, and the situations are extremely dramatic. It was a wonderful subject for the composer. What strong characters to portray! What contrasts to stress! The Duke's cruel, cold cunning, Lucrezia's impassioned vindictiveness and her tender feelings of love—the shameless vices of these illustrious personages,—and the honest candor of Gennaro, the young man cloaked in mystery. What a fertile field for a great composer! What characters for the pen of a Meyerbeer! But Donizetti, writing for the Italian stage, has tailored the work to Italian taste. He has composed pleasant, flowing, and melodious music that one can listen to effortlessly and remember easily; music, that is, that pleases nearly everyone![26]

To cite only one example of it, at the end of the first act or prologue, when the young noblemen introduce themselves to Lucrezia with savage irony and throw her crimes in her face, the first one says, "I am Maffio Orsini, the brother of the man whose throat you ordered cut," and another, "I am Vitelli, the nephew of the man whom you have had murdered," etc., etc. One can hardly imagine a musician setting that terrible confrontation in anything but a strongly accented recitative with broken, declaimed phrases, each reflecting the meaning of the words. Donizetti, however, did not trouble himself much about it; he came up with eight melodious measures that do not express anything, with the result that each character introduces himself in turn much in the same way that a person recites his surname, first name, and occupation when he presents himself at the police station for a passport. Surely it does not take much thought to be shocked by this, but I have since become convinced that I was the only person in the hall who noticed the discrepancy between the words and music. The composers, singers, and public agree totally that it really does not matter whether the opera's recitatives ring true or false, or whether the

25. In Hugo's sensational 1833 melodrama, Lucrezia, having poisoned the wine at the Princess Negroni's banquet, arrives on the scene with a group of chanting monks to collect her victims' dying bodies (except, of course, for Gennaro, who in reality is her own son). As such a scene would have never have passed an Italian censor, Donizetti's librettist, Felice Romani, dispensed with the coffins and replaced the monks with a troop of armed men, who do indeed take Lucrezia's victims into custody.

26. A year or so later, in 1840, Liszt composed an elaborate, extended, two-part fantasy, "Reminiscences," on several of these "flowing and melodious" tunes from *Lucrezia Borgia* for use at his concerts.

unity of character is maintained throughout the drama, etc., etc. I also strongly suspect that if a dilettante ever reads these lines, he will accuse me of wanting to inflict the rules of Aristotle or Bezout[27] on music.

What is there to say about Caroline Ungher?[28] Only that she is one of the finest actresses and most accomplished singers ever to appear on the opera stage. With a voice that is almost unpleasant (and it is well to remember that neither Madame Pasta nor Madame Malibran was gifted with what people popularly call a "pleasant" voice), a voice made supple by years of study, and which she now controls perfectly, she produces effects that the most beautiful voices cannot produce. Her vocalization is perfect, and her manner of phrasing is broad and irreproachable.

Extremely intelligent, she understands and plays her roles not in the way that they have been laid out for her, but as they ought to be played. She brings pathos to the flattest music and gives a sublime lift to the most trite phrases. She is noble, sincere, captivating, and impassioned, and although her exaltation and ardor win us over, it is primarily her great skill, wise heart, and ultimately her art, in the best meaning of the word, that conquer us. From the moment she makes her entrance, the nobility of her bearing and the dignity of her actions command attention. The first notes of her recitative reveal a consummate artist. And the instant she starts to sing, she moves and charms you, making you weep, tremble, yearn, and hope with her.

Mademoiselle Ungher first appeared in Paris about five years ago with little success. Without going into all the reasons behind these unfortunate appearances, we can simply say that her talent at the time was nothing like the ability she has developed since then. Who would think of comparing Mademoiselle Grisi[29] of today with the Grisi of 1832? A similar change has taken place in Mademoiselle Ungher. One can also say that when she appeared in Paris, the first flush of her gifts combined with a lack of confidence, which always pushes singers to

27. Étienne Bezout (1730–1783), a French mathematician who developed a general theory of algebraic equations.

28. Caroline Ungher, actually Unger (1803–1877), Hungarian-born contralto, one of the singers whom Beethoven had selected to sing at the first performance of his Ninth Symphony (1824). She had a highly successful career, mostly in Italy, and retired in 1841 when she married the French writer François Sabatier. She was performing in Venice when Liszt arrived there, and it must have been a very pleasant reunion, since she had sung at his Vienna debut fifteen years earlier, on 1 December 1822, when he was eleven years old. The two of them remained good friends.

29. Giulia Grisi (1811–1869), Italian soprano and younger sister of the mezzo-soprano Giuditta Grisi. She was the unchallenged prima donna at the Théâtre-Italien and, as mentioned, part of the famous "quartet" of singers there.

exaggerate, frequently carried her beyond the limits of refined taste—
that pleasing sense of propriety which the Parisian public demands
above all else. Now that she has learned how to be unrestrained and
controlled at the same time, she possesses such an abundance of varied
gifts—even the contradictory ones that merge to form a well-rounded
performer—that her true place is in Paris. And if I may state my opinion fully, that place should be at the Opéra, not the Théâtre-Italien,
because it is only at the Opéra that she would be able to reveal her
powers to their fullest. The great works of Rossini and Meyerbeer
clamor for her. Her interpretations of Donna Anna, Agathe, Mathilde,
Alice, and Valentine would reveal new beauties to us.[30] The remarkable
polish of her delivery is almost wasted on the Italian stage, where the
music—a series of melodies thrown together at random, so to speak—
does not lend itself to such refined interpretation. The singers, whom
she rouses from their own incompetence for brief periods, are generally embarrassed in the presence of a woman who is so obviously superior to them, since they are unable to see anything in their roles
beyond the *cabalettas* that are to be sung either *piano* or *forte*. Nourrit
was perhaps the only other opera singer who understood art as Mademoiselle Ungher does. The similarity of their gifts is evident. Both
of them developed the interpretation of dramatic music and the power
of declamation to the highest degree of perfection.

There was tremendous excitement in our box. The power of the
dramatic actress had captivated those who did not respond to the
charm and skill of the singer. The full, fresh, and limpid voice of Moriani,[31] the tenor who sang Gennaro, aroused a storm of applause in
the house. I half wished that I could share in this sort of excitement
more often. Unhappily, however, it is utterly impossible for me to enjoy anything that appeals only to my ears, without my mind and my
emotions also taking a part, a very large part, in my enjoyment. In any
event, Moriani, true to Italian custom, has not yet thought of studying
dramatic art seriously. His gestures are always polished, his smile winning, his looks tender, and he spins out sounds with beguiling smooth-
ness. That is enough to insure his success in Italy. If he wanted to
duplicate that success with a less volatile, more reserved audience, he
would have to learn how to make better use of his fine gifts. To be fair,

---

30. The heroines, respectively, of *Don Giovanni, Der Freischütz, William Tell,
Robert le diable,* and *Les Huguenots.*

31. Napoleone Moriani (1808–1878), a dashing hero of the Italian stage who had
made his debut in Parma in 1833. Liszt, for some reason, makes him out to be younger
and less experienced than he actually was.

however, we should say that Moriani is still quite young, that his debut took place only a short time ago, and that he possesses the most beautiful tenor voice imaginable.

A major fault with the opera performances in Italy is the great and painfully evident lack of balance between the number of brasses and the number of strings in the orchestra. The trombones and trumpets (with or without valves, which are much abused today) are not played softly or gently enough to suit the violins and basses, and the result is a frightful racket—music, one might say, that was meant to stir elephants or rhinoceroses. The singers can only make themselves heard by shouting savagely. I doubt that the walls of Jericho were ever subjected to such a pitiless assault.

The performance was over at eleven o'clock, and it led to a discussion with Emilio that put our three friends fast asleep. That did not bother us at all, and the debate, continuing on and off, did not end until we had arrived at Padua, where we were to have a farewell drink while the horses were being changed. It was four o'clock in the morning but the Café Pedrocchi, just like its more modest forerunner, the Café Florian, never closes. No matter what time it is, the place is rarely empty. It is a rendezvous for discussing business matters, for having a pleasant time, or for simply indulging in *dolce far niente*. The women, following Venetian custom, have no qualms about mixing with the men. People talk in loud voices and promenade through the spacious, magnificent rooms. When the upstairs is finished, concerts and balls will be given there. It will be a model *Casino*; Fourier's disciples would be able to claim it as an example of their phalansteries.[32] No ordinary stone or stucco was used in the construction and decoration of the Café Pedrocchi. Its beautiful Greek columns are white marble; the inside walls, tables, and counters are done in snake-stone from Verona and the violet-streaked marble that was unearthed in the excavations they had dug for the café's foundation, which uncovered the ruins of a Roman temple. As the uneven terrain had placed restrictions on the architect Japelli and necessitated an unpleasant irregularity in one of the café's facades, he conceived the odd idea of adding a decorative vaulted arch, which interrupts the smooth lines of the cafe's colonnade and doubtless impresses anyone who sees it as an old Gothic monument he had wanted to preserve.

---

32. According to the precepts of the utopian social reformer Charles Fourier (1772–1837), his followers were to live in complete physical and moral harmony in a building (or buildings) he called a "phalanstery," a neologism he derived from "phalanx" plus "[mona]stery."

Flames flickered on the surface of our punch. Our glasses smoked. Smiling, we spoke of serious things. Our efforts to appear gay only made us feel awkward. The mysterious power of the passage from night to day heightened our awareness of the melancholy of farewells. The moon had called back its beams. The freshness of dawn reached us and announced with painful clarity the return of day, a day that would no longer see us together.

"One last toast, my friends," said the colonel raising his glass and clinking it with ours. "To all outcasts!"

"To all those who love and suffer!" said Emilio.

"To all those who are trying to find their way!" I added.

To Lambert Massart [Part II, Vienna]

[June–July, 1838]

P.S.—I thought that this letter had reached its destination centuries ago, but I found it lying forgotten on my writing table when I returned from a trip, or rather, a flight, that I had made to Vienna, and I do not want to let it go without adding a few words about my stay in Austria.

What a quirk of fate! During the nearly fifteen years that have passed since my father left his quiet home to take me on a journey across the world, since the time he exchanged the obscure freedom of country life for the glorious servitude of an artist's life and settled in France as the best possible place to cultivate the musical instinct that his naive pride called my "genius," I had become accustomed to considering France my homeland, forgetting completely that it was really another country for me.—You know what a man's life is like during his youth, that period in his life that runs from his fifteenth to his twenty-fifth year. It is the time when he is most governed by externals, when people, places, and things exercise their greatest influence over his imagination. Light radiates from his heart, and he is dominated by such an inescapable need to love that he leaves a little part of himself in everything he touches. At that age a young man, reeling from the confusion of his own thoughts, does not live; he aspires to live. He is all curiosity, longing, wild inspiration, and the flux and reflux of contradictory desires. He exhausts himself in the sealed labyrinth of his unruly passions. All that is simple, easy, and natural only brings a smile of pity to his lips. He overdoes everything; he is eager to attack all obstacles; he spurns both the good he could accomplish and the feelings that could make him happy. He is mercilessly tormented by the barbs of youth. I have spent all that time of burning fever, misdirected energy, and vigorous, mad vitality on French soil. It is also the soil that received my father's remains and holds his grave, the holy sanctuary of my first great sorrow!—How could I not believe that I was the child of a land where I had loved and suffered so much! How could I possibly have thought that another land had witnessed my birth, that the blood coursing through my veins was the blood of another race of men, that my own people were elsewhere? . . .

An unexpected event suddenly revived a feeling that I thought was dead but was actually only dormant. Perusing a German newspaper one morning in Venice, I read a detailed account of the disaster that had struck Pest.[1] I was badly shaken by it. I felt an unaccustomed sense of compassion, a vivid and irresistible need to comfort the many victims. "What will I do for them?" I asked myself. "What help can I offer them? I have none of the things that make one a power among men; I have neither the influence of great wealth, nor the power attendant on grandeur." It did not matter. I pushed ahead because I felt that there would be no more rest for my mind, no more sleep for my eyes if I did not contribute my mite to ease that immense suffering.[2] Besides, who could say that heaven would not bless my puny little offering? The Hand that multiplied the loaves in the desert is surely not tired. God has perhaps concealed more joy in an artist's mite than in all the gold of a millionaire.

It was these emotions, these feelings that revealed the meaning of the word "homeland" to me. I was suddenly transported to the past, and upon looking inside myself, I, to my indescribable joy, found there the full, pure treasury of my childhood memories. A magnificent landscape rose before my eyes: it was the familiar forest, ringing with the hunters' cries; it was the Danube, tumbling along its course among the

1. The flood in March 1838 was Hungary's worst natural disaster in modern times. Villages, crops, and livestock were devastated, over 150 people drowned, and half of Pest's some 100,000 inhabitants were forced to flee their homes. Pest's neighbor across the Danube, Buda, which stood on higher ground, escaped severe damage. (Buda and Pest were not consolidated into a single city until 1873.)

2. Liszt must have learned about the calamity about the 1st of April, for he had already decided to go to Vienna by the 2d, when he wrote to a distinguished Hungarian and his former patron, Count Thaddeus d'Amadé, informing him of his intentions: "In seven or eight days I will be in Vienna. . . . Since my stay in Vienna has to be extremely short (because of engagements I have undertaken in Italy in May), my foremost desire will be to give a concert for the flood victims among our unhappy countrymen. For this occasion, I dare to hope that you will be good enough to assist me with your good advice and most efficacious cooperation" (unpublished, The Pierpont Morgan Library, New York).

rocks; it was the vast plain where the docile flocks freely grazed; it was Hungary, that robust and fertile soil that has borne such noble children. It was, in brief, my homeland, because "I too," I cried, in a spate of patriotism that would have made you smile, "I too belong to that ancient and noble race. I am one of the sons of that primitive, indomitable nation, which seems destined for better days!" . . .

The race has always been proud and heroic. Noble sentiments have always found a comfortable place in those ample breasts. Those lofty brows were never made for ignorance and servitude. More fortunate than others, their minds have never been dazzled by false promises. They have not strayed along false paths. Their ears have been deaf to false prophets. No one has ever said to them, "Christ is here, He is there. . . ." They sleep. . . . But let a powerful voice awaken them, and oh! how their spirit will seize the truth! How they will build a formidable sanctuary for it in their breasts! How their brawny arms will defend it! A glorious future awaits them, for they are strong and good, and nothing has sapped their will nor dimmed their hopes.

Oh, my wild and distant homeland! Oh, my unknown friends! Oh, my vast family! your cry of suffering has summoned me to you! My heart has been moved with compassion, and I have bowed my head in shame for having neglected you for so long. . . . Why, then, does a stern destiny restrain me?—Another cry of pain, faint but having all power over me, makes me tremble. It is the voice that I hold dear, the only one that will never call to me in vain.[3] . . . Oh, my grieving homeland! I leave you once more—but this time it is not with the thoughtlessness of a child chasing after novelty, that enticing sprite that seduces and betrays him. I leave with a troubled heart and lowered eyes, because I now know how many pious wishes and noble intentions have been blunted by the pressures of a self-serving, frivolous society, and how many holy thoughts have been swept away by the wind of separation. All I hope to do is to gather my life together again in your virgin solitudes, to strengthen it once more in the simplicity of country life, and to purify it in the oblivion of the crowd, so that I can go to my grave a little less burdened by those shameful lapses that living heaps on a man's head.

I left for Vienna on the 7th of April and planned to give two concerts there: the first to benefit my countrymen, and the second to

---

3. Evidently Marie d'Agoult. She had fallen ill and, as best as we can judge from Liszt's letters, spared him no details of her sufferings while he was in Vienna, even though he did ask her to join him and sent her the money for the trip (*Corres. Liszt–d'Agoult* 1:212–33).

pay for my traveling expenses. After that, I planned to lose myself in the wilder reaches of Hungary, walking alone with a knapsack on my back. But it did not work out that way; my friend Tobias[4] had other plans. So that you understand what sort of a man my friend Tobias is, I will tell you that he is a bit large, a bit fat, but in no way coarse. His round face, reminiscent of Hummel's, is enlivened by two finely shaped gray eyes. The corners of his mouth betray a good-natured but sharp wit. His way of life is peaceful, his manner cordial. Without seeming to trouble himself in the least, he nevertheless manages to expedite a great deal of business and render an enormous number of services. His editions are remarkably correct and carefully done.

I had never met him before, yet he opened his arms to me, welcoming me back like the Prodigal Son. Quickly realizing that my nature was too impetuous, my mind too logical, my character too rigid for the everyday course of life, especially a musical life, he took me under his wing and made me place all my wishes and deliberations in his hands. I saw no harm in it. With his patient perseverence and quiet activity, he overcame all difficulties, saved me from all annoyances, and spared me all the preparations—except that, instead of arranging *one* concert, as we had agreed beforehand, he had surreptitiously taken subscriptions for a *second* concert, and then for a *tenth* one, all within the space of a month.[5] It was enough to weaken, wear down, or destroy a resistance even stronger than mine, since I was to appear at least three times on the program of every concert, but I was so powerfully, so continually supported by the public's warm regard for me that I did not experience any fatigue. Playing for such an intelligent and friendly audience, I was never given pause by the fear that I would not be understood, and without appearing to be foolhardy, I was able to play the most serious works of Beethoven, Weber, Hummel, Moscheles, and Chopin;[6] portions of Berlioz's *Symphonie fantastique*;

4. Tobias Haslinger (1787–1842), a prominent Viennese music publisher and doyen of the city's musical life. Beethoven had been especially fond of him.

5. From 18 April to 25 May, Liszt gave eight of his own concerts in Vienna, including the Hungarian benefit. He also performed at two other major benefits (6 May and 24 May). In addition to these public appearances, he played at the Imperial Court (17 May) and at any number of private soirées. (Press reports of the concerts are given in Dezső Légány, *Franz Liszt: Unbekannte Presse*, pp. 22–58, which also includes portions of this Letter, as translated and published in the Vienna press.)

6. Specifically, the works Liszt performed or took a part in were: Beethoven, Sonata in A-Flat, Op. 26 (the Beethoven sonata he played most often during his later virtuoso tours), Sonata in C-sharp minor, Op. 27 no. 2, and "Adelaïde"; Weber, the *Conzertstück* and the "Invitation to the Dance" (Liszt's own arrangement); Hummel,

fugues by Scarlatti and Handel; and finally, those dear etudes, those beloved children of mine that had seemed so monstrous to the habitués of La Scala.[7]

This I must say: ever since I have been playing the piano and in all my frequent contacts with the music lovers of all nations, I have never encountered an audience as sympathetic as the one in Vienna;[8] it is enthusiastic without being dazzled, difficult to please without being unjust, and its enlightened eclecticism allows for all types of music, for nothing is excluded through prejudice. If the city had a little more life and activity, a little more of that savoir faire that is perhaps too prevalent in Paris, Vienna would unquestionably become the center of the musical world.

Not a year passes that the Viennese are not visited by two or three renowned artists. I saw Thalberg again there, but he had unfortunately decided not to perform publicly. Kalkbrenner had been announced, but we learned to our great regret that when he arrived in Munich he decided to return to France. I was still in time, however, to meet an interesting young pianist, Mademoiselle Clara Wieck,[9] who has secured a very fine and legitimate success for herself this past winter. Her talent charmed me; she possesses genuine superiority, a true and profound sense of feeling, and she is always high-minded. The remarkable way in which she performed Beethoven's famous Sonata in F Minor inspired the renowned tragic poet Grillparzer to write some verses,[10] which I have copied and translated for you:

---

the Septet; Moscheles, etudes; Chopin, etudes from Opp. 10 and 25. Although Liszt does not mention it, six of his programs also included songs by Schubert, with him either performing his own transcriptions of them or playing the accompaniment.

7. Liszt played two of his etudes at the concerts. He also performed a number of his other compositions: the *Grande valse di bravura*; selections from the *Soirées musicales* and the transcription of the *William Tell* Overture; his Fantasy on "Frequenti palpiti" and Fantasies on themes from *I Puritani*, *Les Huguenots*, and *La Juive*; the *Hexameron*; and the *Grand galop chromatique* (a rousing concert-finale).

8. This was an important consideration in Liszt's scheme of things. Writing to Nourrit that summer, 9 July 1838, he mentions "my sojourn in Vienna, where I spent one of the finest months of my life, spoiled, adulated, but better than that, *seriously understood* and accepted by an extremely intelligent public" (L. M. Quicherat, *Adolphe Nourrit* 3:377.)

9. Clara Wieck (1819–1896), daughter of piano pedagogue Friedrich Wieck (1785–1873), and later famous as Clara Schumann, Robert's wife.

10. Franz Grillparzer (1791–1872). His verses "Clara Wieck und Beethoven" were published in the *Wiener Zeitschrift für Kunst*," 9 January 1838.

[Clara Wieck und Beethoven]
Ein Wundermann, der Welt, des Lebens satt,
Schloss seine Zauber grollend ein
Im festverwahrten, demantharten Schrein,
Und warf den Schlüssel in das Meer und starb.
Die Menschlein mühen sich geschäftig ab,
Umsonst! kein Sperrzeug löst das harte Schloss
Und seine Zauber schlafen, wie ihr Meister.
Ein Schäferkind, am Strand des Meeres spielend,
Sieht zu der hastig unberuf'nen Jagd.
Sinnvoll-gedankenlos, wie Mädchen sind,
Senkt sie die weissen Finger in die Fluth,
Und fasst, und hebt, und hat's.—Es ist der Schlüssel!
Auf springt sie, auf, mit höhern Herzenschlägen,
Der Schrein blinkt wie aus Augen ihr entgegen.
Der Schlüssel passt. Der Deckel fliegt. Die Geister,
Sie steigen auf und senken dienend sich
Der anmuthreichen, unschuldsvollen Herrin,
Die sie mit weissen Fingern, spielend, lenkt.

A wizard, weary of the world and life,
locked his magic spells in a diamond casket, whose
key he threw into the sea, and then he died.
    Common, little men exhausted themselves in
vain attempts; no instrument could open the strong
lock, and the incantations slept with their master.
    A shepherd's child, playing on the shore, sees these
hectic and useless efforts. Dreamy and unthinking
as all girls are, she plunges her snowy fingers into
the waves, touches a strange object, seizes it, and
pulls it from the sea. . . . Oh! what a surprise!
She holds the magic key!
    She hurries joyfully; her heart beating, full of
eager anticipation; the casket gleams for her with
marvelous brilliance; the lock gives way . . . .
The genies rise into the air, then bow respectfully
before their gracious and virginal mistress, who
leads them with her white hand and has them do her
bidding as she plays.

At Vienna's Italian Theater, which is quite fashionable, I heard
the Milan opera troupe again. The company now included Poggi,
whose talent and success did not disappoint me. In the salons, it was
with great pleasure and frequently with an intense feeling that brought

tears to my eyes, that I heard an amateur, Baron von Schönstein,[11] sing Schubert's songs. Their translation into French gives a very poor idea of the union of the words, which are generally quite beautiful, with the music of Schubert, the most poetic musician who ever lived. The German language is admirable for conveying emotion, and that is why, perhaps, only a German can fully understand the simplicity and imagination of many of these compositions, with their capricious charm, their melancholy abandon. Baron von Schönstein interprets them with the skill of a great artist and sings them with all the artlessness of an amateur who gives vent to his feelings without being preoccupied with what the public will think. One of the nicest things that I could possibly wish for you, my friend, is that you would come to Vienna, or that he would go to Paris, and that we could have the pleasure of listening to him together.

Do not ask me for any more about Vienna. I would not know what to say about all the people I saw only in passing, or about the things that I did not see at all. Always surrounded by a group of good friends who catered to my every wish, always beset by the sound of the music I made, always on the eve or the morrow of giving a concert, I spent my time in Vienna in a manner that was far too extraordinary to give me the right to add anything else about it, except to say that I came away with the fondest memories of my stay there and the regret that it had been so short.

Adieu one more time. Here is a postscript that is longer than the letter itself. I am rushing to get the whole package into the post so that I will not be tempted to give you a parenthetical account of a voyage to Constantinople.

11. Karl, Freiherr von Schönstein (1797–1876), a lawyer and musical amateur who first met Schubert in 1818. In a later memoir of the composer, Schönstein wrote: "It was Schubert's songs that first awoke in me the love of the German song-style to which, from then on, I devoted myself almost exclusively, and especially to the songs of Schubert. Schubert had grown fond of me and enjoyed making music with me, which he did often; he admitted to me repeatedly that from this time on, in his songs, he generally had in mind only a voice of my range [a high baritone]" (Otto Erich Deutsch, *Schubert: Memoirs by his Friends*, pp. 100–101).

8

GENOA, FLORENCE, AND BOLOGNA

Liszt's trip to Vienna was the beginning of the end for him and Madame d'Agoult, since it exposed a fatal flaw in their relationship that could no longer be concealed or ignored. Essentially, their problem resulted from the traditional conflict between the claims of love and those of a career.

Liszt, despite his immense European reputation, was a neophyte when it came to the musical world beyond Paris. Vienna had been a revelation to him: not only had his concerts there yielded unprecedented financial rewards—no mean consideration for a pianist who had been supporting himself and his parents since he was twelve years old—but the audiences, indeed, the whole populace, had also acclaimed him musically and socially with an enthusiasm he had never experienced before. He was excited, exhilarated. A brilliant career was ready for the taking, and as he was already twenty-six years old, embarking on that career had a now-or-never urgency to it.

The countess was deeply disturbed and challenged by his Viennese success. Having left both husband and child and compromised her social position to be with Liszt, she felt, and with some justification, that she should have first claim to his time and affections. If he took to touring, their relationship was bound to change; the aristocratic art circles upon which much of his success would depend could not be expected to accept their "irregular union," nor was she the type of person to sit demurely by while her lover was off performing at a soirée or at a concert. Hence the dilemma they faced: should Liszt sacrifice or at least restrict his career to accommodate her, or should she, by taking a back seat in his life, free him to pursue that career as he would? We know the ultimate answer, but the working out of it was no easy matter. Love, as Madame de Staël observed somewhere, is basically "égoisme à due."

For the time being, however, Liszt and Marie d'Agoult continued their journey, for there was a lot more that they both still wanted
to see and experience in Italy.

CHRONICLE

June 1838. Liszt and Marie visit Genoa.

July. They travel to the resort town of Lugano.

Mid-July. Liszt hurries back to Milan. A Milanese journal has translated and published his essay on La Scala, and not unexpectedly
a storm of outrage has broken out over what the Milanese see as
a high-handed, disparaging report of their musical and social life
by an opinionated foreigner. Declaring "War on Liszt," the Milanese accuse him of everything from impugning the morals of
Italian womanhood to a total inability to understand the traditions and accomplishments of Italian opera. Liszt, exasperated
by the attack, issues a statement offering to explain his opinions,[1] but as no one is interested in his justifications, he rejoins
Marie at Lugano. It is there, incidentally, that their third child is
conceived.

Late August. Liszt returns to Milan for the coronation of the Austrian Emperor Ferdinand I as King of Lombardy-Venetia. The
ceremony takes place on 6 September.

10 September. Liszt gives a charity benefit concert as a kind of peace
offering to the Milanese. His program includes, among other
pieces, his transcription of the Overture to Rossini's *William Tell*
and a work he improvised for the occasion, a Grand Fantasy,
Reminiscences of La Scala. Later that month he also hosts a lavish dinner for some two dozen friends and supporters in the
city.

Start of October. Liszt travels to the Duke of Modena's castle at Cattajo (near Padua), where he performs privately for the imperial
family.

Early October. Liszt stops off in Bologna en route to Florence.

Mid-October–mid-January 1839. The travelers settle in Florence for
three months, quietly enjoying the artistic treasures the city and
its environs have to offer. While there Liszt performs publicly on

---

1. The translation of Liszt's essay appeared in *La Moda*, 12 and 19 July 1838; *Il
Pirata*, 17 July, is the journal that carried the headline "Guerra al Signor Liszt"; and
Liszt's offer to explain his views was published in *Glissons*, 21 July. See Charles Suttoni,
"Liszt à Milan."

about a half dozen occasions, including galas at the grand-ducal
court (17 November and 12 December) and his own concerts (8
November and 16 December).

23–31 December. Liszt goes to Bologna. He performs at the casino
there on the 25th and gives a concert of his own on the 29th. He
then returns to Florence, where he and Marie await the arrival
of Blandine before setting off for Rome.

All four of the articles relating to this period were published only in
truncated, excerpted form. Further, the one devoted to Genoa was evidently combined with a later account of Florence and published as a
single article in *L'Artiste*. In this chapter, however, the separate halves
of the article have been restored to their proper chronological order.
The two other articles—those discussing Cellini's *Perseus* and Raphael's *Saint Cecilia*—are not so much travel articles as essays which
explore the close relationship that Liszt felt existed between the plastic arts and music.

Genoa and Florence[1] [Part I, Genoa]

[June 1838][2]

The most Italian thing I have seen in Italy so far is Genoa. Situated on
the slopes of the Apennines, whose peaks protect it from the inclement
winds of the North, the prosperous city bathes its marble feet in the
gentle waves of the Mediterranean, while its crown of orange trees,
oleanders, and magnolias floats in a blue sky. Arriving in Genoa, the
traveler's eye is quickly dazzled by the ever-present spell of its past
grandeur. Its vast palaces, with their porticos, colonnades, and soaring
staircases that lead to resplendently gilded rooms decorated with the
masterpieces of Van Dyke, Carraccio, and Veronese, recall both the
splendor of the one-time republic and the wealth of its patrician busi-
nessmen, those conquering speculators who left such names as Doria,
Spinola, and Durazzo to history. Flower-filled terraces rise along the
slopes and perfume the air; beautiful murmuring fountains, falling as
mist for the thirsty plants, charm the ear and add freshness to the sultry

1. *L'Artiste*, 3 November 1839, pp. 153–57.
2. As we do not know when this article was written, this is the date when Liszt
and d'Agoult visited Genoa. It is likely, moreover, that the article on Genoa and Florence, as published, presents excerpts from the two separate essays that Liszt sent Massart on 28 August 1839 for insertion in *L'Artiste* (Vier, *Liszt Artiste*, p. 56.)

atmosphere, while a cicada hidden in the high grass sings his persistent note. At night, thousands of fireflies sketch their fantastic, scintillating arabesques through the darkness.

A singularly colorful native population lives and works among these marble structures and gardens, on this rocky strip of land where nature makes a vain, ostentatious show in an effort to conceal the land's sterility. Even today the dock worker still wears a Phrygian cap, whose purple color gives his manly features an indefinably proud and resolute air. The artisan's wife swathes herself in a long white muslin veil, which, without concealing her face or movements, softens her ruddy complexion and gives her a uniquely dignified appearance. Large groups of monks wearing habits that go back to the founding of their orders seem to be trying, with their unchanging costume, to defy the passage of time and its sway over all things. The Dominican in his spotless tunic symbolizing chastity, the Franciscan girded with a cord to remind him of his obedience, and the mendicant carrying a beggar's sack, the emblem of his poverty, constantly parade their pious idleness through the streets. Little rustic bells warn you that you must yield the center of the road to the mules clambering up the steep streets to deliver the city's provisions. And often, too often, a different, sinister sound mingles with the silvery tinkle that the strong, patient animals make by bobbing their heads: it is the clanking of the chains of the prisoners who are laboring on public works and who, like wild beasts, are under the constant surveillance of an armed guard. Even were it not for the irons that link them together in shame and misery, nor for the infamous blood-colored jacket, crime's livery that they must wear, their faces, brutilized by remorseless crime, would still identify them as prisoners.

All this must surely present a painter with interesting similarities and contrasts, a group of objects that coalesce into an animated, diversified picture; but for a man who sees things not only with his physical eyes, but also ponders them with the eyes of his soul, the initial astonishment, the unthinking delight brought on by the vivid contrast of colors and forms, soon gives way to a deep feeling of sadness. In Genoa the magnificence of the surroundings only makes the degradation of man all the more apparent. Nowhere did human misery impress me as more of a distressing anomaly in our society than it did under this ever-serene sky, and nowhere, perhaps, was it more barefaced and more abject. I cannot tell you how distressed I was when I returned to my hotel—my senses swimming from the thousand delights I have just mentioned, my heart elated by nature's eternal smile—and brushed almost immediately against a beggar covered with ulcerous sores, a convict in chains, and a mendicant carrying his begging sack. There was poverty in its three forms: for the monk, it was voluntary, respected, and somehow sanctified; for the beggar, it was passive, tolerated, and partially alleviated; and for the prisoner, it was defiant, punishing, and a stigma to be borne. These three types of the poor will surely disappear one day—God willing!

Catholicism in the Piedmontese states may not enjoy the allpowerful sovereignty that an active faith had once given it, but it still maintains all its external pomp by force of custom. Hardly a week passes when work is not interrupted by some religious festival, when some parish or other in the city does not hold a procession to honor its patron saint. The houses are then hung with scarlet banners, leafy garlands are strung from corner to corner along the street, and when night comes there are special lights, fireworks, and illuminated transparent screens with holy pictures painted on them. It goes without saying that music plays no part in these solemnities; this is because it is impossible for me to use that honored term to describe the churchsanctioned bellowing of singers accompanied by a serpent, or to place any value on the organists' ridiculous improvisations on themes from an opera that one had heard the night before, and which disrupt your meditation on sacred mysteries by reminding you of the prima donna's deep curtsies or the first tenor's leering smiles.

The Genovese are considered the least musical people in Italy. They are said to prefer the monotonous chink of a piaster against a ducat to the most beautiful tones of Paganini's violin.[3] I will reserve judgment about that charge, as I was in Genoa during what is called the "off-season" (meaning, if you please, the most beautiful time of the year) and met only a few of the natives, although I did, thanks to my lucky star, meet one passionate amateur among them, the Marquis di Negro.[4]

I had a letter of introduction to the Marquis, and I do not know what odd chance, what happy thought made me deliver the letter to his door, because I must confess in passing that I have a quirk about such letters. After many experiences with them, a lot of thought about them, and the conclusions I subsequently reached, I firmly resolved, first, that I would never ask for a letter of introduction from anyone whomsoever to anyone else and, second, in the event that I did accept such a letter out of politeness, absentmindedness, or plain clumsiness,

---

3. Paganini was a native of Genoa.

4. Giancarlo di Negro (1769–1857). He was one of Genoa's more active patrons of the arts and had been influential in launching Paganini's career.

that I would never deliver it, seeing that a letter of introduction is the greatest source of annoyance, unpleasantness, and misunderstanding that an artist of my temperament could ever encounter. When you travel the world, my good friends,[5] you quickly realize that even with moving from place to place, or country to country, or from one type of society to another, you always come across the same three or four categories of people, and that those who fall into any one category are all alike, having the same pretensions, vanities, and peculiarities. One of the most consistent types, moreover, the most insupportable everywhere and the one with whom we musicians must always contend, is the *professional dilettante,* the Maecenas of the sixteenth notes, the pitiless philharmonist. He is the musical dictator of his own little world. He has first and last say about the artists' abilities. He has given advice to Lablache, has encouraged Mademoiselle Ungher, and is going to persuade Rossini to write a new opera; in short, he is an indefatigable busybody, the fly buzzing around Apollo's chariot. Armed as you are with a letter of introduction certifying your virtuosity, you pay him a visit which he does not return, it being understood that he is the patron and you are the protégé thus precluding any question of reciprocal politeness. During that first visit he is at pains to let you know that he has taken an active interest in music all his life. At times he will even sing for you the romance he composed for Mademoiselle————or, better yet—God protect us!—he will play a four-part fugue, a performance which had won unstinting praise from a grand-nephew of Johann Sebastian Bach himself! He will insinuate with greater or lesser (mostly *lesser*) tact that no one in the city besides himself understands anything of music and that his praise and his criticism have the force of law. So there you are, well instructed as to what it means to enlist his support. Two days later he invites you to a soirée. He has told his guests all about you and made a gracious effort to predispose them in your favor. You barely enter the room when you get pushed willy-nilly, like it or not, to the piano or have a violin bow thrust into your hand. There is nothing to be said; the Maecenas has *first* claim to your talent, and he must be able to tell the entire city the following day that you have played *for him, in his home.* This assures his dictatorial standing and renews his credentials as a musical arbiter. I should also add that you will have to give him at least five tickets to your coming concert

---

5. When Liszt sent this text to Massart (note 2 above), he said he had wanted to address it "to my good friends Lambert Massart and Léon Kreutzer," provided they concurred. Presumably they are meant here, even though the published article gives no addressee.

and that he will tell his friends that if you would only listen to judicious advice, do away with certain excesses, and compose in a more correct style, you would unquestionably be a great artist . . . that is your best chance. At times, instead of just one *dictator* you will stumble across *two musical consuls.* Unlucky you! You will then discover that you are the innocent victim who is to be tossed between Capulet and Montague, between Orsini and Colonna, between Fregoso and Adorno, and you will need the astuteness of a Talleyrand to maintain your neutrality between the two powerful warring factions. . . . And all this is precisely why I promised myself never to accept a letter of introduction to anyone.

I must admit, nevertheless, that I failed to follow my own rule when I arrived in Genoa. It was a lucky thing for me, I assure you, because I found the Marquis di Negro to be not only a gracious host but also one of the most interesting personalities I had met in Italy so far.

Di Negro is the sort of Italian gentleman we find portrayed in some novels of the last century. He is perhaps the last of a vanished society, the last representative of a code of behavior that will never return. The scion of an old family and inheritor of a considerable fortune, he nonetheless had a decided penchant for adventure and an artist's life from his earliest days. Endowed with a remarkable natural aptitude for all forms of physical exercise, a sparkling wit, and, above all, a gift for improvisation that is rare even in Italy, he was not content with the plaudits of the drawing room. He wanted to experience the feelings of public success, and taking a leaf from the chronicles of the *minnesingers* and *trouvères,* he traveled throughout Italy mounted on a fine Arabian horse, with his guitar slung from his neck, and followed by a liveried squire. Riding across the green hills and valleys, he would stop at whatever place appealed to him or wherever some pretty peasant lass smiled sweetly at him. . . . Then he would have his squire sound a triple call, just like the dwarf in an enchanted castle, and gather the country people around him, entertaining them in his unusual way with a Vergilian eclogue, or knightly adventures in the style of Ariosto, or even love stories, which, they say, were not to be faulted for their prudery. . . . When his verve was spent, he capped his listeners' excitement by opening a large purse and distributing material riches just as lavishly as he had distributed his poetic treasures. Loud cries of "Hurrah" greeted his bounty, and when he took to the road again, the people would follow him for miles with lively cries of "Long live the famous poet! Long live the great troubador!" At other times, the marquis would go to the most popular café in the area and call for the billiard cue that his squire carried in the guise of a lance; then, challenging the most intrepid local men to a game, he would, to the dismay of everyone present, win all the bets and all the games. But having done so, he never failed to order a score of bottles of the best local wine and invite the losers to drink to his health or offer a toast to his beloved. . . . Upon his return to Italy after traveling throughout Europe, the marquis settled in a villa with such a magnificent location that he was envied by the King of Naples himself (*Villetta* commands Genoa and its entire harbor). To decorate it, he called upon all the arts. His ever-youthful imagination suggested a thousand ways of adding interest and variety to his days, without letting them slip into the dull stupor that prevailed all around him. A fine Erard harp replaced his adventurous guitar, an excellent library was put at his guests' disposal, and the drawing rooms, where allegory and symbolism preside, were adorned with the valuable collections of antique marble pieces, paintings, and engravings he had amassed during his travels. Lastly, even the gardens were decorated with inscriptions and statues dedicated to various great Italians and so became a veritable out-of-doors pantheon. Party after party was given at *Villetta,* and there was hardly a one that did not bear the stamp of originality, with something extraordinary or surprising to offer. One event was an outdoor dinner, with all the tables and chairs placed on swings; another was a cruise on a vessel built as an exact replica of Cleopatra's barge. . . . Thus it is that the Marquis di Negro—philosopher, preacher, poet, historian,* artist, and man of the world—knows how to interest and delight those whose lucky star leads them to *Villetta.* [The text of this Letter continues later in this chapter, p. 157.]

The *Perseus* of Benvenuto Cellini[1]

Florence, 30 November 1838

. . . .

The clock struck two, and I left Prince Poniatowski's ball. The day, which had been as warm as our most beautiful September days in

---

*The Marquis de Negro is the author of a *History of Genoa* and *Lenten Meditations in Tercets.*

1. *Gazette musicale*, 13 January 1839, pp. 14–15. The addressee is not identified, nor is there any clue in Liszt's correspondence as to who it might have been.

Paris rarely manage to be, had been followed by a clear night, one of those Tuscan nights whose majestic beauty defies description. As I could not bring myself to return to where I was staying, I began to walk aimlessly along the Arno. The city slept, the river ran silent; nothing laid claim to my thoughts. I entered the Uffizi arcade and, directing my steps toward the grand-ducal piazza, soon found myself at the foot of Benvenuto Cellini's *Perseus*. The sight of that noble statue, enhanced by the night's spell, made an incomparably strong impression on me. I had often passed nearby without stopping to look at it closely, but this time I felt that I was detained by an invisible force. It seemed as if a mysterious voice was speaking, as if the statue's spirit was talking to me. . . . And while that may strike you as wildly fanciful, the fact is that I sat down on the steps of the *Loggia dei Lanzi* and began to muse.

The story of Perseus is one of the beautiful myths of Greek poetry. Perseus is one of those glorious champions who prevailed in the struggle between good and evil. Perseus is the man of genius, the dual being born of the union of a god and a mortal woman. His first adventures in life were in combat. He slays the Gorgon; he cuts off the head of Medusa, the inert force, that brutal obstacle that always arises between a powerful man and the fulfillment of his destiny. He soars aloft on the winged horse, he is master of his genius; he rescues Andromeda; he seeks to unite himself with beauty, a poet's eternal lover, but this will not take place without further combat. The struggle resumes, but as Perseus is born of woman—as much a man as a god—he is flawed. Fate steps in. He slays the father of Danaë; sorrow and remorse weigh heavily on him. He is slain in turn by Megapenthes, the avenger of Acrisius. After Perseus's death the nations raise altars to him.

A primeval concept! An everlasting truth!

When initially assuming its most abstract form, art reveals itself in words. Poetry lends its language to art; it symbolizes art. In Perseus, antiquity gives us a profound, perfect allegory. It is the first stage, the first step, in the development of the idea. Let us go on.

In modern times and in the hands of a great artist, art takes on a perceptible form, it becomes plastic. The casting furnace is lit, the metal liquifies, it runs into the mold, and Perseus emerges fully armed, holding Medusa's head aloft in his hand, the emblem of his victory.

Glory to you, Cellini! You have completed a difficult task. You too, man of struggle and combat, have vanquished the Gorgon. You too, man of inspiration, have triumphed over the monster, you have secured Andromeda, you have conquered beauty. Your name will never perish.

That is the second stage.

Then in our own times there comes another Cellini, a great artist himself who takes up the idea in its second stage and transforms it even further. By directing himself to the sense of hearing, just as Cellini had directed himself to the sense of sight, he clothes the idea with new splendor and creates a Perseus that is as grand, as complete, and as polished as the first two.[2]

Honor to you, Berlioz, because you also struggle with invincible courage; and if you have not yet subdued the Gorgon, if the serpents at your feet still hiss, threatening you with their hideous forked tongues, and if envy, ridicule, malice, and treachery still seem to proliferate around you, have no fear, the gods are on your side. They have given you, as they did Perseus, a helmet, wings, a shield, and a sword—that is, protection, a quick wit, wisdom, and strength.

Combat, sorrow, and glory: the destiny of genius.

It was yours, Cellini, and it is yours too, Berlioz.

Mysterious conception! Genius giving birth to genius! A divine chain uniting men of ideas across the centuries! Inexplicable connections! A communion of minds! The Breath of God moving through humanity!

My spirit was overwhelmed by these thoughts.

I looked up at *Perseus* again. The strange incidents surrounding the casting of the statue came to mind, and I was struck by a host of curious similarities and contrasts. The casting of *Perseus* was a solemn and decisive event for Benvenuto Cellini. That important moment in the sculptor's life leads, in turn, to a remarkable period in the musician's existence. The inclinations of both men since their boyhood is contrary to their short-sighted parents' wishes, and in this conflict each of them discovers the unmistakable signs of his destiny. It is certainly worth noting that Cellini's father tries to make his son a musician; Berlioz's father tries to make him an anatomist.

This, perhaps, might be the place for some reflections on parental

2. Berlioz's *Benvenuto Cellini* was given at the Paris Opéra, 10 September 1838. Shortly thereafter, Liszt in Milan wrote a friend in Paris: "I learned tonight that Berlioz's opera had no success. My poor friend! The Fates are being hard on him! I am afraid this setback will make him very sad. Did you hear his score? Surely there are beautiful things in it. What a triumph this will be for the mean mediocrities who walk up and down your boulevards. . . . No matter: Berlioz remains nonetheless the most powerful musical brain in France" (to Ferdinand Denis, in *New Letters of Berlioz*, p. 29). Once in Florence, Liszt saw the *Perseus* for himself and must have realized that writing about it would give him a fine and ingenious opportunity to praise Berlioz's effort—sight unseen.

authority and that wonderful influence old graybeards exercise over the young—but let us pursue the parallels between the two artists.

To please his sire, Cellini is forced to play the flute. Berlioz, even more unfortunate, breaks violently away from the distasteful medical amphitheaters. His parents' severe disapproval forces him to give guitar lessons. He struggles miserably to support his glorious way of life and have a few leisure hours to devote to the study of harmony and composition.[3]

Once his father's death frees him from "that damned flute playing" (those are his own words), Cellini applies himself entirely to his calling and soon becomes an accomplished goldsmith, an exquisite metal worker. We then see him being successively courted, pampered, spurned, and persecuted by the princes. A pope has him thrown into prison; a mistress fills him with bitterness.

Popes and mistresses today leave artists in peace, but persecution continues to exist in subtler, less acknowledged forms. Instead of coming from above, it comes from below. The artist's equals and inferiors in the social hierarchy are the people who generally impede and shackle him. They are the ones who first deny him, who then challenge, point by point, his place in the sun, his share of the light. Let Berlioz, like Cellini, write a faithful account of the vicissitudes of his life, and we will be sadly surprised to learn how such a lofty mind and noble heart gave rise to such vile prejudices, and we will refuse to believe that instead of understanding, encouragement, or, at the very least, impartial judgment, the only thing he got from many of his family and colleagues was opposition, injustice, or crass indifference.

For Cellini the precious moment when his talent is to be officially sanctioned comes when he receives a commission from Cosimo I [de' Medici] for the *Perseus,* one of the statues that is to adorn the piazza of the palace. He becomes the rival of Donatello and Michelangelo. Benvenuto the goldsmith, Benvenuto the etcher of metals, is going to become Benvenuto the sculptor.

No longer just a noblemen's favorite, he will be the people's chosen one, the nation's artist. I will not go into detail about the countless obstacles that Cellini and his work had to face. His patience and perseverance were subjected to trials that did not cease, even after his work was a brilliant success. The jealousy of his ignoble rival Bandinelli gave him neither rest nor peace. A mob of mediocre sculptors jeered at him. They defied him to produce a major work. They accused him

---

3. Berlioz gives his own account of this trying period in chapters 10 and 11 of his *Memoirs.*

of bragging and derisively called him *il scultar nuovo,* "the new sculptor." The Grand Duke, shaken by all the clamor, hesitated, made promises, retracted them, and gave Cellini nothing but halfhearted, wavering support.

The very day the statue is to be cast the unlucky artist, broken with fatigue, devoured by rage, and burning with fever, is forced to take to his bed. He cannot supervise the operation. His instructions are not followed. The negligence or malevolence of those whom he had trusted jeopardize everything. They come and tell him that an irreparable accident has taken place, that nothing can be done. Hearing the news, Benvenuto gives a great cry, roaring like a lion. He leaps out of bed and, hardly taking time to dress, runs to the furnace. He sees the danger. He takes command, he gives orders, he sets to work. The dying flame bursts into life; the metal begins to fuse and flow into the mold. Eight days later the statue is raised on its pedestal. The people flock to see it. They admire the work and embrace the artist. His enemies are astounded. His lukewarm friends come to life again. And Cellini's assured place in history begins.

At this point the parallel is all to the sculptor's advantage.

Like Cellini, Berlioz is exposed to countless difficulties. He too has to face rivals devoid of talent but favored by circumstances. He too has been stigmatized by the mob as the "new musician." He too has found nothing but indifference and weakness among those who cannot help but recognize his genius. Berlioz, like Cellini, struggles against blind prejudice, against obstinate ill will, but his work, unlike Cellini's, cannot be presented to an impartial public, to the people, except through the intermediary of the very ones who oppose him. The great majority of his interpreters are hostile to him.

Cellini displays his statue for all to see. His work stands there at any hour or minute of the day, appealing directly to the people. And that is the notable advantage that the plastic arts have over music, which is not permanent and can never have an unconditional effect, since its effect depends to a large extent upon its performance.

All the arts are based on two principles: reality and ideality. Ideality is perceptible only to cultivated minds but the reality of the sculptor can be perceived by everyone because its prototype is the human form, familiar to all. There is not a single artisan who would be any less stirred than a poet by the truth that exists in the works of Phidias and Michelangelo. Each person is equally capable of appreciating the degree of fidelity in the statue's representation of the human body. This, however, is not the case with music: it has no reality, so to speak; it does not imitate, it expresses. Music is at once both a science like algebra and a psychological language that is intelligible only to the poetic consciousness. Hence, like science and art, music remains almost entirely inaccessible to the crowd. The passions and feelings that it is meant to convey certainly exist in the heart of Man, but not in the hearts of all men, while all men can find themselves physically reproduced in a statue. That is why there is a lot more misunderstanding between the public and the musician than between the public and the sculptor.

Yet, despite all, or even in spite of it, the man of genius will have his day. The criticism, obstacles, and injustices that cause the weak man to falter, since he looks to the light of public favor to mark his path, only serve to strengthen the strong. He has his inner light to guide him, and the voice of posterity that speaks softly in his ear.[4] . . .

Genoa and Florence [Part II, Florence]

[December 1838]

It is only a step from Genoa to Florence—Florence, the center of the Italian spirit. You hardly arrive on the Arno's beautiful banks and take your first steps, when the first person you meet—before the porter who carries your trunk, or the valet of the hotel where you are staying, or the friend who is coming to meet you, or even the creditor who is watching for your return—is the young flower girl—the flower seller with her pretty bodice, with her large, finely woven hat flapping in the breeze, with her brisk step and winning words. She carries a wicker basket in which the season's freshest flowers are arranged with the art of a mosaicist, and she offers them to you with a supple gesture, a smile that reveals two rows of pearly white teeth, and a curtsey that is both dignified and awkward. Then, when you open your purse and are about to ask the price of the lovely variegated camelia you are dumbfoundedly holding in your hand, the pretty Florentine has disappeared. But do not dismay, she has not fled forever. You will see her again the following day, every day and at all hours, her and her companions, sisters in dress, behavior, and speech. If you are taking a car-

---

4. On 22 January 1839 Berlioz wrote to Liszt: "Dear friend, I am hurrying to write you to thank you most especially for the article you mentioned. It appeared in the *Gazette musicale* two days after a [fourth] performance of my opera, and I swear to you that it touched me more than I can say" (Berlioz, *Correspondance*, 2: no. 622). The opera, however, was soon dropped from the Paris repertory and languished until Liszt produced the revised versions of the work in March and November 1852 at Weimar.

riage ride with a lady, they, as if divining your secret wish, will deluge you with a scented shower of rosebuds, jonquils, and tuberoses—all the flowers in Florence! It is truly delightful, truly enchanting!

For anyone whose imagination is as nonchalant and as easily seduced as mine, the initial impression Florence makes is so charming and friendly that one is immediately predisposed to enjoy the city, to love it, and to search eagerly through its history and the works of its poets for a thousand additional reasons to love it all the more. But once anyone has started along that path there is no stopping. To know the history of only one of those ancient palaces, whose dark flanks have given birth to so many civil wars, it is necessary to learn the history of the entire city. To understand all the interesting things about only one of its churches, it is necessary to return to the beginnings of art and then follow it through all its later stages of development. The history of Florence is the history of Italy, and the history of Italy is the history of modern civilization.

Yet, forgive me today if I put aside Cimabue, Brunelleschi, Massaccio, Michelangelo, and many other departed artists so that I can tell you about a man who is still alive, one who will certainly not dishonor his renowned predecessors and whose name will resound one day (and may that day be as far off as possible) in the echoing vaults of Santa Croce.* This time I want to tell you about a living artist, the sculptor Bartolini.[1]

I came into contact with Bartolini quite unexpectedly. I had been living in Florence for two months, and let me confess to my shame that I had nearly had my fill of masterpieces by then. I was beginning to think that the Medici *Venus* lacked grace and the *Madonna of the Goldfinch* was a little insipid. I was infinitely grateful to Massaccio for having painted only two frescoes, and I began to pass the *Loggia dei Lanzi* without slowing my pace, something I would never have done in the arcades of the Rue de Rivoli. Enthusiasm is a violent state of the soul; it is agitating and exhausting, and eventually it demands a complete rest, a kind of numbing of the poetic faculty that very few people would dare to acknowledge, although everyone has felt the need for it. I was, therefore, in that shameful state of mind when you won't take a single step to see the most sublime works of God and Man, feeling that you are incapable of appreciating them properly, when a friend arrived one morning and invited me to visit Bartolini's studio with

---

*Santa Croce is, as you know, the Pantheon of Florence. The tombs of Dante [sic], Galileo, and Michelangelo are there.

1. Lorenzo Bartolini (1777–1850), born in Tuscany and trained in Paris.

him. I refused, but he insisted: "You can't possibly leave Florence without seeing the works of the famous sculptor. Besides, he is something of a character and will amuse you. He is strange, cantankerous, and moody. He lives in horror that people will disturb his work, and he sometimes receives his visitors in a very odd way."

"Many thanks!" I said. "You think you can arouse my interest by telling me that I am going to meet some ill-mannered eccentric! And what is more, you know very well that I do not understand anything about sculpture. Even if it were Phidias himself, I would not take the trouble right now to go and see him."

"But," replied my friend, a little annoyed at my lack of interest in his suggestion, "I didn't say that Bartolini was ill-mannered. Come and look at his statues, if only because of what people might think if you didn't. Besides, we will be going with the Duchess of———, who has an appointment with him, and we are sure to be welcome."

"Very well," I said, not wanting to offend him further. Then, too, with grandes dames and pretty women[2] there is never a risk of being unwelcome.

A quarter of an hour later we were at Bartolini's quarters. We were kept waiting for a long time in a very large, cold studio, where five or six apprentices were pointing and scabbling blocks of marble and raising a terrible cloud of dust. The duchess's velvet gown was covered with it in no time. She had had herself announced, but no one appeared. Our situation was beginning to get embarrassing, when a young man with dark eyes and a gentle, shy manner came to us and told us in broken phrases that "the master is extremely sorry . . . he infinitely regrets . . . it is impossible for him. . . ." He was, in short, telling us the most impolite thing possible in the most polite way possible; that is, that Bartolini did not have the slightest interest in seeing us. The duchess, already pale from the cold, turned livid with anger. My friend was mortified. As for myself, I was beginning to form a rather good opinion of an artist who cared so little about maintaining his clientele, and it was with a smile that I followed the dark-eyed young man when he offered to show us the master's work in detail. We went to another room. The duchess and my friend were too incensed to look at anything. I, on the other hand, felt a great curiosity rising within me. The first thing to stimulate it was the beautiful group *Charity*, the original of which is in the Pitti Palace. I was entranced. A standing woman of noble bearing nurses an infant. There is serenity in

2. The gender slips at this point, indicating that the friend in question was probably Marie d'Agoult, who was quite taken with Bartolini's work.

her brow, tenderness in her look. The draperies that veil but do not conceal her limbs are chaste and of classic purity. I had never seen anything truer to nature or more realistic than the infant cradled in her arms. I took care not to communicate my admiration to my highborn companion, who persisted in her foul humor in the presence of *The Nymph of the Arno* [*La Arnina*], *The Nymph of the Scorpion,* the group *Misericordia,* and *The Grape Crusher* [*Il Bacchino*]; but I did interest her in glancing over the collection of contemporary busts, which we were given to understand was unlike anything in the world. Bartolini, as even his critics readily admit, is a master at reproducing nature and working in marble. For more than thirty years he has continued to sculpt, in addition to his larger works, a great number of busts, which, independent of their artistic merit, have the virtue of faithfully repro-ducing the features of interesting and famous people: Lord Byron, Madame de Staël, Countess Guiccioli, Cherubini, Rossini, Prince Met-ternich, Count Orlov, Casimir Delavigne, Ingres, Countess Aurore de Démidoff, and many other celebrities have posed for Bartolini. . . . We were perusing this group of renowned heads one by one when, to our great astonishment, the sculptor appeared at the door of the studio. His appearance and outfit were very "artistic," as they say today. He was wearing a fine white woolen smock, longer in front than in the back, which had been scorched in two or three places, and a velvet skullcap, which he seemed to doff more often than he actually did, covered his head with its fringe of fine, silky white hair. Bartolini is of medium stature and already somewhat stout in his middle age. His face is full, his complexion fair, his lips thin and caustic, and his blue eyes flash at times with an indescribable expression, both vexed and com-manding.

Tipping his velvet cap as I have just described and without offer-ing a single word of apology to Madame de————, who was now wearing her duchess smile as she approached him, he brusquely ad-dressed my friend: "You have seen my colossal statue of Napoleon? That is the only work that I am sorry to see still here in my studio. . . . It belongs on Saint Helena. My God! If it were placed on top of one of the cliffs along the coast, it would create a marvelous effect. . . . When the sunlight strikes that polished marble, it will be visible for fifty leagues at sea. . . ."[3] Thereupon the sculptor nodded his head and retired to his private workroom without further ceremony, leaving us dumbfounded. . . .

3. Standing 18 feet high, Bartolini's statue portrays the emperor as a toga-clad, chisel-featured Olympian.

"Now that is what I call an impolite man," cried the duchess. "Apparently his mother neglected to teach him his manners. The only thing that will get him," she added in an irritated tone, "is that I will now have someone else do the bust that I was about to commission from him for 300 louis d'or."

"I am afraid, considering what we have just seen, that Madame will find it difficult, even in Italy, to replace Bartolini. . . ."

"Good Lord, sir!" she cried. "So there is only one Bartolini in the world! Marchesi, Finelli, and Pampaloni are just as good, and you won't deny that Thorwaldsen is far better. . . ."

"That is not what artists think," I replied.

"Artists! Artists! It's common knowledge that there are no worse judges of works of art! Besides, even if someone sculpted a statue for me that had ears under the mouth and eyes on its back, I would rather have it that way than have anything to do with such a boor."

There being nothing further to say, I remained silent.

Two days later I gave a concert,[4] and I sent Bartolini a ticket. I did not know if he liked music, but on the off-chance he did, I was glad to make the polite gesture. I did not see him in the hall during the concert, and so I was more than a little surprised to see him hurrying towards me as I was leaving the stage. He extended his hand and said: "How much longer, sir, will you be staying in Florence?"

"Two weeks at most," I replied.

"That will be enough," he said. "Tell me, would you consider it a bore if I did a bust of you?" Dumbstruck by that brusque, terse approach, I managed to stammer a few words of thanks.

"It's set, then," he continued. "If you could give me a dozen sittings, we can begin tomorrow. There is something about your head . . . something that interests me . . . I will do my best not to make a mess of it."

The following day, as you might imagine, I arrived promptly at the agreed time, curious to take a closer look at a man whose unusual behavior was the equal of his prodigious talent. This time he welcomed me most charmingly and we chatted away, since he works with wonderful ease and never has his models "pose" for him. He must have taken his inspiration from some bump or other that he discovered on my forehead or whatever sympathetic feeling he developed for the

---

4. Most likely on 16 December 1838 at the Teatro Cocomero. Liszt played his Fantasy on "Frequenti palpiti," improvised on a theme from *La Sonnambula*, and was then joined by five colleagues for the twelve-hand, three-piano transcription of the Overture to *The Magic Flute*.

angle of my jaw. In no time at all we were talking quite freely. He told me the story of his life, and I came to know one of the greatest and most beautiful artistic natures that ever I was privileged to meet and admire.[5]

The *Saint Cecilia* of Raphael
To Joseph d'Ortigue[1]

[December 1838–early 1839][2]

As soon as I arrived in Bologna, I sped off to the museum. I hurried right through three galleries filled with the paintings of Guido Reni, Guercino, Carracci, Domenichino, etc., as I was very anxious to see the *Saint Cecilia*. It would be difficult, even impossible, for me to make you understand everything I felt when I suddenly found myself in the presence of that magnificent canvas where Raphael's genius appears to

5. Liszt's bust was finished early in 1839, and although there was some talk of exhibiting it in that year's Paris *Salon*, it apparently languished in Bartolini's studio until Liszt eventually wrote to the sculptor, asking him to send it to Paris for the *Salon* of 1846. At that time Liszt also ordered a bronze cast of it, which was to be sent to him in Vienna (Mario Tinti, *Lorenzo Bartolini* 2:68). Bartolini also sculpted a bust of Marie d'Agoult, completing it in the autumn of 1839.

1. *Gazette musicale*, 14 April 1839, pp. 115—17. Joseph-Louis d'Ortigue (1802–1866), a musical journalist and scholar who is remembered mostly for his studies of opera and Gregorian chant. A friend, he was also the author of Liszt's first published biography, which appeared in the *Gazette musicale*, 14 June 1835. Writing to him sometime in the late summer of 1839, Liszt remarked: "I am very glad that my Saint Cecilia did not displease you. I could not have addressed that letter to anyone but you. It was written under the inspiration of your compelling ideas" (Constantin Photiadès, "En Avignon, avec Liszt et Berlioz," p. 27).

2. It is difficult to ascertain when Liszt first saw the painting or conceived this article. He passed through Bologna on his way to Florence in October 1838 and may have been inspired by the *Saint Cecilia* at that time. On the other hand, it is more likely that his return there in December gave him a better opportunity to study the painting. His letters to Marie do not mention this, but one to Pierre Erard implies as much: "Since you last received news from me I have spent eight days in Bologna and three months in Florence. I will not tell you about the *Saint Cecilia*, the Medici *Venus*, or the *Fates* of Michelangelo. Not that I have not studied and admired these masterpieces as best I could, but that it would require of me, and you too, far more leisure time than we have at the moment. We shall save this for our future dinners" (1 February 1839, in Pincherle, *Musiciens*, p. 96). This implication, coupled with the fact that the article was not published until April, strongly suggests that Liszt conceived and produced it in December 1838 and early 1839.

us in all its splendor.[3] I knew the masterworks of the Venetian school. I had recently seen the Van Dykes in Genoa, the Correggios in Parma, and in Milan the *Madonna of the Veil,* one of Raphael's most sublime creations. But much as I admired the boldness, brilliance, truth, and polish of these paintings, I never felt that I had penetrated the intimate meaning of any of them. I was always an onlooker. Not one of these lovely works seized me, if I may put it that way, with the force that the *Saint Cecilia* did. I do not know by what secret magic that painting made an immediate and twofold impression on my soul: first, as a ravishing portrayal of the most noble and ideal qualities of the human form, a marvel of grace, purity, and harmony; and at the same instant and with no strain of the imagination, I also saw it as an admirable and perfect symbol of the art to which we have dedicated our lives. The poetry and philosophy of the canvas were actually so visible to me that its abstract sense of line and its IDEAL beauty gripped me as forcefully as did its beauty as a painting.

Raphael has chosen to depict the moment when Saint Cecilia is preparing to sing a hymn to the Omnipotent God. As she is about to rejoice in the glory of the Most High, the Comfort of the Just, the Hope of Sinners, her soul trembles with that same mysterious trembling that seized David when he played on his blessed harp. All at once her eyes are flooded with light, her ears filled with harmony. The clouds part and choirs of angels appear, their eternal *hosanna* resounding through the firmament as the virgin's gaze rises toward heaven. Her posture conveys ecstasy, her arms fall loosely at her sides as if they were about to drop the instrument on which she performs her holy canticles. One senses that her soul is no longer on earth, that her beautiful body is about to be transfigured. . . .

Tell me, my friend, wouldn't you have seen in that noble figure, as I did, a symbol of music at the height of its power? Of art in its most spiritual and holy form? Isn't that virgin, ecstatically transported above reality, like the inspiration that sometimes fills an artist's heart— pure, true, full of insight, and unalloyed with mundane matters? Those eyes fixed on the vision, the unutterable rapture that floods her fea-

---

3. Marie d'Agoult, who had passed through Bologna a short time before Liszt in October, saw the painting in a rather different light: "Nice day. Arrival in Bologna. First impression, disappointment. Town badly built, poorly paved, ugly arcades, very choice art gallery. *Saint Cecilia* less admirable than I had expected. I am beginning to think that Raphael's reputation is somewhat overrated. There are many pictures by Titian, Correggio, Veronese, and Leonardo that I find more appealing" (d'Agoult, *Mémoires,* p. 158).

tures, those languid arms bending beneath the weight of a mystically blessed state—isn't this the very expression of human powerlessness in wrestling with the desire for and the perception of the divine? Isn't it the most poetic idealization of the discouragement that seizes the poet during his participation in the abundance and plenitude of divine mysteries, when he knows full well that he will not be able to give other men an account of the celestial banquet to which he had been invited?

To the right of Saint Cecilia, facing her with an expression of chaste tenderness, Raphael has placed the figure of Saint John—Saint John, "the disciple whom Jesus loved," the one to whom He entrusted His mother when dying, the one who by placing his head on the Master's breast learned the secrets of boundless charity and of a love that will endure "until the end of time," as the Scriptures say. Saint John is the perfect symbol of human affection purified and sanctified by religion, by Christian sentiment—tender and profound, yet strengthened by the salutary lessons of sorrow.

On the other side of Saint Cecilia, also there to hear the holy canticles, is Mary Magdalene in all the glitter of her worldly attire. There is something haughty and profane about her bearing, and her whole figure has a voluptuousness that smacks more of Greece than Judea, more of paganism than Christianity. The Magdalene also represents love, but a love born of the senses and attracted by visible beauty. She is, therefore, farther from Saint Cecilia than Saint John, as if the painter had wanted to make it clear that she does not share as fully as he does in the divine essence of music, and that her ear is captivated by the sensual appeal of sound instead of her heart being stirred by supernatural emotions.

Saint Paul stands in the foreground in a state of profound meditation, his head leaning on his left hand. His right hand rests on a sword, the symbol of those militant and compelling words with which he dispelled people's ignorance and conquered souls for the unknown God. Saint Paul was the first of the apostles to use eloquence and philosophy to establish the religion and propagate the faith. It was he who first brought reasoning and dogma to a belief where only feelings had previously existed. For him, music is still a form of eloquence. He sees it as a means of teaching by intuition, a veiled but no less powerful form of preaching that attracts hearts, opening them to the truth. Consequently, the expression on his face is one of deep thought rather than rapture. One sees that he is trying to fathom the mystery of a language that is new to him, that he is trying to understand the effects of this "word," and that he envies the young virgin because she did not have to labor or suffer persecution and captivity, as did he, in order to acquire the gift of persuasion and the power to move hearts.

Behind Saint Cecilia, Saint Augustine seems to be listening with more reserve. His face is serious and grieved. One sees in him a man who has erred for a long time, who has transgressed a great deal, and who is suspicious of even the most saintly emotions. Having waged a constant war against his senses, he is still fearful of the fleshly snares hidden in the appearance of a celestial vision. As one who found the truth only after he had exhausted himself on the paths of doubt, as one who had been seduced and transported far from God's way by the lure of paganism, he is asking himself if there might not be some secret poison in this sublime music and whether these harmonies that seem to descend from heaven are not actually deceptive voices—a contrivance of the devil, whose power he knows only too well.

Thus it was that the four persons grouped with inimitable simplicity around Saint Cecilia struck me as the supreme prototypes of our art; they epitomize the essential elements of music and the different effects it has on the heart of man.

At Saint Cecilia's feet, the painter has placed the instruments of her torture. Isn't this to remind us that genius and dedication—that genius of the heart—always entail some form of visible or hidden martyrdom? And that suffering and atonement have throughout history always either preceded or followed one's initiation into divine mysteries?[4]

But, you may well ask, do you really believe that Raphael actually intended to do all that you claim he did? Did he really mean to symbolize music, or was he merely conforming to the custom of his day by following instructions he had received? In his time the communities and individuals who commissioned an artist's work were usually motivated more by a sense of piety than by the love of art. When they engaged a Perugino or a Raphael to paint a picture they were less concerned about owning a masterpiece than with gratifying their own particular devotion, and as a result they specified even the smallest details of the work. Typically, it had to be a Madonna or a patron saint surrounded by other saints and martyrs for whom the Maecenas had been named. In this way he hoped to do earthly honor to his heavenly protectors so they would be predisposed to intercede for him when death summoned him before the tribunal of the Supreme Judge. This

---

4. However laudable the point Liszt wishes to make, the instruments grouped about the saint's feet are in fact musical instruments.

is what explains the illogical relationships and anachronisms found in most of the paintings of the period.

Yet it is really not important to know if Raphael had found a deep meaning in his subject, or whether he was as great a poet and philosopher as he was a painter. He created a marvelous painting of irreproachable composition and color. What more can we ask of him? His painting, like all works of genius, stirs the mind and excites the imagination of all those who ponder it. Each of us sees it in his own way and, depending upon his own makeup, discovers a novel form of beauty there, something new to admire and praise. And that is precisely what makes genius immortal, what makes it eternally young, fertile, and stirring.

I, for one, saw *Saint Cecilia* as a symbol, and that symbol is very real to me. If this is an error, it is in any case a pardonable one for a musician to make, and I would love to believe that you share it with me.

Adieu, my friend. Love me and pray to Raphael's Saint Cecilia for me.

9

FROM FLORENCE TO ROME

By the time Liszt and Marie d'Agoult left Florence at the beginning of 1839, it had already been decided that he would begin his tours when the concert season opened that fall and that they would separate at that time. This, therefore, was to be the last spring and summer they would spend together in Italy.

CHRONICLE

16 January 1839. Blandine, now three years old, is delivered to her parents in Florence, and the little family group soon leaves for Rome, traveling via Pisa and Siena.

ca. 5 February. Arrival in Rome. They rent a furnished apartment on the via della Purificazione.

The following essay is, as its title indicates, basically a correspondent's report of musical life as Liszt found it south of the Alps. It adopts a more temperate tone than the one Liszt, no doubt chastened by his experience with the Milanese, had taken in the earlier articles.

(To the Editor of the *Gazette Musicale* [Maurice Schlesinger])
Musical Conditions in Italy[1]

[Florence–Rome, early 1839][2]

You have asked me to send you a precise account, a detailed review, of all the interesting musical events in Italy. I am, you say, in a better

---

1. *Revue musicale*, 28 March 1839, pp. 101–5. For a time in 1839 the *Revue et Gazette musicale* was published as a semi-weekly: the *Gazette* on Sunday, the *Revue* on Thursday, each separately paginated.

2. Ramann, in *Gesammelte Schriften* 2:229, dates this Letter "Florence, Novem-

position than anyone to keep you up-to-date on the news pertaining to our art. As I have been treading this classic soil and living in this land of music, as they call it, for over a year now, I must surely have faithfully attended all the theaters, heard all the new operas, gone to all the concerts, come to know all the musicians, and kept an eye out for all the important publications. . . . That is true and could not be truer. But the result of it all is exactly the opposite of what you would think; that is to say, I have nothing, or virtually nothing, to tell you.

From what I can see, my dear Schlesinger, you, in common with many other people, are harboring a strange misconception. You think that Italy is still the center of today's musical world, that a lot of activity takes place here, and that art in the land of Rossini and Paganini, those two supreme personifications of composition and performance, has a powerful driving force behind it. Disabuse yourself of this notion. There is, to be sure, a great deal of musical activity in Italy; but that activity is only concerned with operatic music, for one thing, and for another I would surely say that the activity at this time is merely sterile agitation, a static movement that one perhaps would have every reason to consider regressive.

As I have already had occasion to observe when writing you from Milan, there can be no question whatsoever of instrumental music when talking about music in Italy. That is not to say that there is not a number of remarkable instrumentalists here. But these isolated artists cannot, for all the pleasure the public takes in hearing them, contribute very much to progress. In music, as in everything else, associating with others is the only principle that produces great results. It is only "there, where several are gathered together," that the spirit manifests itself. One person is not really effective unless he can gather other individuals around him and communicate his feelings and thoughts to them. Alone, he will astonish and charm, but the effect he produces will be transitory. If others do not join and work with him, the wind will disperse the seeds he has sown, and he will exert no lasting influence. Further—and this is absolutely true—there is not a single group of artists in any of the Italian cities I have visited who has either the requisite ability or desire to perform the symphonic works of the masters. Quartet music is totally neglected; and except for the opera overtures that one hears in the theaters, where they are performed without style, precision, or ensemble, and are in any case nearly drowned out by the

---

ber 1838," but internal evidence (see notes 17 and 21 below) indicates that it was not written, or at least not finished, until the early part of 1839 when Liszt was in Rome.

noise of conversation, it is virtually impossible to hear even the most trifling piece of orchestral music.*

As to instrumental music, then, there is nothing—absolutely nothing. Whether this is the result of an inherent antipathy in the national character toward this species of music, whether it should be attributed to the absence of artists who have sufficient determination, authority, and perseverance to elevate public taste little by little and direct it towards serious matters, or whatever the cause might be, the fact remains that the result is deplorable. Consequently, any such paragraph in my weekly article must necessarily always be left blank.

Let us turn to the theaters.

Italy, as you know, has three principal opera houses: La Scala in Milan, La Fenice in Venice, and the San Carlo in Naples. The San Carlo, which I have not yet attended, resounds with Nourrit's growing success, and I have nothing to add to that. I would, however, like to tell you a little anecdote, as it will give you some idea of our tenor's exquisite tact and the opinion the Italians have of their own musical supremacy. Since many people had expressed their admiration of Nourrit and stated that they were glad he was to appear on the Italian stage, he told them, no doubt with a wry smile, that he was all confused by a welcome that so exceeded his talent and that he had come to Italy "to learn how to sing." This charming exaggeration, this amiable pleasantry was taken seriously by the dilettants. They interpreted it literally, and on many an occasion since I have heard it said that Nourrit settled in Naples "to study singing." What saintly simplicity!**

In a letter that I sent you from Venice,[3] I told you in detail about La Fenice—that remarkable hall, so harmonious in its proportions, and decorated with such taste and elegance—and about the elite opera troupe that was delighting the Venetians at the time. I attended the early performances of Mercadante's new opera *Le due illustri rivali*.[4] It is a skillful, conscientious score; a number of its ensembles are truly remarkable, and as a result it enjoyed complete success. There is no

---

*In Italian the same word is used to designate an overture and a symphony (*sinfonia*). The true meaning of the word "symphony" is generally unknown.

**It is worth noting that the most popular theatrical artists here at present are foreigners: Mademoiselle Ungher is German, Madame Schoberlechner is Russian, Madame García and Nourrit are Parisian. Mesdames Spech, Schütz, Méric-Lalande, Dérancourt, Olivier, Pixis, Castellan, Miss Kemble, and Henequin (actually Inchindi) also do not bear Ausonian names.

3. *L'Artiste* had not yet published that Letter.

4. (The Two Illustrious Rivals.) Its first performance was at La Fenice, 10 March 1838.

question that Mercadante's most recent works are the best conceived and composed of any operas in the current repertory.

Unhappily, once the season at La Fenice ended I again found myself in a total musical wasteland, and since I, like Brid'oison,[5] realized that I did not know what else to tell you, I hit upon the idea of lengthening my letter by including some words about painting. I ventured to mention Titian and Veronese, and if I am not mistaken, I allowed myself to give you some of my personal impressions of the lagoons, the Moorish palaces, etc. But you then accused me of becoming "too literary" (which, upon my honor, is the last reproach that I think I should ever deserve!). You claimed that your subscribers could and should not hear about anything but a diminished seventh chord or an F double-sharp. You shamefully rejected my poetic hen scratches, you scuttled my gondola in the moonlight, and you irritatedly asked me what Giambellino, Donatello, and Sansovino had to do with the editor of the *Gazette musicale*. It is not my fault, therefore, that your readers do not know what is currently taking place at La Fenice.

As to La Scala, allow me to remind you that I have already written to you about it in the most detailed fashion. You also know, to some extent at least, about the churlish interpretations that were put on my observations and all the unpleasantness the letter caused me. The incident gave me another chance to think about criticism in general and music criticism in particular. My thoughts, supported by many personal experiences and a host of well-known facts, went round and round in the same circle and always led me back to the same conclusion, one that I was, however, loath to reach: namely, that the critic's task—which I consider useful, laborious, difficult, and consequently worthy of respect so long as it is done in a sincere, fair, knowledgeable, and proper manner—is either a demeaning career because of the way it is carried out or an act of heroic devotion because of the persecution it entails for anyone who wishes to be conscientious and impartial. As for myself, I have never worried about it as a career, since I have, thank God, something else to do; as for being heroic, I am beginning to tire of it and, strictly between us, would much prefer to reserve that attribute for other matters.

When a critic is not an artist, when he does not practice the things he claims to be informed about, people accordingly—and apparently with great justification—reject his authority. They deny his

---

5. Brid'oison is a self-aggrandizing, ignorant magistrate in Beaumarchais's *Le Mariage de Figaro*. In Da Ponte's libretto for Mozart's opera, he appears very briefly as "Don Curzio."

ability to appreciate and evaluate results since he is unfamiliar with the procedures involved in obtaining them, and if his words are harsh they only laugh at what they regard as his impotent rage. The artists resent him, and no matter what approach he takes, he incurs not only the hatred but the scorn of all those upon whom he does not lavish the most exaggerated praise. As for the artist-critic, his situation is ten times worse. If, in good conscience, he allows himself to criticize the things that seem flawed in the works of great composers, his presumption is intolerable. If he attacks his equals and contemporaries, he is consumed with envy. Those whom he knows personally accuse him of ingratitude, while those whom he has never met ask themselves what they have ever done to him to deserve such treatment. Thus, although he only meant to raise a question of art, he finds that he has raised a hundred questions of personality and made as many enemies as these people have spouses, brothers, cousins, patrons, and sometimes even countrymen!

In summary, then, that eternal dilemma: either *criticism* is powerless or else it is given in bad faith; or, to put this another way, either the *critic* is unintelligent, insolent, and absurd, or else he is envious, prejudiced, and full of rancor and annoyance, etc. Hence, let me ask you: if one is faced with these alternatives, isn't it more prudent and profitable to remain silent?

All I have just said is especially applicable to Italy, where high-minded criticism and serious artistic analysis are totally beyond the usual workings of the press. Composers and performers have their friends and enemies, their promoters and detractors among the journalists. The former take every occasion to praise them to the skies, while the latter insult them grossly. Praise, however, predominates by far, and it must be absolute and unrestricted: "Madame——is marvelous, divine; she created a *sensation;* Maestro——is an incomparable genius" are the typical formulas critics employ. The essential principles of beauty and truth are never mentioned or discussed. Criticism caresses the artists' vanity instead of stimulating their self-esteem. It follows the current fashion instead of illuminating good taste, and it habitually plays the role of a *cicerone* who pompously gushes with admiration over everything he shows you.

In addition to the three big opera houses mentioned, there is not an Italian town—no matter how small the black dot representing it on a map may be—that does not also possess a theater, which is almost always spacious, architecturally well designed, and quite comfortable. Each of these theaters takes on special importance at specific seasons of the year and becomes a first-class theater. In Bergamo, Brescia, Senigallia, Piacenza, Livorno, Lucca, etc., when the fairs are held or the ruling prince is in residence, the best performers are hired and paid the same fees that they receive in the biggest cities. It is then, and for a very brief time, that each town which was empty and silent becomes animated, high-spirited, and alive. People who live isolated lives during the rest of the year, without entertainment and almost without any interests, suddenly find themselves assembled in the same hall every night, taking excited sides for or against the same performers and works, comparing and sharing their feelings, their reactions. The incredibly low price of the tickets makes the pleasure of going to the theater accessible to everyone. This is something that is almost unknown in other countries: a center of entertainment that brings all classes of society together; a communal hall where there is life, passion, and enthusiasm; a civilizing force which, like an ever-flowing spring, is constantly spreading through every branch of society.

What a pity that this custom, so beneficial to the cultivation of art, results in nothing today but a host of ephemeral productions and the fleeting emergence of some names and works that are destined to return almost immediately to the oblivion whence they came! The public, lacking any comparison, accepts these things, listens to them out of habit, and then praises them out of patriotism, since national pride is a highly sensitive issue in Italy and is beginning to take hold in those areas where it absolutely would not seem at first sight to apply.

The operas that comprise most of the current repertory making the rounds of the various theaters are *Marin Faliero, Lucrezia Borgia, Parisina, L'Elisir d'amore,* and, above all, *Lucia di Lammermoor.*[6] As they have all been presented in Paris, there is no reason to analyze them here for you. Besides, the manner in which they were conceived would make such a task unappealing and difficult for me. Occasionally the faint breath of Rossini can still be heard giving some semblance of life to these soulless bodies. Their pleasant melodies—which fill the air in Italy just as we say that cleverness fills the streets in Paris—are placed here and there in the action and caress the ear agreeably. But anyone looking to these operas for ideas, inventiveness, proper recitative, dramatic expression—in a word, for art, in the serious and universal meaning of the term—would, I think, be wasting his time and effort.

Understandably, the study of these compositions hardly ever produces first-rate actors and singers. Beautiful voices are relatively common in Italy compared to other countries. People are born in this privileged land with a natural aptitude for the arts. They have the fiery

6. All operas by Donizetti.

look, the lively gesture, and the enthusiastic nature that make an artist. Yet the number of distinguished singers, male and female, is very small. The carelessness of the composers inspires carelessness in their interpreters. Roles that have not been thought out seriously by the former are surely not studied seriously by the latter. Everyone here has adopted a standard procedure, a conventional manner for rendering all feelings and situations. The public, which is quite familiar with the stereotypes, has also developed the habit of invariably applauding the effects. Typically, they are: violent and sudden contrasts of *pianissimo* and *fortissimo,* whether motivated or not; quasi-convulsive accents in the singing; and terrible cries at the end of a piece when the character's situation has become pathetic and the action turns to combat, vengeance, or despair. The Grand Cry is indispensable to anyone who aspires to become a *cantante di cartello.*[7] An actress would not know how to fall to the floor or into an armchair without her Grand Cry. The Grand Cry is a useful replacement for the chromatic scale, the leap of a tenth, and the improvised cadenza, all of which have been declared overly fussy and in poor taste today. Scales, difficulties, and bravura are no longer in fashion. Many people credit Bellini's music with bringing about the change, taking it to be progress, a welcome revolution in the arts. I must confess that it is difficult for me to share that view. The "progress" from Rossini to Donizetti has not been clearly demonstrated to me; and as for the revolution that substituted mawkish sentimentality for agility and cheap effects for lavish profusion, I doubt that it will ever be very gratifying—except, of course, to those lazy Ladies and Gentlemen, the singers.

Among the women who play starring roles in Italian opera houses there is one who stands apart, and nothing I have just said applies in any way to her. Mademoiselle Ungher,[8] endowed with profound feeling, remarkable intelligence, and such boundless if not actually excessive energy, has after ten years of serious continuous study developed the finest dramatic talent to appear on the stage since Mesdames Pasta and Malibran. Always sincere, noble, and moving, she penetrates to the heart of her role, and by breaking through, if I may put it that way, those icy barriers that the platitudes of an inane libretto and insipid score can raise between her and the audience, she becomes sublime where one would have thought it impossible to be anything

---

7. A singer (*cantante*) whose name is prominently featured on the opera poster (*cartello*): a star.

8. See "Venice," chap. 7. As Liszt evidently had some doubts about that article being published, he repeated his views here. He does the same for Moriani below.

more than pleasing. She can create the liveliest feelings at those times when anyone else would barely conceal the disparity between the words and the music. It is both curious and sad to see this fine genius of a woman held captive by the mediocrity of her assignments. I often think of her as a bold swimmer floundering miserably in a shallow little stream of water. At times she also reminds me of the great Mozart forced to play the piano with his hands covered by a handkerchief in order to amuse the ladies of the court, or, even better, the young Michelangelo hired by the magnificent Cosimo de'Medici to sculpt a snowman in his garden. Mademoiselle Ungher's voice is extensive in range, true to pitch, and flexible. A consummate musician, she is quite prepared to undertake any role. The comic repertory is as familiar to her as the tragic, and the breadth of her talent is as exceptional as its profundity.

Mademoiselle Garcia,[9] a far more recent arrival on the dramatic scene than Mademoiselle Ungher, is still at that happy point in her career where an artist can appeal to future criticism. Young enough so that her remarkably pure, full-bodied, and fresh voice has nothing to fear from age for a good long time to come, she can only profit from more experience. A little carelessness mixed with some hesitancy in her acting, some unevenness in her usually charming voice, and even some poor choices of costume (a matter to which the Italian public pays little attention) will doubtless disappear when she appears before the Parisian public, that most demanding audience of all in matters of taste. And it is to them that she will turn next for guidance, encouragement, and reward. The name she bears augurs brightly for her future.

Having decided not to give you any reports based purely on hearsay, I will merely remind you of Mesdames Boccabadati, Giuditta Grisi, and Schütz.[10]

9. Pauline Viardot-Garcia (1821–1910), Maria Malibran's younger sister, a mezzo-soprano. Liszt's notice is really a friendly puff for his then seventeen-year-old former pupil. (She was an excellent pianist and could easily have made a career of the instrument had not the Garcia family tradition dictated that she go on the opera stage.) She was not appearing regularly in Italy, but she and her mother, Joaquina Garcia, were traveling through it on their way back to Paris in the autumn of 1838 when they happened to meet Liszt by chance in Padua. Pauline's formal operatic debut was as Desdemona in Rossini's *Otello* at Her Majesty's Theatre in London on 9 May 1839. Years later, in 1859, Liszt devoted an essay to her wide-ranging, extraordinary talents. (Liszt, *Ges. Schriften*, 3:121–35.)

10. Soprano Luigia Boccabadati (1800–1850); mezzo-soprano Giuditta Grisi (1805–1840), elder sister of the famous Giulia; soprano Amalia Schütz-Oldosi.

I have already given you my opinion of Madame Schober-lechner.[11] Her recent marital devotion deserves all manner of praise: with a prolonged swoon, she brought the unyielding audience back to a more compassionate point of view and thus saved her husband from the horrors of the unmitigated *fiasco* that was threatening him, the composer of *Maria Tudor*.

The tenor who is all the rage at the moment is Moriani.[12] He is quite young. If he consented to work hard, he would after only three more years on the stage unquestionably join the ranks of the great singers. But that is precisely what he has not done, does not do, and will, I fear, never do. His fine voice, absolutely the most beautiful that I have ever heard, is enough to insure his success. Many a time I have seen him on stage with Mademoiselle Ungher, looking as if he did not grasp the pathos of the scene or the great actress's skillful declamation. After listening to her, a smile befitting a refined young tenor on his lips, he approached the footlights when his turn came and sang his part of the duet, whatever the dramatic situation, with the same melancholy tenderness, the same lack of dramatic intensity, and, it must be admitted, in so heavenly a manner that he roused the public to passionate applause. He probably then asked himself what was the purpose of all those terrible, lacerating vocal inflections, those stifled notes, and that declamation modulated according to the meaning of the words and the feelings they expressed. Moriani sings easily and effortlessly, he charms and captivates all those who hear him. What more can he want?

Another tenor, Salvi,[13] whom I heard in Genoa and who is now in Naples, possesses an equally remarkable voice. His singing is moving, his voice production big and pure, and his delivery and gestures have a faultless ease and nobility about them.

Add to these names those of Coselli (primo basso), an intelligent and distinguished artist, and Donzelli, who made his debut in Paris,[14] and you will be almost as up to date as I about the *personnel* of the Italian theaters.

A number of the ruling princes in Italy have a decided taste for music. Her Majesty Marie Louise, a very fine pianist herself, welcomes

11. See "La Scala," chap. 6.

12. See "Venice," chap. 7.

13. Lorenzo Salvi (1810–1879), noted for his limpid, mellifluous voice.

14. Domenico Coselli (1801–1855), Italy's leading bass-baritone; Domenico Donzelli (1790–1873), tenor.

artists with the most gracious kindness. The Grand Duke of Lucca maintains a pianist, Doehler,[15] in his household, and His Royal Highness [Leopold II], Grand Duke of Tuscany, arranged for several concerts in the large, well-proportioned rooms of the Pitti Palace when Prince Frederick of Prussia visited Florence. Mademoiselles Ungher and Francilla Pixis and Moriani and Coselli did the honors. It was there that I also had the pleasure of hearing Giorgetti,[16] a fine violinist and distinguished composer. Unfortunately, he has several painful infirmities that prevent him making a European tour, which is so necessary today for a performer's reputation. Since Jules Janin has told you with as much wit as grace about His Highness's generous act, for which I was glad to serve as the reason or the pretext, I shall refrain from repeating it here.[17]

Florence, like Milan, takes justifiable pride in several socially prominent amateurs with quasi-professional skills. As in Milan, a privileged family with an illustrious name includes such an assembly of talent that no other example of it comes to mind. All the Poniatowskis,[18] like all the Belgiojosos, sing and sing well. The similarity of their

15. Theodore Doehler (1814–1856), born in Naples of German parents, pupil of Czerny, and a polished "salon pianist" in the best sense. The Duke of Lucca had virtually adopted Doehler when he was thirteen years old and remained his lifelong patron.

16. Ferdinando Giorgetti (1796–1867).

17. The incident took place at one of the musicales at the Pitti Palace (possibly 11 December). Janin's account appeared in the *Journal des débats*, 14 January 1839, under the heading "Liszt and the Grand Duke of Tuscany." After rhapsodizing about the setting—Raphael's *Leo X* to Liszt's left, Allori's *Judith* to his right, Michelangelo's *Fates* in front of him, Titian and Rubens above his head, etc.—Janin went on to write: "Among the many foreigners who live in Florence as pensioners of the Grand Duke was a Hungarian nobleman, a poor gentlemen with a family to support, but ruined by the wars, and that very morning the Grand Duchess had asked her august husband to increase the Hungarian's pension. When Liszt had finished playing the Grand Duke was standing, leaning on the back of the Grand Duchess's armchair. They looked at one another with the expression of those who are in love and content, and who can convey all their happiness in a single glance. A long silence, and then: 'What is his nationality, and what shall we do for him?' asked the prince of the happy woman who was listening to him. 'My Lord,' replied the Grand Duchess, 'Liszt is a Hungarian.' Leaning toward her, the Grand Duke said even more quietly to his wife, 'Do you know what we must do for Liszt? We must double the Hungarian's pension.' And that is how the Grand Duke and Duchess of Tuscany that day gave the noblest and most touching of rewards to Liszt, the Hungarian." Berlioz in a letter dated 22 January 1839, had alerted Liszt to Janin's article (*Correspondance* 2: no. 622).

18. Among the Poniatowskis, Liszt met young Prince Joseph-Michael (1816–1873), an aspiring and trained tenor. As a kind of professional-amateur in Florence and later in Paris, the prince was a devoted operamane who produced, staged, and performed in operas, including several that he himself had composed.

musical tastes and the happy circumstance of a familial bond that facilitates their studying together allow them to present several remarkably well performed operas each year. Another delightful little opera company, also sponsored by a musical amateur, [Newland] Standish, gives five or six performances during the winter that attract the most elegant Florentine society as well as the many foreigners who for a thousand different reasons are drawn to and detained on the banks of the Arno. A kind of "European" applause thus crowns the efforts of that young and graceful company. Notwithstanding the impropriety of any sort of criticism under such circumstances, I cannot help but regret the fact that a broader and more comprehensive way of thinking does not determine the choice of operas presented at Standish's theater. Last winter, for example, as benefits for the orphanage, they presented *Otello, Barbiere di Siviglia,* and *L'Elisir d'amore.* The first two are masterpieces, and the third is one of Donizetti's best works. But *Otello* and *Barbiere,* given for the past fifteen years with huge success by all the opera companies of Europe, operas that the most eminent artists sing in competition with one another, *Otello* and *Barbiere,* works that children know by heart and that people hum in the streets, no longer need the limited exposure provided by an amateur theater. *L'Elisir d'amore* has also enjoyed a fashionable success and is the order of the day in all the opera houses. Thus it strikes me that one or two more performances of these operas do not produce any substantial benefit for art. Isn't there a nobler aim that might be proposed to these amateurs whose position puts them above financial considerations and public demands, something besides mere entertainment and the legitimate satisfaction of their vanity? That aim would be to introduce the Italians to excellent works which seem fated, because of a deplorable chain of circumstances, to remain unknown to them for a long time to come; to take up the works of Mozart, Weber, and Meyerbeer courageously; to transplant these products of a foreign muse to well-prepared soil; and to make them appreciated and liked by presenting them initially to well-bred society, since they exercise such a great influence in every land, and in this way gradually stimulate the general public's desire to become familiar with these renowned works.

I place less faith than anyone in sudden revolutions or in changes wrought by a magic wand. In the realm of art and intellectual activity, above all, nothing happens by leaps and bounds, and I am not naive enough to think that if Prince Poniatowski or anyone else were to produce an opera by Weber or Mozart in Italy, the taste for genuinely dramatic music would suddenly be reborn as if by magic. On the contrary, I believe that in order to make such an attempt, one would have to be armed with a great deal of determination and to be resigned not only to listen to an infinite number of absurd comments but also to have a miniscule number of supporters for a long time to come. But when one combines an artist's taste and talent with the advantages of an independent social position, there can be no more laudable endeavor than trying to initiate, stimulate, and encourage in every possible way an operatic reform, without which Italy will soon find itself completely outside the progressive movement that is taking place in other countries.

As I am talking to you about reform, I cannot remain silent about the one now being proposed to the Holy See by an artist whose long and brilliant career gives him every right to speak with authority. After an absence of some thirty years, Spontini,[19] seeking some rest and perhaps sensing the need to breathe his native air, has asked his noble patron the King of Prussia for permission to return to Italy. No doubt—and I do not believe I wrong him by making this supposition—he was also secretly drawn here by a desire to settle his debt to his homeland, to pay his tribute to Italy with the product of his labors. No doubt it pleased him to think that his compositions, enthusiastically greeted as they were throughout Europe, would be welcomed on his native soil and lovingly received by his compatriots. But whatever his desires, plans, and illusions might have been in this regard, he can only have abandoned them very quickly. I saw him when he first returned to Italy, and I happened to be with him when he first attended a performance at La Scala. That very night he was able to convince himself that music, as he understood it and wanted it to be, was an unintelligible language this side of the Alps, that the great school of dramatic declamation founded by Gluck and which he helped to perpetuate was unknown to this audience, that the artists' habitual manner of singing made them incapable of performing works composed in this style, and that the public was totally unprepared to appreciate them. Although Spontini never uttered a word to betray his feelings, we might be permitted to suppose that he was painfully saddened by the realization that as an artist he would always be an outsider among his own people, and that the homage his homeland paid him was due solely to his reputation in other countries. No doubt he must have felt

19. Gaspare Spontini (1774–1851), an important but rather contentious composer whose career in Italy, Napoleonic Paris, and Berlin was dogged by controversy, much of it his own making. In addition to a goodly amount of vocal and church music, he wrote about twenty operas, of which *La Vestale* (Paris 1807) is his acknowledged masterpiece. (See also Berlioz's remarks about Spontini, app. C.) Spontini's wife Marie-Celeste, was the sister of Liszt's old friend and piano supplier, Pierre Erard.

and thought at the time that the fame foreign lands had justly lavished upon him could not replace the intimate and profound joy of seeing his works appreciated, understood, and loved in his homeland. That moment of internal *resignation* must have been a bitter one.

Yet however disappointed he may have been, Spontini did not abandon the idea of being useful to his homeland. Although he had correctly assessed the operatic situation and given up the impossible task of attempting to regenerate the theater, he was also struck by the sorry state into which church music had fallen and decided to propose its reform, since such reform depended, after all, upon the will of a single individual.

Shocked and scandalized—as are all those who add an artistic dimension to their religious sentiments—at hearing nothing but ridiculous and disconcerting operatic reminiscences during the church Office and the celebration of Mass, irate at hearing the huge pipes of the organ, that majestic voice of cathedrals, resound with nothing but the latest cabalettas, he conceived the noble idea of ridding the Church of the scandal and reinstating the austere and solemn music of such composers as Palestrina, Marcello, and Allegri.[20] Strongly supported by the Bishop of Jesi (the town in the Papal States where Spontini was born)—who quickly issued a ban on the use of opera music in his diocese, citing the decrees of councils and popes who had at various times castigated the abuse and condemned its perpetrators to severe punishment—Spontini sent the Holy Father a report about the many defects and difficulties that currently exist. He concluded by proposing the most efficacious means of rooting out the abuse and by recommending the establishment of a new school of sacred music.[21]

His Holiness [Gregory XVI] has granted Spontini several audiences. He has apparently listened to the plan with favor and has honored the renowned composer with the Order of Saint Gregory the Great. . . .

But all this, perhaps, will not prevent the reform plan, which Spontini also intends to publicize as widely as possible in France and Germany, from sleeping forgotten in some file drawer in the pontifical chancellery.

---

20. Giovanni Pierluigi da Palestrina (ca. 1525–1594), Benedetto Marcello (1686–1739), Gregorio Allegri (ca. 1582–1652). Years later when Liszt was living in Rome, he transcribed Allegri's nine-part *Miserere* in combination with Mozart's motet *Ave verum corpus* and published the resulting piece as *Â la Chapelle Sixtine* (1865).

21. Spontini submitted his "Report regarding the Reform of Sacred Music" in January 1839. (Paolo Fragapane, *Spontini*, pp. 74–75.)

On that note, my dear Maurice, do sleep peacefully and do not, above all, reproach me any more for being too literary, since I have not allowed myself to write a single word today that does not conform to your editorial policy.

10

ROME AND SAN ROSSORE

CHRONICLE

Mid-February 1839. Liszt takes part in a concert by Francilla Pixis and her father.

8 March. Liszt introduces a far-reaching innovation in the way concerts of his time are normally organized, that is, with a featured performer (the concert-giver) and assisting artists. Marie provides the details: "Franz is giving *monologues pianistiques* here. Concerts are forbidden during Lent, but the foreigners absolutely wanted to hear him. The Russian ambassador [Prince Dimitri Gallitzin] and two or three others offered him their salons. Last Friday 200 people gathered in the Gallitzin apartments [in the Poli Palace]. They were the fine flower of all the aristocracies. Franz played the Overture to *William Tell*, etudes by Chopin and Moscheles, and two of his own fantasies. *Furore, fanatismo,* that goes without saying. The Romans are completely astonished that anyone would pay two piasters to listen to a pianist *all alone,* without the accompaniment of a flute, an oboe, without the 'Casta diva,' without the duet 'Dei palpiti.' "[1] A

1. Letter to Hiller, 17 March [1839] (Chantavoine, "La Comtesse d'Agoult," p 581). If the date is correct, a performance "last Friday" would mean the 15th, but that date conflicts with a report in the *Rivista teatrale* (Rome) which indicates that Liszt had actually played the previous week, presumably the 8th. That journal also gives a more detailed listing of his program, which was: his piano transcription of the Overture to Rossini's *William Tell*; Fantasy on Bellini's *I Puritani*; an etude by Moscheles; two etudes by Chopin; and Schubert's "Serenade" (Francesco Attardi, *Roma musicale nell'800,* p. 81). This report is quite possibly a truer reflection of what Liszt played at his "monologues" than his well-known later and quasi-bantering letter to Cristina Belgiojoso (*Letters* 1: no. 18), in which he remarked that "le concert c'est moi" and mentioned only his works.

single performer without assisting artists! Liszt's innovation was the beginning of the modern solo recital.[2]

1 May. Liszt gives an organ concert, including works of Bach, during a celebration honoring Louis-Philippe at the Church of St. Louis of France.

9 May. Marie d'Agoult gives birth to their third child, a son, who is baptized Daniel-Henri. He, like his sisters, is quickly given over to a nurse, a comely peasant woman in the nearby town of Palestrina.

Mid-May. Liszt gives a concert at the Teatro Argentina. The program includes the tried and true *Conzertstück* by Weber.

These months in Rome give Liszt his first, and virtually only, experience at being a father. He is enchanted with Blandine. Her rapt attention as he plays the opening bars of Schumann's *Scenes from Childhood* over and over again for her delights him,[3] and he even composes a song in her honor, "Angiolin dal biondo crin" (Little Angel with Blond Hair).

Mid-June-August. The Liszt party leaves Rome to pass a quiet summer in the gentler climes of Tuscany. After stopping briefly in Florence, they spend about two months at the Villa Massimiliano in the fashionable resort of Lucca.

11 August. Berlioz's article, titled simply "To Liszt," is published in the *Gazette musicale*.

September-mid-October. Liszt and Marie move to San Rossore, a village on the Ligurian Sea and close to Pisa. (His article below is written there.)

19 October. Madame d'Agoult returns to Paris. She takes Blandine and Cosima with her (Daniel will remain in Italy for two more years). Once back in the French capital, she gives the girls over to the care of Liszt's mother and mostly forgets about them as she sets about reestablishing the independent social and literary life she had cultivated before leaving Paris with Liszt four years earlier.

Mid-October-November. Liszt, alone in Florence, gets ready for his coming tours: traveling, as most artists did, with only a general schedule in mind, he plans to make a sweep of Austro-Hungarian and German cities and to be back in Paris the follow-

---

2. Liszt introduced his new form of concert to the public on 9 June 1840 at the Hanover Square Rooms in London. At that time he revised the designation of his performance from "monologues" to "recitals"—note the plural form.

3. See n. 12 below concerning a letter to Schumann, 5 June 1839.

ing spring. He pays a sentimental visit to Venice and then journeys on to Trieste. He gives two concerts there, assisted by
Ungher and Moriani, on 5 and 11 November, after which he
leaves for Vienna.

19 November. Liszt gives a concert in Vienna, the start of his virtuoso
tours. His aim is to capitalize on his reputation, amass a fortune,
and retire within a few years.[4]

The following Letter, written in response to Berlioz's article (app. C),
marks the end of Liszt's Italian experience, that vague yet intense
yearning he shared with other Romantics to know "das Land, wo die
Zitronen blühn." Its countryside was rich and hospitable, its visual
arts unsurpassed, but the musical life he found there fell far short of
the ideal he envisioned for this noblest and most mystic of arts. By
urging Berlioz to join him in German lands, he was clearly pinning
his hopes for musical progress to the north, and it is perhaps not surprising that Liszt, leaving Lombardy-Venetia in November 1839,
would not have the occasion to return to Italy for over twenty years.

To Hector Berlioz[1]

San Rossore, 2 October 1839

If there is one place on earth where the hubbub of worldly cares does
not penetrate, an isolated spot that is not troubled by pointless disputes and childish ambitions, it must surely be the place from which I
am writing, the isolated spot where I am now staying in order to say
goodbye to Italy and enjoy the ineffable beauty of this sunny land one
last time.

4. In Rome that past summer Liszt made the following candid assessment of
his musical future: "My place will be between Weber and Beethoven, or rather, between Hummel and Onslow. Maybe I am a would-be genius, that is something that
only time can tell. I feel that I am certainly not a mediocrity. My mission, as I see it, is
to be the first to introduce poetry into the music of the piano with some degree of
style. The most important thing to me is my *Harmonies* [*poétiques et religieuses*]; that
will be my serious work, and I will sacrifice nothing in it for the sake of effect. When I
have finished touring as a pianist I will no longer perform, except for my very own
public. I will shape it, I will elevate it, and then, in four or five years perhaps, I will try
my hand at writing an opera. As one who has never laid claim to anything, I am more
than content to be the second, at least, or half of the first in the world's opinion—it is
the grand prize that Thalberg and I share" (d'Agoult, *Mémoires*, pp. 164–65).

1. *Gazette musicale*, 24 October 1839, pp. 417–19.

Leaving Pisa by the Cascine gate, after having skirted the green square surrounded as if by enchantment by those four monuments of bygone days—the cathedral, the baptistery, the campanile, and the *Campo Santo*—the traveler takes a straight road cutting through vast pasture lands and soon arrives at the forest of San Rossore.[2] This lovely forest spreads its trembling, gently sea-blown pine tops beneath the sun and answers the hollow rumbling of the waves breaking at its feet with a continuous sigh. Skittish herds of deer dart through its sandy, sunlit clearings, while camels and buffaloes quietly graze on the scented grass or, at the woodcutter's bidding, carry away the cast-off branches of the ancient trees. An isolated house two hundred paces from the beach is my retreat. It is built of wood, like the chalets of Oberland. Its inhabitants cannot imagine what led me to seek refuge here. The good people are unaware of the profound poetry which surrounds them. They cannot understand the pleasure I take in lying in the sun on the deserted beach, nor why I am always looking towards the fiery band of light on the horizon for that barely perceptible black speck, the island of Elba.

I had been living here for a month, completely isolated from the outside world, when someone who knew that I hold you dear sent me your letter of 6 August. That letter, so concerned with a world that has become alien to me, touched me in a most remarkable way. I felt as if I had suddenly been summoned by the force of circumstances back to a milieu I had voluntarily put aside; I sensed the sadness and weariness hidden beneath the *indifference* with which you cloak yourself; I understood, too, that our being apart has not changed anything between us and that we will again be the brothers that we were in those days you recalled to me. However, we will be considerably older then, Berlioz. All that young, heartfelt impatience, that urge to conquer which would subjugate or destroy everything, that mad love for art which was so indignant about not being understood, those youthful illusions and

2. Although Liszt biographies typically describe San Rossore as a fishing village, according to Valery the area actually was more of a seaside cattle and horse ranch. The Versailles librarian goes on to note: "The principal curiosity of the domain of San Rossore is the herd of camels, whose ancestors were brought to these shores during the crusades . . . by a grand prior of Pisa of the Order of Saint John. A score of these camels are employed in the work of the farm and lodge in the stables; more than sixty stray through the pine forests or along the sands that border the sea. . . . These sands, with the sea, the camels, the purity and brightness of the sky, the solitude and silence give this picture something oriental, novel and poetical, which pleases the fancy and transports it to the desert" (Valery, *Travels in Italy*, p. 411).

the senseless efforts they entailed, they have all vanished, never to return. Experience has made you heed its stern voice. Your dealings with men have taught you more than one severe lesson. You have learned to conserve your strength and to proceed slowly along your difficult path. The proud and joyful young artist fresh from the Apennines, who picked a fight with everyone who did not adore his muse, is now pensive and dejected, dispassionately watching the distracted crowd rush back and forth from the true to the false, from an idol to a god, from art to delusion. Much like a farmer who sows seed in the earth and then withdraws to his humble cottage to let the winter do its work, you have sown your grain and can now confidently await a gentler day when it will flourish and ripen. As for myself, your junior, realizing more readily that I did not understand the ways of the world and that I surely had not been called to the glorious sufferings of a noble destiny, it is possible that the years may not have passed entirely in vain. There is a voice in solitary places that speaks clearly to those who ask questions of it. Ancient forests are always oracles of wisdom, and the pines of San Rossore have long known all about human folly and the inevitable course of fate.

During these past two years I have been alone much of the time and have not taken any part in what I would hasten to call the musical "free-for-all". The few concerts that I gave on rare occasions, in order not to forget my calling completely, did take me back to the artistic world, but I then returned to my retreat. You have chided me for saying so little about the state of music in Italy, but there are several reasons for my silence. Apart from the operas—and there is nothing to say about them, since you can see and hear the best productions of them at the Théâtre-Italien in Paris—the current musical scene, in my opinion, is totally lacking in interest. At most, I could mention the names of some solitary, disheartened artists or tell you about the noble efforts of some distinguished amateurs to produce a fine work like Haydn's *The Creation,* for example, at the Palazzo Vecchio in Florence,[3] and that would be all.

As I had decided to visit all the major Italian cities in turn without settling in any one of them, it would have been folly to suppose

3. Liszt is a little misleading here. It was the director of the museum in Florence who initiated the performance of Haydn's *The Creation*—a German work sung to celebrate the birth of a prince in Tuscany's German ruling family. Four hundred professionals and amateurs took part in the performance, and as the tickets were free, the event was a resounding success. The *Gazette* had already carried the news item on 18 July.

that I could have exerted any lasting influence; it would have been foolish of me to try to sway others and to waste my energies on a task that could have no positive results! I have, therefore, limited myself to a little daily study and to my own projects. There being nothing to discover about present-day Italy, I began to investigate its past; there being very little to ask of the living, I questioned the dead. A vast field of endeavor opened to me. The music of the Sistine Chapel—music that is decaying and disappearing day by day along with the frescos of Raphael and Michelangelo—led me into an extremely interesting field of study. Once I embarked on it, it was impossible to limit myself or stop. I certainly did not want to send you any hasty judgments on that great school of sacred music about which we know so little in France, and so I waited. But too many other things had to be attended to; the time was too short, the field too large. One has to look, listen, and think before writing.

The beautiful in this special land became evident to me in its purest and most sublime form. Art in all its splendor disclosed itself to my eyes. It revealed its universality and unity to me. Day by day my feelings and thoughts gave me a better insight into the hidden relationship that unites all works of genius. Raphael and Michelangelo increased my understanding of Mozart and Beethoven; Giovanni Pisano, Fra Beato, and Il Francia explained Allegri, Marcello, and Palestrina to me. Titian and Rossini appeared to me like twin stars shining with the same light. The Colosseum and the *Campo Santo* are not as foreign as one thinks to the Eroica Symphony and the Requiem. Dante has found his pictoral expression in Orcagna and Michelangelo, and someday perhaps he will find his musical expression in the Beethoven of the future.[4]

One of the luckiest encounters of my life also helped in no small way to strengthen both my intimate feelings about these matters and my fervent desire to increase my understanding and knowledge of art. A man whose genius, abetted by exquisite taste and virile energy, has

4. Whether or not Liszt is styling himself as the "Beethoven of the future" here is a moot point. The two artists he mentions did, however, inspire Dantesque musical thoughts in him during those years (d'Agoult, *Mémoires*, p. 180); Michelangelo's statue for Lorenzo de' Medici's tomb in Florence became the basis for the dark, brooding *Il Pensieroso* in the *Années de pèlerinage: Italie*, and the Orcagna work, the fresco *Triumph of Death* (now attributed to Francesco Triani) in the *Campo Santo* at Pisa was the stimulus, in part at least, for his *"Dante" Sonata* in the same collection (Sharon Winklhofer, "Liszt, Marie d'Agoult and the 'Dante' Sonata"). Liszt's fullest "musical expression' of the poet, the Dante Symphony, was probably also conceived at this time, but it was not actually composed until the mid-1850s at Weimar.

produced the finest examples of contemporary painting, Ingres[5] extended his friendship to me so warmly in Rome that I still recall it with pride. He was everything that his reputation had led me to expect, and even more. Ingres's youth, as you know, was a time of constant study and courageous struggle. He overcame obscurity, misunderstanding, and poverty only by working determinedly and by dedicating himself stubbornly and heroically to his unshakeable convictions. Now that he has reached his later years, he humbly enjoys the fame he has earned so honestly. This great artist, for whom antiquity holds no secrets and whom Apelles could have called his brother, is an excellent musician as well as an incomparable painter. Mozart, Haydn, and Beethoven speak to him in the same language as do Phidias and Michelangelo. He seizes beauty wherever he finds it, and his impassioned veneration even seems to enhance the genius to which he turns. One unforgettable day we visited the halls of the Vatican together. We walked through the long galleries filled with innumerable art works from Etruria, Greece, ancient Rome, and Christian Italy, passing respectfully before those yellowing marble figures and partially effaced paintings. Ingres spoke as he walked, and we listened like rapt disciples. His glowing words gave new life to all those masterpieces; his eloquence transported us back to bygone centuries; line and color came alive before our eyes; forms that had been damaged by the passage of time or a profaner's hand were born again in all their pristine purity and displayed all their young beauty for us. A mystery of poetry stood before us fully revealed: it was the genius of modern times evoking the genius of antiquity. That evening when we returned, after having discussed these marvels heart to heart at length sitting beneath the live oaks of the Villa Medici, I took the initiative and led Ingres toward the open piano, gently chiding him: "Come now, master," I said, "we cannot forget our beloved music. Your violin is there,[6] and the A-minor sonata on the music stand is tired of waiting for us.[7] Let us begin."

Oh, if only you could have heard him! The religious fidelity with which he played Beethoven's music! The firm, fiery way he handled

---

5. Jean-Auguste-Dominique Ingres (1780–1867), painter. He was the director of the French Academy at the Villa Medici in Rome from 1835 to 1841.

6. Ingres was a fine violinist who had played professionally in theater orchestras during his student days. He was so well known for his playing that the phrase "le violon d'Ingres" came to mean a second profession, an important avocation.

7. Beethoven's Violin Sonata, Op. 47, a favorite piece. That spring, 1 March 1839, Liszt had written Massart: "I often see Ingres, who is very kind to me. We make a lot of music together. . . . We plan to go through everything by Mozart and Beethoven" (Vier, *Liszt Artiste*, p. 51).

the bow! What purity of style! What integrity of feeling! Despite my deep respect for him, I could not help throwing myself into his arms, and the fatherly affection I felt as he pressed me to his breast made me very happy.

Soon I will leave Italy. I am going to Vienna. They are going to perform Mendelssohn's *Saint Paul* on the 10th of November, and I want to be there.[8] Why not come too? Why not have your symphonies presented in German lands,[9] where they will be understood and loved? Germany is their true homeland. They are hardy, northern plants that demand a robust terrain and will not display all the richness of their powerful and somber foliage growing in the lighter soil. Germany is the country for symphonists; it is yours. Your symphonies may be greeted as passing novelties everywhere else, but it is only in Germany that a profound sense of understanding awaits them and can offer them a home. Although the current Italian style has alienated the social world from serious music, as it has done in France, a large and knowledgeable audience exists there for serious music. The study of art is usually less superficial, the emotions truer, and the customs stronger. The traditions of Mozart, Weber, and Beethoven have not been lost. These three geniuses have planted vigorous roots in German soil.

Beethoven! Can what I read possibly be true? The fund-raising appeal for a monument to the greatest musician of our times produced all of 424 francs 90 centimes in France! What a disgrace! What a calamity for us! This state of affairs surely cannot continue, isn't that true? Beethoven's memory cannot be buried because of this slow and parsimonious fund-raising. It cannot and will not be! You know that the finest sculptor in Italy, Bartolini,* is a friend of mind.[10] He is a noble

---

*Contemporary sculpture is indebted to Bartolini for its most beautiful works. The only ones I will cite here are *The Nymph of the Scorpion*, bought by the Prince de Beauveau; the *Trust in God*; the group *Charity* in the Pitti Palace; the monument for [Niccolò] Demidoff and the one for Alberti in Santa Croce in Florence, etc. I have given many details about the life and works of Bartolini in a recently published biographical account.

8. Mendelssohn's oratorio (1836) was to be the featured work at the annual festival concert of the Gesellschaft der Musikfreunde. By tradition a "monster" event, the concert boasted a chorus of 700, an orchestra of 300, with the imperial family in full attendance and over 6,000 people in the audience. But as Mendelssohn himself did not attend, Liszt tarried on his way to Vienna and did not reach there until 15 November.

9. Again a reminder that the term "Germany" (*l'Allemagne*) embraced all German-speaking lands, including Austria-Hungary.

10. Although the article Liszt wrote on Bartolini, evidently an extension of his remarks in the article about Florence, was submitted to *l'Artiste* for publication, it ran

artist who has also experienced the vagaries of fate and the thankless-
ness of man. He is as indignant as I am about the insult to Beethoven's
memory and has promised me to begin work immediately on a marble
statue, which can be completed in two years. I have just written to the
Beethoven committee, asking them to suspend the fund raising and
offering to make up the amount still needed. I certainly do not mean
to step on anyone's toes, and I do not want to deprive those who have
already given money of any of the honor of contributing to the monument. All I want to do is supplement the sum collected so far in order
to expedite the completion of a project that I regard as a duty for us.
The sole privilege I ask is that of naming the sculptor: entrusting
Bartolini with this task is a sure guarantee that it will be worthy of
Beethoven.[11]

---

into trouble there—several of the manuscript's pages were lost, editorial tempers
flared, etc.—all with the result that that article and one devoted to Rome were never
published and have now disappeared (*Corres. Liszt–d'Agoult* 1:318, 322–23).

11. Liszt's letter to the Beethoven Committee in Bonn reads:

Gentlemen,
As the subscription for the monument to Beethoven is progress-
ing so slowly and as the completion of that monument is, as a result,
indefinitely delayed, I have the honor of making a proposal to you, the
acceptance of which would make me happy.
I offer to complete the entire sum needed to raise a monument to
Beethoven, asking no privilege in return other than that of designating
the artist to whom the work is to be entrusted. That would be Bartolini
of Florence, whose works are familiar to you and whom Italy honors as
her greatest sculptor.
I have had a talk with him about this matter, and he has assured
me that the statue done in marble (whose cost would be 50,000 to
60,000 francs) could be finished within two years and that he is ready to
begin work immediately.
I have the honor, etc., etc.

Notwithstanding the generosity and sincerity of Liszt's offer, this letter—like
the Thalberg review or his account of La Scala—smacks of an overbearing approach
that was sure to provoke controversy, especially since Liszt made his offer to the committee public by having the letter published in the *Gazette musicale* (20 October 1839),
a few days, in fact, before this Letter to Berlioz appeared. Paris was up in arms; Marie, writing from there to Henri Lehmann, noted: "You can just imagine all these
bullfrogs croaking against the project for the Beethoven monument. All the musical
riffraff is indignant about it, complaining loudly what bragging, what humbug, what
impudence! What an imitation of Paganini! (3 November 1839, in Solange Joubert,
Une correspondance romantique, p. 67). The last charge must have been painful, since

He should give me his proposal very soon, and I will send it to you. Vast sums will not be needed to accomplish the project. Three concerts, in Vienna, Paris, and London, should suffice to cover just about everything. The remainder will come, with God's help, from the pocket of the "indefatigable vagabond," as you call me. Barring any obstacle over which I have no control, therefore, the monument will be erected in two years.

I would like to give you some news, except that I hardly have any. Francilla Pixis sang quite successfully in Naples and has been hired for Palermo. Hiller, who is working on a new Italian opera, was suddenly called to Frankfort because of his mother's death. Schumann, our *inspired* Schumann, has composed some ravishing *Scenes from Childhood* for the piano. Schumann is a poet of considerable sensitivity and a great musician.[12] A young Polish pianist, Schwarzbach, has sent me some delightful mazurkas.

I have just attended a Mass of the Holy Spirit that was sung in the cathedral of Pisa to open a congress of learned men, and it was truly a mass "for the learned." They also dedicated the statue of Galileo to *wisdom*. The renowned Professor Rosini[13] gave a speech that was roundly applauded. The pope has forbidden his learned subjects to attend the congress. Today, though, they claim that he has lifted the ban. . . .

Adieu, my friend. I hope to see you soon in Vienna. My best to you, everywhere.

Liszt himself had been incensed by the public manner in which Paganini's gift of 20,000 francs to Berlioz was treated (d'Agoult, *Mémoires*, p. 160). Be that as it may, the committee for the monument eventually replied in mid-December, thanking Liszt for his offer but postponing any decision about the sculptor until Bartolini submitted a model for approval. (The *Gazette* published this reply on 2 January 1840; it also appears in the *Corres. Liszt–d'Agoult* 1:334–36.)

12. Liszt, writing to Schumann on 5 June 1839, told him how much he enjoyed playing the *Scenes from Childhood* for Blandine. He also said: "At the risk of appearing monotonous I will tell you again that the last pieces you were kind enough to send me in Rome [*Scenes from Childhood*, *Kreisleriana*, the C-major Fantasy] impressed me as admirable in both inspiration and composition" (*Letters* 1: no. 19).

13. Evidently Giovanni Rosini (1776–1855), writer, poet, and professor of Rhetoric at the University of Pisa.

II

HAMBURG, COPENHAGEN, AND THE RHINE

The last of the travel articles skips ahead to the summer of 1841. By that time Liszt, his virtuoso career in full swing, had been touring almost incessantly for a year and a half, performing in Vienna, Pressburg, and Pest (where he was fêted as a conquering hero), Prague, Dresden, Leipzig, the Rhine spas, Brussels, and Paris. During this period he also made three extensive tours of the British Isles. When the last of them ended he turned his attention across the Channel to Hamburg and the other events his describes in his Letter.

CHRONICLE

5—8 July 1841. Liszt attends and performs at the music festival in Hamburg. It is his first experience with such a gathering.

9 July. He gives a concert in Hamburg.

14–26 July. Liszt pays his first visit to Copenhagen. He performs several times for the King of Denmark and gives at least two concerts of his own.

ca. 29 July. The steamer on which Liszt is returning to Hamburg is forced to seek refuge at the little German coastal town of Cuxhaven.

31 July. He gives another concert in Hamburg.

Early August. Liszt sails to Amsterdam and travels thence to Rotterdam, where he boards a steamer for a leisurely trip up the Rhine.

ca. 10 August. Liszt reaches the Rhine isle Nonnenwerth (just south of Bonn) and joins Marie d'Agoult, who has been awaiting his arrival there. This is the first of three summer holidays they will spend on the little island.

22 August. Liszt, in Cologne, gives the first of his several benefit concerts for the completion of its cathedral.

Whether this late-blooming Letter to Kreutzer was actually an attempt to revive the *Bachelier-ès-music* series is difficult to say. It is, in any case, the last of the travel articles, a pleasant piece of occasional journalism.

To Léon Kreutzer[1]

[Nonnenwerth, August 1841][2]
I arrived in Hamburg on 5 July, the festival there having begun the day before. Until you have been to Germany, my dear Léon, you can only have a very vague idea of what these large musical celebrations can be, exciting the whole population as they do, uniting all classes of society, even if only for a few days, in a communality of enjoyment and freeing them with a spontaneous burst of energy from the monotony of their work or idleness. In France it is difficult to understand the impact that these sorts of gatherings can have, and even if they were to be copied there I doubt that they would ever play as significant a role in national life.

The festival in Hamburg was the third sponsored by the Association of North-German cities.[3] No effort was spared to insure that it came off brilliantly and splendidly. Foreign artists and amateurs had been invited well in advance to take part in it. The number of performers exceeded six hundred. A large and richly decorated hall (*Festhalle*) had been built especially for it and held about six thousand people. Concerts, balls, and banquets followed one another without interruption for eight days. It was a very lively event; however, a certain sense of reserve that extends even to the Germans' liveliest moments consistently set the tone of the numerous gatherings, and there was not, as far as I know, the slightest incident or bit of trouble at any of them.

1. *Gazette musicale*, 19 September 1841, pp. 417–20. Léon Kreutzer (1817–1868), pianist, composer, and critic, nephew of violinist Rudolph Kreutzer and a close friend of Lambert Massart.

2. Liszt sent the manuscript or proofs of this Letter to Schlesinger on 8 September 1841 with the note: "Have the *Bachelier* carefully corrected by Mormais [Monnais?] and let the varied fragments . . . be separated by dotted lines, or any type of line of separation, as I've indicated" (Alan Walker, *Franz Liszt* 1:22n).

3. Norddeutschen Musikfest-Verein, founded in 1838; its two earlier festivals had been held at Lübeck and Schwerin.

On the 5th they performed Handel's *Messiah* at Saint Michael's Church under the direction of Schneider, music director to the reigning Duke of Anhalt-Dessau.[4] A huge crowd filled the church and listened attentively to the great work, which was conducted competently and performed remarkably well by the chorus and orchestra.

The 7th was devoted to secular music. The Eroica Symphony opened the concert, followed by the Fantasy for Piano with Chorus.[5] Then, Madame Schroeder-Devrient, that lovely, pathetic Leonora for whom Paris yearns, sang a Mozart aria in her inimitable manner, a manner that surpasses all others.[6] The Overture to *Oberon* and the one to *William Tell*, a vocal selection by Madame Duflot-Maillard,[7] several choruses, and a Fantasy on Themes from *Robert le diable*[8] completed the program.

A second sacred concert at Saint Michael's closed the festival. It included a mass by Mozart, a choral piece by J. S. Bach, Schubert's "Ave Maria," and lastly, the lovely chorus from *The Creation*, "The heavens are telling."

All this may strike you, perhaps, as an enormous amount of music. It would be difficult to hold the attention of a Parisian audience for so long a time with a program of such serious works. But the Germans' particular virtue is their perseverance, and they even approach their entertainment conscientiously. Once they are convinced that they are listening to a fine piece, they would not dare to allow themselves to think that it was too long. They listen intently, their attention never flags. They are endowed with more resilience regarding their pleasures than I have ever encountered anywhere else . . . .

. . . .

A musical court! A king who loves and listens to music! Truly, this is a rare phenomenon in our times, and one that was well worth the trouble of being the sea's plaything for twenty-four hours, even when one is, like myself, susceptible to that pitiable sickness for which there is no cure but "the resignation of a fateful smile."

So saying, I boarded the ship, and the following day I was at the

---

4. Joh. Chris. Friedrich Schneider (1786–1853), teacher, composer, and one of the most experienced choral conductors of the day.

5. Beethoven's Fantasy for Piano, Chorus, and Orchestra, Op. 80. Liszt was the soloist.

6. Wilhelmine Schroeder-Devrient (1804–1860), the celebrated soprano. She had created the role of Leonora in the 1822 revival of Beethoven's *Fidelio*.

7. Hortense Duflot-Maillard, soprano. Remembered as the first to sing the role of Marguerite in Berlioz's *The Damnation of Faust* (1846).

8. It was Liszt's own fantasy.

Danish court, where I played [Beethoven's] *Pastorale Symphony* and the sonata dedicated to your uncle. It was a real joy for me, I swear, to see how these great and favorite works of ours were received so intelligently and understood so well by a king who knows how to find in the art of noble recreation feelings which, if I can trust my artist's instincts, can only have been translated into kindly deeds on more than one occasion. Several times His Majesty deigned to discuss old and new music with me. He was remarkably knowledgeable in pointing out the differences and similarities that one finds in the genius of great composers. The superior manner in which he discussed questions that his royal duties would hardly have allowed him time to study in depth astounded me. The great benevolence with which His Majesty was pleased to welcome me and to place both the court and city theaters at my disposal for my concerts filled me with gratitude.[9]

It is truly a shame that crowned heads are usually so little concerned with the course the art of music is taking in their countries. I could expand at great length on this subject, and I might even be quite eloquent about it, but I cannot ignore a small, traitorous voice that keeps reminding me of that profoundly wise line from the great and witty Molière: "You are in the trade, my dear sir."[10] How should I continue after that?

Instead of music, let me talk to you about an art which is not mine but one whose ability to endure is something I envy, and about a man who has left a glorious example of his inspiration to Copenhagen, a man who has built an everlasting monument of love and gratitude on his native soil. When I entered the Church of Our Lady a feeling of profound admiration and spontaneous reverence filled my heart. That church, as you know, has been entirely decorated by Thorwaldsen alone. A Christ in white marble rises on the altar, and the statues of the twelve apostles, their backs against the pillars of the nave, seem to guide the faithful and teach them the way leading to the Man-God. A magnificent bas-relief depicting the road to Calvary forms the arch of the choir.[11] It is all simple and grand. Its unity of thought and execution creates a striking and lasting impression. One God, one art, one man; or, as one might say, a profound, solemn discussion between

9. Christian VIII. Liszt showed his gratitude by dedicating his *Reminiscences de Don Juan* to him.

10. "Vous êtes orfévre, monsieur Josse." Literally, "You are a goldsmith, Mister Josse," but which, understood in context, indicates special pleading for one's profession.

11. Thorwaldsen's *Christ and the Twelve Apostles* was created in 1821–1827.

Jesus and the artist, as well as the glorification of that mystic conversation, that wonderful flow of words whose secrets are revealed to us as if we were reading a book of marvelous simplicity!

Oh! How is it possible to look at the stability, the permanence of the plastic arts, the human immortality which accompanies the works of the painter and sculptor without being envious? How is it possible not to be devastated by the inability of our own art to create and establish enduring monuments? Thorwaldsen, Rubens, Michelangelo, great artists and fortunate men, you completely fill a church, a city, a whole country with your ideas! Your inspiration, clothed in imperishable forms, perpetuates itself throughout the ages and shines forever on your homeland! You are identified with it, you are its representative for all posterity! Copenhagen is Thorwaldsen, Antwerp is Rubens, Rome is Michelangelo!

But alas, even if a musician as powerful as Michelangelo, as pure as Raphael, and as brilliant as Rubens were to come along, he still would not be able to produce anything that time will not efface; his work, ephemeral and fleeting, would only see the warm understanding of it grow cooler day by day. Soon it would barely be known at all, even to those pitiful scholars who rummage through the past in order to display their fruitless learning, who see nothing in a masterpiece but a means of proving their own pedantry, and who, in this respect at least, are like Cleopatra, happily dissolving the pearl of genius in the vinegar of their criticism. Palestrina! Gluck! and even you, oh divine Mozart, with your ashes still warm, what meaning do you have today for the masses who have been swept away by the melodies of Rossini? And Rossini, he too, doesn't his eagle eye see that his last wave of harmony is already moving closer and closer to that sinister beach, where indifference, like the arid sand, is lying in wait for genius and fame in order to make them vanish into its oblivion!

I was silently pondering these ideas when the church suddenly shook with a long, powerful shudder. It was the organ vibrating under its master's fingers, and its sound was like a solemn and piercing reproach to my doubts and frailty. I listened for a long time in silence. The organist, Weyse,[12] who was giving voice to these lonely walls, knew how to recapture the learned inspirations and enduring solemnity of Johann Sebastian! I was nearly moved to tears several times as I listened. The double fugue in five-quarter time [five voices?] that he improvised and that lasted, without exaggeration, nearly half an hour

12. Christoph Ernst Friedrich Weyse (1774–1842).

filled me with admiration. Never before had the organ revealed the fullness of its grandeur and magnificence to me like this. But then, I have not yet heard Mendelssohn perform. . . .

. . . .

A storm at sea drove me to Cuxhaven. Maybe you have noticed a little black dot bearing that name on detailed maps, but have you ever thought what it would be like to find yourself stranded there by the wind and tides for twelve hours? It is enough to infuriate you or drive you mad. I could well understand the sacrifice Iphigenia made. The day passed quickly enough: there was correspondence to catch up on, people whom you have not thought of in three years to write to; you try to convince your friends that you are mending your ways and becoming a zealous correspondent. But the evening! The evening in Cuxhaven! Fortunately there is a Providence that never completely abandons unlucky people. Quite by chance we learn that a troupe of actors, driven by the most evil of stars, is there and has nothing to do—certainly not for any lack of desire on their part, but for the lack of an audience. We quickly organize a subscription. All the passengers on the *Beurs* buy tickets, and a number of the natives, succumbing to our bad example, also indulge in the same mad extravagance. The hall is swept, the orchestra takes its place; the musicians are served some wine; the basses are in fine spirits, the violas reconcile themselves to life, the bass drum feels unusually energetic; the lamps are lighted, and we light our cigars. Several young ladies—attracted by curiosity and restrained by propriety, that mother of all boredom—enter, leave, return, and finally sit down when they realize that there are enough of them to form a solid front. The play begins: it is *The Father of the Debutante.*[13] Vernet is missing, but the actors are pleased and laughing. The public laughs to see them laughing, and everyone looks at his neighbor as if to say, "Well, isn't it amusing to see us all here together?" When the comedy is over no one makes a move to leave. Where is one to go in Cuxhaven at half-past eight at night? But the orchestra knows Strauss waltzes. A wonderful idea! We will dance. Dance! Really! In a public theater with foreigners and strangers! "Why not, ladies? I am Hungarian. My name is Franz Liszt. I play the piano fairly well. My manners are no worse than anyone else's, and I answer for my companions as I do for myself—that is, not at all!"

They have no ready reply to that little speech. Besides, the or-

13. *Le Père de la debutante*, comedy-vaudeville in five acts by Théolon de Lambert and J. F. A. Bayard. First performed, Paris, October 1837.

chestra is warming up; the rhythm grows more and more insistent; it quickly wins over the most recalcitrant wills, convinces the most reluctant minds! And soon—oh, great Strauss!—all the pretty young Cuxhaven girls place their blond heads on the castaways' shoulders and abandon their slender bodies to their strong arms. One more hour, just one, and every Don Juan would have found his Heidi! Why did the storm subside so quickly? Why did the north wind stop blowing?

. . . .

To the Rhine! To the Rhine!

Between Coblenz and Bonn, at the foot of the Seven Mountains, the Rhine lovingly cradles a green and flowered isle. At one time it was a retreat, a pious sanctuary from which the hymns of virginity and the canticles of divine ecstasy rose to the heavens. Only one building, green and white and surmounted by a steeple, can be seen there. A copse of birches and hazel trees shields it on the south, a curtain of poplars veils it on the east. A large hedge of brambles and some clematis surround its tufted lawns, where one can see some scattered fruit trees and larches with the wind playing on their trembling leaves, sending their plaintive endearments and fugitive farewells to the river passing nearby. The island is Nonnenwerth; the building was once a convent. Not long ago, the chaste, veiled daughters of Saint Benedict walked beneath its porticoes. A scapular rested on their breasts, the rosary's black beads glistened in their pale hands, silence sealed their lips, and obedience, that silence of the will, was in their hearts. From any of the covered walks the nuns could see the cemetery,* their final resting place. The path from the altar to the tomb was short, familiar, straight, and direct. Their faith having marked this certain destination for them, their renunciation drew an unalterable line to it.

Today, a worldly clamor fills these walls which are watched over by the statue of a bishop who, crozier in hand, still seems to want to drive away the profane. It is no longer the penitent who comes to this holy place to beg the charity of a prayer from the abbess; it is the traveler, driven hither and thither by his inconstant will, who stops here for a moment, only to resume his journey as quickly as possible. It is no longer a solemn procession that makes the flagstones ring with its measured pace; it is now a spritely dance, a wild waltz. It is no longer frugal bread and limpid water that are served in the silent refectory; it is wine that flows freely, bringing unguarded remarks to people's lips. Today, the inn has replaced the convent. Our age has

---

* *Gottesacker.*

overrun the cloister. *Harold*[14] has passed where Hildegonde once prayed;* the pilgrim of doubt has sung his song in the ruins where a martyr to an eternal love had entombed her living self.

It was to Nonnenwerth that I came for a few hours to lay aside my care-laden cloak and the vagabond's staff that always seems to be urging me to "Move on, move on!" It was there one day that I found shade that refreshes, water that quenches one's thirst, and a mysterious echo that answers one's thoughts and completes the sentence that has yet to be spoken.[15] . . .

Yesterday I passed the foot of the Lorelei's Rock. She has disappeared, that wonderful fairy creature who combed her golden hair in the sunshine and sang such a powerful, enticing song that the fascinated river pilot, raising his eyes to her, forgot his tiller and was wrecked on the reefs. She is no longer there, that Teutonic siren with her heaven-colored eyes and her wave-colored sash. She has left this region that has been overwhelmed by our barbaric civilization. The black smoke of our steamers dulled the brilliance of her gown, and the noise of our machines drowned out her sweet voice. Moreover, if you look down there on the other bank, you can see the stern, menacing figure of the man who destroyed the legends, along with the marvels and enchantments she carried in her fertile breast. At the sound of Gutenberg's voice, the startled bevy of water sprites, fairies, and sirens fled in search of younger lands, natural sites that were more impenetrable. And yet, oh beautiful Lorelei, you still return they say to this old world of ours. You are called the *ideal*! Invisible to the crowd, you appear to the poet; he sees you, he hears you! Enthralled, ecstatic, he takes up his lyre and strikes the chords that harmonize with your heavenly voice.[16] He is enflamed by a fatal love for you. You move away,

---

*According to legend, the beautiful Hildegonde, on hearing the news of Roland's death at Roncevaux, had a convent built on Rolandswerth (Nonnenwerth today), and there she dedicated her life to God. But the report was false, and Roland returned, full of life and love. Learning that Hildegonde was now lost to him forever, he retired to the top of the mountain overlooking the convent—a place where the ruins of Rolandseck can still be seen today—and spent the rest of his life there in contemplation and in the constant hope of hearing Hildegonde's voice rise above the choir of nuns and ascend to him.

14. Byron, *Childe Harold's Pilgrimage*, canto 3, stanzas 50–60 describe Harold's passage through the Rhine country, but the poet does not mention Nonnenwerth specifically.

15. Liszt first visited Nonnenwerth briefly during his tour of the Rhine spas the previous summer (1840).

16. Liszt, incidentally, composed his setting of Heine's "Die Lorelei" in November 1841, two months after this article was published. It was written "for Marie."

and he follows you. You smile at him, and he thinks he can reach out and touch you. His hand is already grasping at the folds of your trailing gown. But you disappear, and *reality*, that reef where all enthusiasm is dashed, displays its naked face and fleshless flanks to him.

I do not know whether it is because "music is the architecture of sounds"* or because "architecture is solidified music"**—I am not even sure that there is a special affinity between the two arts—but the sight of an old cathedral has always moved me deeply. I love the dark depths of those huge vaults that generation after generation have crossed with bowed heads. I love those massive pillars whose echoes have resounded with the misery of man, his unassuageable sighs, and the anguish of his desires. I shudder when I contemplate the arrows that pierce naked flesh, that sublime effort of human genius to draw nearer to heaven, where it seems to want to wrest a glance, a bit of hope from God! Thus when some people arrived from Cologne to tell me that they wanted to finish their cathedral, I could not keep myself from exclaiming: "And I too will contribute my grain of sand. It is a matter of raising millions, but accept my poor little artistic mite first. Accept it before you accept the gold of others, for art ennobles everything. Besides, it is our privilege as artists to contribute whenever and wherever we can, even though we ourselves possess nothing."

Two days later the roar of a cannon startled the winged inhabitants of Nonnenwerth. Joyful cries and hurrahs filled the air. Rockets lit up the night sky and made the river appear red. A boat decked out with flags had come to fetch me and take me to the doors of the cathedral. A warm cordiality united us all in the thought of art and possibly in hesitant faith! . . .

*Madame de Staël.
**Victor Hugo.

EPILOGUE

As Liszt's travels continued, his career as a virtuoso reached its apogee in 1842. He gave twenty-one concerts in Berlin early in the year, arousing such a frenzy of acclaim that Heine coined a new word, "Lisztomania," to describe it. He was awarded a doctor's degree in music by the University of Königsberg. He totally conquered St. Petersburg, and that November he was appointed *Hofkapellmeister* on a part-time basis in the little grand-ducal city of Weimar.

The more he toured, however, the more his relationship with Madame d'Agoult disintegrated. Their attempts to patch over the differences that had led to the separation in Italy proved futile: he was caught up in his tours, while she was then wholly absorbed in cultivating her salon in Paris and her budding career as a writer. Her social position as Liszt's occasional mistress became increasingly uncomfortable and untenable for her, and in the end it was she, in May 1844, who insisted they put a formal end to their affair.

Inevitable though it was, the break with Marie disturbed Liszt profoundly. Thenceforth he avoided Paris, even though his mother and children lived there, and he intensified his efforts to find a suitable retirement position. He hoped that it would be in Vienna, but when an appointment failed to materialize, he turned increasingly to Weimar. The tours, nevertheless, continued for several more years— until 1847 when Liszt finally decided that he had had more than enough of his nomadic life. It was time to stop: that February in Kiev he had met and become involved with the Polish-born Princess Carolyne Sayn-Wittgenstein (1819–1887). In September at Elisabethgrad in the Ukraine he gave his last concert as a professional pianist. He was thirty-five years old at the time.

The following year Liszt, accompanied by Princess Carolyne, settled in Weimar to take up his full-time duties as music director of the court. Life in the Thuringian capital where Goethe and Schiller once lived and worked was not just a complete change for him; it was also his first opportunity to create and experience a feeling of artistic community, that spirit of association, which he believed was so necessary to the progress of art. Everything that he had held in abeyance, so to speak, during his virtuoso years came to life in Weimar. He composed, revising early works and writing new ones. He attracted a group of the brightest young musicians Germany had to offer: Hans von Bülow, Joachim Raff, Joseph Joachim, and Peter Cornelius among them. Having an opera theater and concert hall at his disposal, he utilized them to produce and conduct the works that he felt represented the best in modern music. The then little-known works of Wagner, Berlioz, Schumann, and Schubert, for instance, were given an honored place in the Weimar repertory. And when Liszt turned writer again, this time with Carolyne's help, he used both his pen and his prestige as Europe's most renowned musician to champion the cause of those whose works deserved a wider hearing.

Even though Weimar was basically a stodgy, tradition-bound town whose conservative bureaucracy eventually prevailed over Liszt's dreams for a "New German Music," forcing him to resign his position, there seems little doubt that the decade he spent there was the most fruitful and productive period of his life. It gave him the opportunity to practice, as best he knew how, his "mission" in life, that ever-present and unstinting commitment to art he had made years earlier under the guidance of his mentors in Paris. Perhaps the best way, then, to conclude this presentation of his *Lettres d'un bachelier ès musique* is to return to the younger Liszt and his *Album d'un voyageur*. It was a work which he conceived during the idyllic days spent with Marie d'Agoult and which, in many ways, presents a musical parallel to the ideas and sentiments expressed in the Letters. When the *Album* was published in 1842 it opened with a preface[1] in which he stated:

> Having traveled of late through many new lands, many different places, many locations consecrated by history and poetry, having felt that the diverse sights nature afforded and the scenes related to them did not pass before my eyes as meaningless images, but that they stirred profound emotions within my soul, that there

---

1. The preface, or at least the initial version of it, was written in the fall of 1837. (For the complex publishing history of the *Album* and its eventual transformation into the *Années de Pèlerinage; Première année, Suisse,* see Humphrey Searle, *The Music of Liszt,* pp. 23–29, and György Kroó, "Ferenc Liszt: dall'Album alla Suite.")

existed between them and me a vague but direct relation, an indefinite but real connection, an inexplicable but sure communication, I have attempted to render some of my strongest sensations, my liveliest impressions in music. . . .

The inner and poetic sense of things, that ideality which exists in everything, seems to manifest itself pre-eminently in those artistic creations that arouse feelings and ideas within the soul by the beauty of their form. Even though music is the least representational of the arts, it nonetheless has its own form and has been defined not without reason as an architecture of sounds. But even as architecture not only has Tuscan, Ionic, Corinthian, etc., orders, but also embodies ideas that are pagan or Christian, sensual or mystic, war-like or commercial, so too, and even more perhaps, music has its hidden meanings, its sense of the ideal, which the majority of people, truly speaking, do not even suspect, because where a work of art is concerned, they rarely rise above the comparison of externals, the facile appreciation of some superficial skill.

The more instrumental music progresses, develops, and frees itself from its early limitations, the more it will tend to bear the stamp of that ideality which marks the perfection of the plastic arts, the more it will cease to be a simple combination of tones and become a poetic language, one that, better than poetry itself perhaps, more readily expresses everything in us that transcends the commonplace, everything that eludes analysis, everything that stirs in the inaccessible depths of imperishable desires and feelings for the infinite.

It was with this conviction, this inclination, that I undertook the work which is published here today. I direct it to the few rather than the many. I do not seek success, but rather the approval of a small number of those who think that art has some purpose other than idly passing time and who ask of it something more than the trivial distraction of a fleeting entertainment.

APPENDICES

A

GEORGE SAND: LETTER OF
A VOYAGER TO LISZT

George Sand—Aurore Dudevant, née Dupin (1804–1876)—first came
to the attention of Parisian readers in 1832 with the success of her second novel, *Indiana,* a mostly autobiographical tale whose heroine, as
Sand explains in her preface, "is woman herself, that frail creature
charged by the author to represent those passions which are repressed
or, if you prefer, suppressed by social laws. She is free will grappling
with necessity; she is love butting her head blindly against all the obstacles placed before her by civilization."

As Sand's career, her literary and personal reputation, continued
to flourish with each succeeding work, it became inevitable that she
and Liszt would meet. Not, though, just as highly visible celebrities
on the Parisian scene, but more as a writer and a musician who were
sympathetically attuned to each other. She had always had a deep, enthusiastic interest in music, a craving almost to be a musician, though
she lacked the technical training for it, while Liszt, for his part, had
been one of her devoted readers from the very start. Even before they
met, he had written to a former pupil who was then in Italy: "Did
you happen to come upon a Madame George Sand (Madame Dudevant) in Naples or in Rome? She is . . . a woman with a genius that is
most extraordinary, quite bitter and quite painful in its force. No
doubt you have read *Indiana, Valentine,* and, above all, *Lélia,* but perhaps you have not come across *Leone Leoni* yet and that marvelous
letter about Italy she has recently published in the *Revue des deux
mondes.* I strongly urge you to read them when you return. . . . There
is, without doubt or comparison, no woman who is as 'strong' (in the
biblical sense) or more astonishingly gifted [than Madame Sand]."[1]
Strong sentiments indeed.

1. Letter to Valérie Boissier, in Bory, "Diverses lettres," p. 16. Bory dates the

Liszt and Sand were finally introduced to each other some time around the beginning of November 1834. Their friendship got off to a slow start, since each seemed to be taking the other's measure, and she was also in the last throes of her problematic affair with poet Alfred de Musset. With time, however, a deep, easy intimacy, a kind of "creative comradeship," developed between them, particularly in the weeks just prior to Liszt's leaving Paris. (Sand was one of the very few people who knew about the flight to Switzerland and the reasons behind it.)

When Liszt said that her Letter about Italy was "marvelous," he was clearly not alone in his opinion, since that article and the eleven others Sand wrote under the general title *Lettres d'un voyageur* were among the most sensationally successful of her writings.[2] Parisian readers doted on their idiosyncratic mixture of travelogue, personal reflection, social commentary, and high-class gossip. Concision, though, was a virtue that they never possessed; Sand, like most writers who were paid by the line for their efforts, never used one word where three would do. It seemed advisable, therefore, when presenting her Letter to Liszt within the context of this volume, to condense it by summarizing those portions of it which do not pertain in some way to music or to him.

On Lavater and a Deserted House
[To Franz Liszt][1]

[July-August 1835]

As I do not know where you are at present,[2] my dear Franz, nor even where I will be going, I am sending you my news through your oblig-

---

letter "Spring 1834," but the internal evidence indicates that it was written about 1 July of that year.

2. Sand's *Lettres* were written 1834–1836 and, with one exception, published in the *Revue des deux mondes*, to whom Sand was under contract at the time. The collected edition of them appeared in 1837.

---

1. *Revue des deux mondes*, 1 September 1835, pp. 551–86. Liszt's name was not included when the article was originally published. It first appeared in the collected edition of the *Lettres* although it had been abundantly clear to all who "mon cher Franz" was.

2. A bit of subterfuge; Sand knew exactly where Liszt and Marie d'Agoult were and had been corresponding regularly with them, but she respected their wish to keep their precise whereabouts a secret.

ing Genevan friend. I think that he will be able to discover your retreat before I can, confined as I am to mine for some days to come.

I need not tell you how sorry I am about not being able to come and join you. Your mother, I see, is setting forth, as well as Puzzi and his family.[3] I presume that you are going to establish a holy colony of artists in beautiful Switzerland or verdant Bohemia. Happy friends! How noble and sweet is the art to which you have dedicated yourselves! How dry and disagreeable is mine by comparison! I must work in silence and solitude, while the musician lives in harmony, sympathy, and union with his pupils and colleagues. Music is taught, is revealed, is disseminated and communicated. Doesn't the harmony of sounds demand a like harmony of wills and feelings? What a wonderful republic is created when a hundred instrumentalists gather in a common spirit of order and love to perform a great master's symphony! When Beethoven's spirit soars above that sacred chorus, what fervent prayer rises to God! And last spring when you merged your magic language with Urhan's viola and Batta's cello, what implacable skies would not have opened to allow that sublime trio to ascend to heaven![4]

Yes, music is prayer, it is faith, it is friendship, it is the preeminent form of association. There, where only three of you are gathered together in my name, Christ said as he was leaving his apostles, you may be sure that I will be with you. The apostles were soon dispersed, condemned to travel, to labor, and to suffer. But when they met at times between prison and martyrdom, between the chains of Caiaphas and the stones of the synagogue, they knelt together beside the road, in some olive grove, or on the outskirts of some town, in an *upper room,* and they spoke about their master and friend Jesus, the Brother and the God to whose worship they had dedicated their lives. Then, after each had spoken in turn, the need to call in unison upon the spirit of their dear Friend must surely have inspired them to think of singing. Surely too the Holy Spirit, which descended upon them in tongues of fire and revealed the unknown to them, must have given them the gift

---

3. Sand is again deceptive; Madame Liszt never left Paris. She had such difficulty, in fact, accepting the role that Marie d'Agoult had assumed in her son's life that she steadfastly refused to consider even visiting the couple in Geneva. On the other hand, Liszt's favored, fourteen-year-old pupil Puzzi, accompanied by his own mother and brother, did move to Geneva in mid-August 1835 to continue his lessons (see below, note 10).

4. The only trio performance by these three that Sand could have heard took place on 7 May at a concert given by soprano Madame Duflot-Maillard. They played a trio by Joseph Mayseder (1789–1863). Urhan, for one, was especially fond of Mayseder's music and made a special effort to promote it in Paris.

of that sacred tongue which belongs only to the elect. Oh! you can be sure that if some beings were great enough in the sight of God to merit the sudden acquisition of new faculties, if their minds were opened, their tongues loosened, divine songs must have flowed from their lips, and that first, harmonious concert must have ravished men's ears.

What a unique event in the history of mankind—and one that I cannot keep from venerating when I think about it—was that retreat the apostles made for forty days, that fervent union, that untainted purity of twelve believing and devoted souls who withstood the trials of being together for so long! If I ever doubted that miracles would result from it, I would not say so, and neither would you, isn't that so? If it were proved to me that these men were very accomplished physicians and alchemists for their time, I would say that that in no way detracts from the reality of a Divine Man nor from the existence of a race of saints powerful enough to walk on water and to raise the dead. The miraculous power faith grants to men is, to me, indisputable. Thus, even if it were demonstrated that the apostles had to have recourse to the tricks that were then called magic, I would think that it was a time of doubt and suffering during which the heavenly power in them had ebbed. Let someone find twelve men among us, I would respond, who were superior to the apostles in the intensity of their faith and the sanctity of their lives, twelve men who could spend forty days confined under the same roof without wrangling among themselves or trying to lord it over one another, who were concerned solely with prayer, asking God for knowledge of the truth and the strength of virtue without being halfhearted or ostentatious, without giving in to spiritual fatigue or the presumptuous urgings of the flesh—Oh! have no doubt it my friends—we would see miracles, new sciences, unprecedented capabilities, and a universal faith. Man, *made divine again,* would emerge from that gathering one fine spring day with a flame on his brow, with the secrets of life and death in his hand, with the power to make tears of charity flow from a stone, with the knowledge of tongues that people still unknown to us speak, but above all, with the gift of that most perfect and divine of languages; music raised to the zenith of its eloquence and persuasiveness.

Because, when the wondrous descent of the Paraclete took place, the heavens opened above the heads of Jesus' disciples and they must have heard and retained in some hazy fashion the songs of the fiery seraphim and the sounds of the golden harps held by those beautiful crowned elders who later reappeared to John of the Apocalypse, allowing him to hear their heavenly chords above the winds of a stormy night on the deserted sands of his island.

Oh! you who perceive holy mysteries in the silence of the night; you, my dear Franz, whose ears have been opened by the spirit of God so that you might hear heaven's concerts from afar and transmit them to us—we who are so weak and forsaken—how fortunate you are to be able to pray during the day with hearts that understand you! Your work does not condemn you, as mine does, to solitude; your fervor is rekindled at that congenial hearth where everyone who loves you brings his tribute. Go on then, pray in the language of angels and sing God's praises on those instruments set vibrating by the breath of heaven.

As for me, a solitary traveler, things are not like that. The roads I take are deserted, and I look for a refuge within silent walls. I had started out to join you last month, but a quirk of fate or a caprice shunted me from my path.

[Sand goes on to say that she had not been feeling well and stopped to rest in a city "on the banks of the Loire." There she happened to meet an old friend who offered her the use of a ramshackle, deserted old house he owned in the outskirts of the city.[5] She describes the house and its overgrown garden: in all, it is a poetic, mysterious place, still populated by ancient woodland spirits. She continues:]

Yes, Franzi, I am still in that deserted house; alone, absolutely alone, never opening the outside door except to admit a cenobitic dinner, and I cannot recall having known sweeter and purer days. It is a great comfort to me, I assure you, to realize that my spirit has not kept watch for so long that it has become inured to the joys of its vibrant younger days. If vast dreams of virtue and fervent aspirations to the heavens no longer fill my contemplative hours, I, at least, still have consoling thoughts and religious hopes; but then I am no longer devoured, as I once was, by the impatience to live. The closer I get to life's decline, the more I savor, piously and justly, the generous and providential things that it has to offer. On the far side of the hill, I pause and descend slowly, casting a loving, admiring glance at the beauties of the place I leave behind and which I did not really appreciate when I was at the summit of the hill and could have enjoyed it fully.[6]

5. The "old friend" was Sand's relatively new lover, Louis-Chrysostom Michel, known as Michel de Bourges (1798–1853), an attorney, spellbinding orator, and champion of Republicanism. She spent most of the summer—actually with him—at his house in Bourges.

6. In view of these anile comments, it is worth nothing that Sand has just turned thirty-one years old. She was a year and a half older than Marie d'Agoult.

You, my child, who have yet to arrive at the summit, do not proceed too quickly. Do not be too lighthearted about scaling those sublime heights from which one can only descend, never to scale them again. Ah! your fate is better than mine. Enjoy it, do not disdain it. As a man, you have the treasure of your best years at hand. As an artist, you serve a more fertile and delightful muse than mine. You are her darling, while mine is beginning to find me old and has, moreover, condemned me to melancholy, lonely dreams that would destroy your precious poetry. Go on then, live! The brilliant flowers of your crown demand the sun. The ivy and bindweeds of mine, symbols of the wild freedom with which the ancient woodland deities girded themselves, grow in shadow and among ruins. I am not complaining about my destiny, and I am glad that Providence has given you a happier one; you deserve it, and were it mine, Franz, I would yield it to you.

And so I have remained at ————; at first because I had no choice; at present because I love the reading and the solitude; and later, perhaps, I will stay here because I am lazy and would like to get out of myself and forget the hours flying by. But I want to share with you some good luck I had in my retreat which contributed greatly to my liking for this place.

You, who read a great deal, even though you do not have the same respect as I do for books (and you are right, since your art must make you disdain ours)—you, I say, who grasp things quickly and devour volume after volume—you have no idea how important slow and attentive reading is for a mind as lazy as mine.

[Sand discusses reading in general, especially the joys of her childhood reading. Among the books that made a lasting impression on her were those by the physiognomist Lavater (1741–1801). She continues:]

The day I arrived here I opened a cupboard filled with books, and the first thing I picked up was the works of Johann-Caspar Lavater, minister of the holy gospel in Zurich; published in 1781, the three folio volumes are translated into French, with plates, etchings, etc. You can just imagine my joy, and I can assure you that I have never read anything more pleasant, instructive, and beneficial. Poetry, wisdom, profound observation, goodness, religious feeling, evangelical charity, morality, fine sensitivity, nobility, and simplicity of style—those were the qualities I found in Lavater, when I was only looking for some physiognomical observations and conclusions, erroneous perhaps, but at least tentative and conjectural.

Since you ask for a long letter and are very taken up with intellectual works, I will talk to you about Lavater. It would, moreover, be difficult for me, considering where I am and the life I lead, to tell you anything about the more recent books. I want with all my heart to create a desire in you to get to know this old guest, this venerable friend I have just discovered here.

Further, as you, following the example of the proud innovators of our time, may have so far scorned the science of Lavater as a tissue of dreams based on a false principle, I would also like to have the pleasure of changing your mind. Today we regard physiognomy as a science that has been judged, condemned, and buried. Upon its ruins another science has arisen, phrenology, which has yet to be judged but which is now deemed worthier of study and attention. I hate the scorn and lack of appreciation with which our generation overthrows the idols of its fathers and how, after having crucified the doctors and the masters, it flatters the disciples. To prefer Schiller to Shakespeare, Corneille to the Spanish tragedians, Molière to the writers of Greek and Latin comedy, La Fontaine to Phaedrus or Aesop, strikes me not just as an error but a crime.

[The bulk of Sand's letter follows: she extols Lavater, admires his modest attitude and perceptive analyses, and quotes paragraph after paragraph from him. She observes that Lavater "is a Christian and a believer in spiritual values. He thinks, as do you and I, that man is *free,* that he has received from the hands of Providence his ever-equitable share of the great legacy of good and evil that He left to the first man." At one point Sand singles out the portrait of a painter, Henry Fuseli (1741–1825), and remarks on its striking similarity to Liszt's "best friend," leaving it to him to judge its "ethical resemblance." The engraving and Lavater's analysis of it would seem to suggest that she was thinking of Chopin, but it is not possible to be certain. She then returns to more personal observations:]

For my part, I have always felt that certain human constitutions were so finely wrought that they possessed quasi-divinatory powers. Their earthly covering is so ethereal, so diaphanous, so sensitive that their animating spirit seems able to peer through and penetrate the material substance that covers or comprises the external world. Their fiber is so delicate and fine that everything that escapes the coarser senses of other men causes them to vibrate, just as the slightest breath causes the strings of an aeolian harp to stir and tremble. You, my dear Franz, must be one of those perfected, quasi-angelic beings. Your physiognomy, complexion, imagination, and genius disclose those capabilities with which heaven endows its *elected ones*. As for me, I am one of those who sleep by night and who walk and eat by day. I have one of those constitutions that are active, robust, carefree, inured to fatigue, and insensitive to all the delicacies of perception and the revelations of magnetic attraction. I have been too much the peasant, the bohemian, and the warrior. I have thickened my shell. I have toughened the skin of my feet on the stones of all the roads, and I am astonished to recall those childhood days when the slightest disturbance or expectation would have made me shrivel like a sensitive plant. Why have I turned to stone? . . .

Had I known him, Lavater would have exercised great influence over me; even from the depths of the tomb his intellectual prowess combined with his great virtue and deep wisdom make a lively and indelible impression upon my heart. Since being confined to this retreat, I find that the memories of all those I hold dear have only come to me through the magic mirror he has set before my eyes. Seeing you, my dear phantoms, oh my friends! my masters! I salute the wealth of greatness and goodness that is in you and which the finger of God has inscribed in sacred characters on your noble brows! The immense vault of Everard's bald head,[7] so handsome and so large, so finished and perfect in its contours that there is no way of knowing which one of his wonderful faculties rules over the others; the nose, the chin, the eyebrows that would tremble with energy were it not for the exquisite delicacy of intelligence found in the nostrils, the superhuman kindness of the gaze, and the tolerant wisdom in the lips; the head, which is that of both a hero and a saint—all these things have appeared in my dreams beside the stern and awesome face of great Lamennais.[8] His brow is a solid wall, a sheet of steel, the seat of indomitable strength, and like Everard's, as Lavater writes, it is "furrowed between the eyebrows with those incisive perpendicular marks that belong exclusively to those of great capacity, whose ideas are sane and noble." There is no doubt that the stark profile and the sharp angularity of the face bespeak his inflexible integrity and hermit-like austerity, and the constant activity of a mind as glowing and vast as the heavens. But the smile that

7. Michel de Bourges.
8. Liszt had introduced Sand to Lamennais at a small dinner party he gave for them in May shortly before he left Paris.

suddenly humanizes that face changes my awe into confidence, my respect into adoration. Can't you just see them taking each other by the hand, these two men with their frail constitutions, who nonetheless appeared to be giants to astonished Parisians when the defense of a holy cause recently summoned them from their retreats and raised them atop the Mount of Jerusalem, there to pray and to threaten, to bless the people, and to strike fear into the pharisees and doctors of the law, even unto the synagogues.[9]

I see them constantly as I wander at night through the large, dimly lit rooms of my deserted house. Behind them I see Lavater with his direct, open gaze, his pointed nose indicating subtlety and sensitivity, his ennobling resemblance to Erasmus, his fatherly attitude, and his warm and compassionate words. He tells me: "Go, follow them. Try to emulate them. Behold your masters, behold your guides. Give ear to their counsel, follow their precepts, repeat the holy words of their prayers. They know God and will teach you His ways. Go, my son; may your injuries be healed, may your wounds be closed, may your soul be purified and don a new robe, may the Lord bless you and return you to His flock."

But I also see other phantoms, less imposing yet full of grace and charm. They are my comrades, my brothers. It is you, above all, my dear Franz, whom I place in a picture flooded with light, a magic vision surging through the dark shadows of my contemplative evenings. In the candlelight, through a halo of admiration that crowns and envelops you while your fingers fashion new wonders from the wonders

9. The "holy cause" Sand mentions is to be found in one of the most sensational trials in French political history. Briefly, in May 1835, 120 leaders of the Republican party (i.e., the moderate to radical left) were indicted on charges of fomenting insurrection and/or belonging to radical societies. These charges stemmed from the party's alleged role in inciting the violent riots that had broken out among the workers of Lyons in April 1834 and had spread to other cities, including Paris. While there was a large element of truth in the charges, the trial itself was a patent attempt by Louis-Philippe's conservative government to discredit the Republicans. It was this aspect of the case, not just the criminality, that summoned such liberals as Lamennais and Michel to Paris; Lamennais to lend whatever support he could, and Michel to participate directly as one of the defense attorneys. To heighten the significance of the proceedings, the Conservatives staged the mass trial—"le procès monstre," as it was called—in a large wooden pavilion erected for the purpose at the Luxembourg. The trial lasted for three months, and when the verdict was handed down on 13 August all the defendants were condemned, some to prison, some to exile. The condemnation might not have been so wholesale and so harsh, perhaps, had not a particularly horrifying attempt been made on Louis-Philippe's life while the trial was in progress (see note 17 below).

of Weber, I love to see your affectionate gaze as it descends towards me and seems to say, "Brother, do you understand me? It is to your soul that I am speaking!" Oh yes, young friend, yes, inspired artist, I do understand that divine language, even though I cannot speak it. Would that I were at least a painter, so that I could capture those flashes of lightning that embrace and illuminate you when heavenly inspiration descends upon you, when a bluish flame courses through your hair, and the purest of muses beams smilingly over us.

But were I to paint that picture, I would not want to omit your charming and favorite pupil, Puzzi.[10] Raphael[11] and his young friend Thebaldeo never possessed more grace in the eyes of God and men than did you, my dear children, when I saw you one night across a hundred-piece orchestra, the hushed audience waiting to hear you perform, and when the boy standing behind you—pale, visibly moved, still as a statue and yet trembling like a flower about to drop its petals—seemed to imbibe the music through his every pore and open his chaste lips to drink the honey you poured out to him.[12] They say the arts have lost their poetry, but truly, I have scarcely noticed it. Have Italy's bright days ever produced a holier, more dedicated artistic existence than yours, Franz? And setting aside several people whom we know and esteem, has heaven ever fashioned a more beautiful soul, a subtler mind, a more interesting face than that of our Hermann? That is to say, our Puzzi, since he must for many years to come bear that delightful nickname you sanctified in your own youth and which brought you happiness.

Well, now! Haven't we spent beautiful mornings and lovely evenings in my blue-curtained garret, that humble studio close to the snow on the roof in winter and hot as the leaden dungeons of Venice in the summer?[13] But what did that matter? A few engravings after

10. Puzzi—that is, Hermann Cohen (1820–1871), or simply "the pianist Hermann" in professional terms (see E. H. M. von Asow, "Hermann Cohen").

11. Earlier in the Letter, Sand had quoted Lavater's comments about Raphael: "Raphael is and always will be an apostolic man, which is to say that painters regard him in the same way that the general run of men regard the apostles of Christ, and just as his works show him to be superior to all the artists of his class, so his beautiful face distinguishes him from ordinary men.—Where is the mortal man who can compare to him? Whenever I want to fill myself with admiration for the perfection of God's work, I need only recall the figure of Raphael!"

12. Sand is probably thinking of the orchestral concert given by the "Gymnase musical" on 23 May 1835, at which Liszt performed a "piece by Weber," surely the *Conzertstück*.

13. Sand's widely known and frequented studio on the Quai Malaquais—"la mansarde bleue."

Raphael, a mat of Spanish jute to stretch out on, some good pipefuls, the clever little cat Trozzi, flowers, some well-chosen books, and above all, poetry (oh, language of the gods that I also understood but cannot speak!), isn't that enough for an artist's loft? Read poetry to me, go to the piano and improvise those wonderful pastorals that make old Everard and me sob as they remind us of our youth, our hills, and the goats we tended. At such a moment, let me savor the rapture of latakia tobacco or fall ecstatically into a corner behind a pile of cushions. Haven't we known beautiful days? Haven't we been the dutiful children of a God who blesses simple souls? Haven't we seen the hours fly by without wanting to hurry their course as the men of our time do in order to pursue who knows what miserable ambition or personal gratification? Do you remember Puzzi sitting at the feet of the Breton saint,[14] who said such wonderful things to him with the kindness and simplicity of an apostle? Do you remember Everard, deep in melancholy rapture while you played, suddenly rising to tell you in his deep voice, "Young man, you are sublime!"? And my brother Emmanuel hiding me in one of the huge folds of his great coat in order to sneak me into the Chamber of Peers,[15] and how, when we returned to my house, he set me upon the piano, telling you "The next time you will have to put a paper cone on my dear brother's head so that he doesn't muss his hair"? Do you remember the blond peri in an azure gown,[16] a kind and noble creature who descended from heaven to the poet's loft one evening and sat between us, like one of those marvelous princesses who appear to poor artists in the delightful tales by Hoffmann? Do you remember that other, less fanciful but patently ludicrous visit, when we behaved like such impudent schoolboys that I still laugh about it, alone in the shadows of the night. . . . Hush! the echoes of the deserted house, unaccustomed to such unseemly behavior, are waking and responding to me in an irritated tone. The household gods are looking at one another in astonishment and considering driving me away.

14. Lamennais.

15. Emmanuel Arago (1812–1896), a young lawyer and later diplomat, who had come under Sand's spell that spring. He was evidently with her on 20 May when she, donning men's clothes, brazened her way into the exclusively male gallery of the Chamber of Peers (the trial chamber) to observe "le procès monstre."

16. Marie d'Agoult is meant, but it is not clear whether Sand actually met Madame d'Agoult in Paris at this time or whether she was just being gracious, since a later letter of Sand to d'Agoult, September 1835, begins: "My beautiful countess with the golden hair, I do not know you, but I have heard Franz speak of you and I have seen you." The ladies' first face-to-face meeting is a point that various biographers still disagree about.

[Sand then returns to ruminating about the deserted, crumbling house, the solitary life, and her advancing years. She concludes with the following, which is set off by a row of dots as a kind of epilogue.]

Last night a great hubbub interrupted my sleep. The police rang as if to shatter the bell, they knocked as if to break the door. Finally they shouted to me through the slot in the door, like a Molière comedy, "Open, in the name of the King!" This time I was not afraid; what is there to fear when one has a valid passport in one's pocket? The police found mine in order. However, the shafts of light that people sometimes noticed in the windows of this uninhabited house and the daily Pythagorian dinner delivered through the slot in the door had made some of the neighbors very fearful and apprehensive. At first the light made me seem like a ghost, but the dinners, by disclosing my corporeal existence, made me seem like a conspirator. This morning I had to go and give an account of my behavior to the magistrates. My innocence was quickly established, but in the process I learned that the face of France had changed during my retreat. The explosion of an *infernal machine,* the results of which had been tragic enough in themselves, had given the despotic regime some supposed rights over the purest and most peaceful of our brothers.[17] Savage acts can be expected from that insolent power that styles itself law and order. Well, so be it! Life is life, Franz; there will be suffering, there will be work to be done, just as there will be life to live. Will one disaster more or less change

17. Sand is referring to the attempt that was made on Louis-Philippe's life during a review of the National Guard held on 28 July 1835 to mark the fifth anniversary of the July Revolution. A Corsican-born adventurer, Joseph Fieschi (1790–1836), devised the "infernal machine"—two dozen rifles, each loaded with ball and shot, mounted on two wooden racks, and linked together with gun powder so that they would fire simultaneously. It was installed at a window overlooking the king's route, and when Fieschi fired it he exacted a grisly toll. Louis-Philippe escaped with a slightly grazed forehead, but forty others among his party and those lining the parade route were not so lucky: eighteen were killed and twenty-two wounded (Andre Castelot, *The Turbulent City,* pp. 205–10). The vicious attempt not only horrified France but, coming as it did during the mass trial, it also elicited a stern and harsh response from the government in the form of the so-called "September laws." These laws, among other things, created special courts to try, even *in absentia*, all those who were seen as a threat to the security of the state. They also severely curbed the press by imposing punitive fines for "seditious" articles.—Although it may be difficult under the circumstances to condone Sand's casual remark about "one disaster more or less," she was not the only one to sense a real danger in these laws: Liszt, for instance, wrote to Lamartine that September to compliment him on the plea he had made for continued freedom of the press, "the holiest of causes, the most imperishable of doctrines" (Jacques Vier, "Liszt et Lamartine," p. 181).

that? Man is free because of God's will. The body can be chained and destroyed, but moral man cannot be subjugated. They say that there will be sentences of death or banishment passed against our friends. We ourselves have nothing to do with politics, but we are the children of those whom they want to strike down. I know whom you would follow to the scaffold or into exile, and you know for whom I would do the same. So, Franz, when we see each other again, it will perhaps no longer be as happy travelers, no longer as carefree artists in the delightful valleys of Switzerland or in the concert halls or in a pleasant Parisian garret, but rather on the other side of the ocean or in prison or at the foot of a scaffold—because it is easy to share the fate of those one loves once one has firmly decided to do so; and however weak or obscure a person may be, he can always count on an enemy's compassion to kill or imprison him. They seek to create martyrs, people say: The Lord be praised! Our cause has been won before the tribunal of posterity! Greetings, brother Franz, let's be cheerful. As long as one can sacrifice oneself for someone and die for a cause, these are not desolate times. What can they deny us, we who have never asked anything of the world? Do we have some insane ambition that must be cured, some greedy thirst that must be slaked? People with possessions are wretched; they can never prevail over those who shun such things. Will they deprive us of one another? Can they keep us from living for our brothers and dying with them? . . .

While I was out, my friend, the owner of the deserted house returned from the country. He had the grass in the courtyard cut, the vines pruned. The windows are open, the daylight and the flies enter the rooms. The house, in his opinion, has been put in order; in mine, it has been devastated. These mutilations, this vandalism, are they an omen of what is to happen in France? Let us go and see. I am leaving. Where will I go? I do not know—somewhere where one of our kindred spirits will have the need for a person like me who has no need of anyone, only of God!

I received news of you in a letter from Puzzi. You have a piano done in mother-of-pearl; you play beside a window that faces the lake overlooking the sublime snows of Mont Blanc! That is beautiful and good, Franz. Yours is a noble and pure life. But if our saints are persecuted, you will leave the lake, the glacier, and the mother-of-pearl piano, just as I am leaving Lavater, the leafy vines, and the deserted house, and you will take up your pilgrim's staff and sack just as I am doing now by embracing you and saying adieu, my brother, until I see you again!

B

HEINRICH HEINE:
CONFIDENTIAL LETTER

Heinrich Heine (1797–1856) came to Paris in 1831 to escape the constraints that he, a politically liberal, baptized Jew, had experienced in his native Germany. He loved the city, thrived in its liberal atmosphere, and took an immediate, active interest in the Saint-Simonians meeting at the Salle Taitbout, which is probably where the renowned poet and young Liszt first met.

Settling in the French capital, Heine produced a steady flow of journalistic reports about Parisian life for the German press, articles in which he discussed the leading French artists, the Paris Salon, and French political conditions. Then in 1837 he wrote the account of Berlioz, Liszt, Thalberg, and Chopin which concerns us here. It first appeared as the last of a series of ten "Letters on the French Stage" which were published that year in the *Allgemeine Theater-Revue* in Stuttgart. Liszt, in Italy at the time, evidently knew nothing then about the article. Some months later, however, the *Gazette musicale*[1] published a revised, translated version of Heine's typically fanciful and mordant article,[2] and that is how it first came to Liszt's attention, prompting his response in chapter 7.

---

1. The *Gazette musicale* actually published two of Heine's *Briefe über die französische Bühne*: the ninth, discussing Meyerbeer, which appeared as "Lettres confidentielles 1" on 21 January 1838, and the tenth, discussing Liszt et al., which followed two weeks later.

2. The French article, which is the one translated here, differs in many particulars from both Heine's original German text and its subsequently revised version as reprinted in his collection *Der Salon*. For a comparison of these texts, see Heine, *Historiche-kritische Gesamtausgabe*, vol. 12/1, pp. 496–502.

Heinrich Heine: Confidential Letter 2[1]

. . . .

The foregoing should provide an understanding of the present spirit of French grand opera.[2] It has signed a truce with the enemies of music, and the affluent middle class, seeing that the aristocracy had ceded the field to them, has invaded the Royal Academy on Rue Pelletier [the Opéra] as it did the Tuileries. The elite of fashionable society, which is known for its rank, education, birth, elegance, and idleness, have taken refuge at the Théâtre-Italien, that musical oasis where the great nightingales of art still sing, where the magical springs of melody yet flow, and where beauty's palms waft their proud fronds . . . while nothing but a sterile desert, a musical Sahara, lies all around them. Some isolated concerts surge at times like freshets through the arid land, bringing extraordinary refreshment to music lovers. Among such events this past winter, one can note the Sunday Concerts at the conservatory, some private soirées on the Rue de Bondy, and above all the concerts of Berlioz and Liszt. These two men are quite the most remarkable phenomena in the musical world.

We will soon be having an opera by Berlioz. Its subject is an episode in the life of Benvenuto Cellini, the casting of his *Perseus*.[3] It is expected to be something extraordinary, for this composer has already done extraordinary things. His particular turn of mind leads him to the fanciful, combined not with tender simplicity, but with a sense of passion. He has a great affinity with Gozzi and Hoffman. Even his physical appearance announces something out of the ordinary. It is a pity that he has trimmed his monstrous, antediluvian head of hair, a shaggy mop that he combed forward over his forehead like a primeval forest towering on a rocky cliff. That was how I first saw him six years ago and is how I will continue to see him in my mind's eye. It was at the Conservatory where they were performing a big symphony of his,[4] a strange, tenebrous work, shot through at rare intervals with the vision of a woman's sentimentally white gown fluttering here and there, or with a sulphurous flash of irony. One of the best sections, or at least the one that struck me the most, is a Witches' Sabbath, where the devil

---

1. *Gazette musicale*, 4 February 1838, pp. 41–44.

2. The *Gazette* did not include the "foregoing." In the original article Heine had been having some heavy-handed fun with the way the Opéra's management catered to its star performers.

3. Berlioz's *Benvenuto Cellini* was first performed at the Opéra on 10 September 1838. See "The *Perseus* of Benvenuto Cellini," chap. 8.

4. The *Symphonie fantastique*, a performance given in December 1832.

chants the mass and the music of the Catholic Church is parodied with the most horrible, the most outrageous mockery. It is a farce, in which all the serpents we secretly hide in our hearts rear up hissing with pleasure and bite off their tails in a paroxysm of joy.

My companion in the box, a talkative young man, pointed out the composer to me. He was at the rear of the orchestra playing the timpani; that is his instrument. "Do you see that pretty English woman in the proscenium box?" continued my neighbor. "That is Miss Smithson,[5] whom the French actresses have imitated so. For three years Berlioz has been madly in love with her, and it is to that passion that we owe the savage symphony we are hearing today." I looked at the celebrated actress from Covent Garden in the proscenium box. Berlioz, for his part, made no secret of looking at her constantly, and every time their eyes met, he pounded furiously on the drum. Miss Smithson has since become Madame Berlioz,[6] and her husband has had his locks trimmed. Last winter when I attended another performance of his symphony, I saw him at his accustomed place behind the timpani at the rear of the orchestra. The pretty English woman was again in front of the proscenium. Their eyes met, but he no longer pounded the drum with such fury.*

Liszt is the man who relates most closely to Berlioz and knows best how to perform his music. I need not tell you about his talent; his reputation is European. In Paris he is, without doubt, the artist who has the most dedicated admirers as well as the most vigorous detractors. The fact that no one talks indifferently about him is in itself significant. Without some personal value, there is no way on earth to excite friendly or hostile emotions. Fire is needed to inflame people, for hatred as much as for love. The most telling factor in Liszt's favor is the true esteem with which even his enemies regard him as a person. His character is unsettled,[7] but as a man, he is noble, impartial, and

---

*This letter was originally written in the early spring of 1837. Since then a transformation has taken place in Berlioz's music, the proof of which can be found in the more *melodic* and gentler character of his Second Symphony [Harold in Italy], as well as in his latest work, the Requiem in honor of those who died at Constantine, a work whose style differs essentially from that of his previous works and whose reputation has resounded throughout Europe.

5. Harriet Smithson (1800–1854). Berlioz first saw and fell in love with her when she was performing with Charles Kemble's Shakespearean company in Paris in September 1827.

6. The marriage took place on 3 October 1833. Liszt was one of the witnesses to the ceremony.

7. *Mal assis*, literally, "poorly or badly seated." In the German publication, Heine had described Liszt's character as *verschroben*, "confused, wrong-headed."

straightforward. His intellectual proclivities are quite remarkable; he has a very lively taste for speculation and is less preoccupied with his own artistic interests than with the investigations of the various schools of thought dealing with the great questions of heaven and earth. For a long time he was full of enthusiasm for the sketchy pronouncements of the Saint-Simonians. Later he lost himself in the spiritual, or rather the nebulous, ideas of Ballanche.[8] Today he raves about the Catholic-republican doctrines of one Lamennais, who has placed a Jacobin cap[9] on the cross. . . . Heaven only knows in what philosophical stable he will find his next hobbyhorse. Yet it is impossible not to praise that indefatigable thirst for enlightenment and divinity which manifests itself in his predilection for sacred and religious matters. Given such a restless mind, torn in every direction by all the doctrines and the miseries of our time, feeling the need to torment himself over all the interests of humanity, loving to stick his nose into all the pots in which God is cooking up the future of mankind, it is easy to understand why Franz Liszt is not the placid pianist to entertain peaceable citizens and sensible cotton bonnets. When he sits down at the piano, sweeps his long hair back several times, and starts to improvise, he often hurls himself furiously at the ivory keys, creating a towering wilderness of chaotic thoughts throughout which flowers of the sweetest sentiment disperse their fragrance. He overpowers and inflames you at one and the same time, but the feeling of being overpowered predominates.

I must confess that despite my friendship for Liszt, his music does not affect my feelings in an agreeable way, especially since I, unfortunately, am visually minded and see the phantoms that other people can only hear. You know that each tone on the piano leads my imagination to conjure up the image corresponding to that tone; that music, in a word, is visible to my mind's eye. I am still stunned by the recollection of the last concert at which I heard Liszt perform. It was at that concert for needy Italian émigrés given at the residence of the

8. In an earlier article (May 1836) describing an elegant soirée, Heine had noted: "They began with music. Franz Liszt, having allowed himself to be drawn to the piano, swept back his hair from his gifted forehead and served up one of his most brilliant battles. The keys appeared to bleed. If I am not mistaken, he played a passage from the *Palingénésie* by Ballanche, whose ideas he translated into music—a very useful thing for those who are incapable of reading the works of the renowned writer in their original form" ("Les Nuits Florentines II," which was reprinted in vol. 3 (1837) of Heine's *Der Salon*).

9. During the Revolution the Jacobins, under Robespierre, were the most extreme of the revolutionary groups.

beautiful and noble princess who truly personifies her twofold home-land, Italy and heaven.[10] In Paris, you have no doubt seen that slim and elegant figure, which is but the earthly prison in which a divine soul languishes. . . . Yet what a beautiful prison! . . . Thus it was this past winter at that concert for unfortunate Italians that I last heard Liszt play—who knows what? But I would surely have bet that he improvised on themes from the Apocalypse. At first I could not see the four mystical beasts distinctly; I only heard their voices; the roar of the lion especially, and the cry of the eagle. As for the ox with a book in his hands, I could make him out quite plainly. The Valley of Jehosha-phat was what Liszt rendered best. The lists were set out for a tourna-ment, and the spectators who thronged about the huge space were the resurrected nations, deathly pale and trembling. First to enter was Sa-tan, who galloped into the arena clad in black armor and mounted on a blood-red steed. Death followed slowly, riding his pale horse. Finally, Christ appeared clad in golden armor on a white charger. With a thrust of His lance He drove Satan to the ground and Death after him, while the spectators cried out with joy. They enthusiastically applauded the performance of the gallant Liszt, who rose exhausted from the piano and bowed to the ladies. . . . On the lips of the most beautiful of them there was a sweet, melancholy smile that recalled Italy and hinted at heaven.

That concert was also a particularly interesting one for the public. The newspapers, as you know, have been more than filled with the misunderstanding that developed between Liszt and the Viennese pi-anist Thalberg, with the uproar that Liszt's article against Thalberg raised in the musical world,[11] and with the part that their enemies and fanatical partisans played in the matter, to the detriment of criticism as well as to the parties involved. Even at the early stages of that scandal-ous collision, the two heroes of the day had agreed to perform in turn at the concert I just mentioned. They put aside their personal resent-ment, and the audience, whom they provided with an instant compar-ison of their respective skills, gave them the unstinting approval they both had earned.

One need but compare the musical character of the two to be convinced that only malice or ignorance would praise one at the ex-pense of the other. Their technical prowess was evenly balanced, and as for the spirit of their playing, it is impossible to imagine a sharper

10. Princess Cristina Belgiojoso. The concert was her charity gala on 31 March 1837, at which both Liszt and Thalberg performed. See p. 26.
11. Liszt's review in the *Gazette musicale*, 8 January 1837.

contrast than between Thalberg—noble, sensitive, intelligent, tender, serene, German, or even Austrian—and Liszt—possessed, tempestuous, volcanic, and as fiery as a titan.

The comparison between these two musicians is usually based on an error that existed for a time in the art of poetry; that is, the principle of "the difficulty overcome." But once we realized that metrical form serves a completely different purpose than merely demonstrating the poet's adroit handling of language and that we do not consider a verse beautiful simply because it took a lot of trouble to write, we can likewise realize that it is quite enough for a musician to be totally able to convey through his instrument all that he feels and thinks, or that others have felt and thought, and that all those virtuoso tours de force whose only merit is the difficulty overcome should be rejected as empty, useless noise and relegated to the realm of carnival tricks along with juggling, death-defying leaps, sword swallowing, and dancing on a tightrope or on eggs. It is enough for a musician to have total control over his instrument so that one can ignore the technique completely and listen only to the spirit of the playing. Moreover, since Kalkbrenner[12] has raised piano playing to such a height of perfection, pianists should not be overly conceited about their manual dexterity. Only intrigue and ill will could have spoken pedantically of a revolution that Thalberg was supposed to have brought about on his instrument. People did that great and excellent artist a disservice when, instead of praising the youthful purity, finesse, and charm of his playing, they portrayed him as a Christopher Columbus who had discovered a pianistic America while other pianists were arduously thumping about the Cape of Good Hope searching for musical spices. How curiously Kalkbrenner must have smiled when he heard all the talk about the new discovery.

It would be wrong on this occasion not to speak of a pianist whose renown is second only to Liszt's: Chopin, who can, with justification, serve to prove that the ability to rival the most accomplished performers in the perfection of technique is not enough for an extraordinary man. Chopin's satisfaction surely does not come from having the dexterity of his hands applauded by other hands. He aspires to a higher type of success; his fingers are but the servants of his soul, and

12. Friedrich Kalkbrenner (1785–1849), German-born pianist trained at the Paris Conservatory. Active as a teacher and composer, he was regarded as the smoothest, most accomplished technician of the Hummel-Moscheles generation. Chopin made his Paris debut in 1832 under his aegis, and Liszt found his piano *Method* (1830) very useful for polishing his own technique (*Pages romantiques*, p. 40).

his soul is applauded by those who listen not only with their ears but also with their own souls. Hence, he is the favorite of that elite who seek the most elevated intellectual pleasures in music. His success is of an aristocratic sort. His fame, one might say, is perfumed by the praises of polite society; it is elegant, as he himself is.

Chopin was born in Poland of French parents, and his education was completed in Germany.[13] The diverse influences of these three nationalities made him into a most remarkable person. He has appropriated the best qualities which distinguish the three nations; Poland has given him her chivalrous feelings and historic suffering; France, her smooth elegance and grace; Germany, her dreamy profundity . . . but Nature gave him a slender, stylish, and rather frail figure, the noblest of hearts, and genius. One must surely grant that Chopin has genius in the broadest sense of the word. He is not only a virtuoso, but very much a poet as well. He is able to reveal the poetry that lives in his soul. He is a poet-musician, and nothing can compare with the delight he gives us when he improvises at the piano. At such moments he is neither Polish, French, nor German, but discloses a nobler origin: he comes from the land of Mozart, Raphael, and Goethe—his true homeland is the land of poetry.

When he improvises he seems to me like a compatriot who has just arrived from my country to tell me about the strangest things that have happened during my absence. . . . At times he tempts me to interrupt and ask: "And what of the beautiful Ondine who used to arrange her silver veil so coquettishly about her green hair? Is that white-bearded sea god still pursuing her with his silly, superannuated passion? Do our roses at home still have their proud, fiery brilliance? Do the trees still sing their lovely songs in the moonlight?" . . .

Alas! I have not seen my country for a long time, and my strange homesickness sometimes makes me feel like the Flying Dutchman and his crew, eternally sailing the seas and longing vainly for peaceful ports, tulips, maidens, clay pipes, and Delft porcelain. . . . "Amsterdam! Amsterdam! When shall we return to Amsterdam!" they cry desperately during a storm whose howling winds keep tossing them back upon the damnable waves of their watery hell. I fully understand the sorrow that one day led the captain of the accursed ship to say: "If I ever return to

13. Chopin never studied in "Germany" as we know it today. In this period, however, all German-speaking lands went by that general name, and Chopin did visit Vienna on two occasions in 1829–31. Since he met both Czerny and Hummel there, he may have taken some coaching from either or both of them.

Amsterdam, I would rather remain there as a stone marker on a street corner than ever leave the city!" Poor Vanderdecken![14]

My dear friend,[15] I hope that these letters find you happy and gay on the rosiest day of your life and that I will not suffer the fate of the Flying Dutchman, whose letters were usually addressed to persons who died long ago. Alas, how many of those who were dear to me have died since the ship of my life was driven to foreign seas by the storms of fate. I am starting to feel giddy, and I think I see stars flicker and trace fiery circles in the sky. I close my eyes, and wild dreams gather me into their long arms, transporting me to unknown lands filled with horrible anguish. . . . You have no idea, my dear friend, of the bizarre, wonderfully exotic landscapes I see in dreams or of the fearful sufferings that assail me even in sleep.

Last night I found myself in an immense cathedral pervaded by a gloomy twilight. . . . In its upper reaches, in the galleries rising above the first rank of pillars, all I could see was the flickering light of processional lamps; choir boys in red surplices carrying immense candles, standards, and crosses; then monks in cowls and priests in brilliantly ornamented vestments. . . . And the procession proceeded with a sinister magic around the galleries under the dome. . . . I fled blindly down the nave of the church holding a woman, the unlucky companion of my dreams, in my arms. . . . I cannot remember what terror pursued us, but we ran, our hearts pounding horribly, and tried to hide behind the gigantic pillars, but in vain. Gripped by an even greater fear, we tried to flee, for the procession was now descending a curved flight of steps and coming towards us. . . . There was a chant whose sadness was inconceivable, and even more inconceivably, a tall, pale woman whose aged face still bore the traces of great beauty, walked at the procession's head and approached us with a measured pace, much like that of a ballet dancer. She carried a bouquet of black flowers and offered it to us with a theatrical gesture, as immense, genuine sorrow flooded her large, brilliant eyes with tears. . . . But then the scene changed: we were no longer in a gloomy cathedral, but in a field, where the surrounding mountains took on all sorts of human postures, where the trees covered with flame-colored leaves appeared to burn, and actually did burn, because after the mountains had gone through

---

14. Heine's *Aus den Memoiren des Herrn von Schnabelewopski*, with its tale of the Flying Dutchman (the one that prompted Wagner's opera), was published in 1834.

15. Presumably August Lewald (1792–1871), editor of the *Allgemeine Theater-Revue*, Stuttgart.

the most grotesque contortions and sunk completely out of sight, the trees burst into great flames and fell to ashes. . . . In the end, I found myself all alone on a vast plain, with nothing but yellow sand beneath my feet and a bleak, desolate sky overhead. My companion had disappeared, and as I searched uneasily for her, I found a statue of a woman in the sand. She was wonderfully beautiful, but her arms were broken off like *Venus de Milo*, and the marble was sadly discolored with age in some places. I stood for some time in melancholy contemplation before the fragment until a horseman came riding by. It was a large bird, an ostrich, ludicrously galloping on a camel. He also stopped before the broken statue, and for a long time we talked about art. "What is art?" I asked him, and he answered, "Ask that of the great granite Sphinx who lies in the courtyard of the Museum in Paris."

Do not laugh at my nocturnal visions, my dear friend; or might you, by some chance, be one of those common people with a prejudice against dreams? Tomorrow I return to Paris. Adieu!

C

HECTOR BERLIOZ: TO LISZT

During their years together in Paris, Liszt and Berlioz were more than friends; they were mutually supportive professional comrades. Liszt, who regarded Berlioz both as an admired older brother and as the embodiment of modern genius struggling for recognition, did all he could to promote his friend, performing at Berlioz's concerts, transcribing his works for piano, and championing him in his writings.[1] Berlioz reciprocated: as a working journalist and critic, he regularly reviewed and lauded Liszt's concert performances and leapt to his defense during the fretful affair over Thalberg.[2]

In the summer of 1839, Berlioz, faced with the task of summarizing the musical news in Paris and giving the *Gazette*'s readers a preview of the coming musical season, hit upon the ingenious and attractive idea of casting his article in the form of an affectionate open letter to the long-absent Liszt. The result is a typically droll and delightful piece of Berlioziana.

Hector Berlioz: To Liszt[1]

Paris, 6 August 1839

I would have liked, my dear friend, to tell you *absolutely everything* that is happening in our musical world, or at least everything that I

---

1. In addition to the article "The *Perseus* of Benvenuto Cellini" (chap. 8), Liszt had taken up the cudgels for Berlioz in his essay "On the Situation of Artists" (*Pages romantiques*, pp. 26–29) and in a review of his works—the *Symphonie fantastique* and Harold in Italy—performed in concert at the Paris Conservatory (*Le Monde*, 11 December 1836).

2. See n. 4 in chap. 3 above concerning Berlioz.

---

1. *Gazette musicale*, 11 August 1839, pp. 297–99.

know about—the business that is being transacted, the sales that have been made, the ins and outs of the shady deals that are being considered, the banalities that are taking place—but I really do not think my account would stand a chance of interesting you. It would have nothing new to offer. Your study of Italian musical customs has made you blasé about such refined matters, and what is happening in Paris is *exactly* like what you experienced in Milan. Besides, you would not have the heart to laugh about it. You are not one of those who are amused by the insults that the muse we serve has to suffer. You, on the contrary, would do everything possible to hide the dirty stains on her virginal gown and the sad rents in her divine veil. Let us not talk, then, about the outrages that would irritate you just as much as they do me, and against which we are not even free to protest, for reasons that you know or that the most recent and terrible book by *Balzac*[2] will, if necessary, explain to you. All I intend to do, therefore, is to give you a superficial idea of what is happening at our concerts and opera houses and with our virtuosos, singers, and composers, and to do it without any comments or emotion, neither praise nor blame—that is, with the calm monotony of an adept of that celebrated school of philosophy we founded in Rome in the Year of Grace 1830, and which is called the "School of Absolute Indifference in Universal Matters."[3]

The advantage of this approach is that I can dispense with theories and explications and let the *facts* speak solely and brutally for themselves, without concerning myself about the consequences. Putting chronological order aside, I shall begin with the most recent events.

The day before yesterday, while I was as usual smoking a cigar on the Boulevard des Italiens, someone grabbed my arm; it was *Batta*, back from London. "What are they up to in London?" I asked. "Absolutely nothing; they despise music, poetry, drama, and everything there. Except for the Italian Opera, which attracts a crowd because the queen attends it, all the other musical establishments are empty. I consider myself lucky that I made my traveling expenses and was applauded at two or three concerts. That is all I got from British hospitality, but I arrived too late in the season, and the same was true of

---

2. *Un grand homme de Province à Paris* (*Illusions perdues*, part 2.) (I am indebted to Frédéric Robert, editor of the Berlioz *Correspondance générale*, vol. 2, where this letter is reprinted as no. 660, for a number of points in these annotations, this one among them.)

3. "A transcendental doctrine which aims to produce in man the sensitivity and rounded perfection of a stone" (Berlioz, *Memoirs*, p. 203).

Artôt. A violinist named *David*[4] had managed to attract the attention of London's small musical audience; he was fashionable and no concert took place without him. As a result, *Artôt*, despite his success with the Philharmonic Society and the incontestable beauty of his playing . . . became very bored there." "And *Doehler*?" "*Doehler* is bored too." "And *Thalberg*?" "He is cultivating the provinces." "And *Benedict*?" "Encouraged by the success of his first score,[5] he is writing a new English opera." "And Madame *Dorus-Gras*?" "Madame *Gras*[6] became fashionable within a few days, matching the Italians in popularity; she sang everywhere, and her name no longer appeared on the posters without the phrase THE INCOMPARABLE SINGER printed in great big letters. They say that she was booed and hissed in *William Tell* when she returned here." "That's true." "What happened? Why?" "Would you like a grog?" "No, I'm going. Come to *Hallé*'s tonight. We'll have a drink and make some music there." "That's fine."

Hallé[7] is a young German pianist who has long blond hair, is tall and thin, plays magnificently, and grasps the music more by intuition than by study; in other words, he is much like you. At his place I also saw his countryman *Heller*.[8] A serious talent with a huge amount of musical intelligence, a quick intellect, and great technical skill—those are the qualities as a composer and performer that all who know him well attribute to him, and I am one of them.

Hallé and *Batta* played the Sonata in B-flat Major by *Felix Mendelssohn*.[*] It was generally admired for its classical structure and forceful style. *Heller* declared it the work of a great master, and we all seconded the opinion by drinking beer. Then came Beethoven's Sonata in A major,[9] whose first movement moved us to shouts, oaths, and cries of enthusiasm. Its menuet [i.e., the scherzo] and finale only doubled

---

* Sonata for Piano and Violoncello or Violin, Op. 45.

4. Belgian violinist Alexander Artôt (1815–1845); Ferdinand David (1810–1873), close friend of Mendelssohn's and the first to perform his Violin Concerto (1845).

5. Julius Benedict (1804–1885). His opera was *The Gypsy's Warning*, first performed in April 1838, Drury Lane, London.

6. Julie Steenkiste (1805–1896), known as Madame Dorus-Gras, soprano. She had sung the role of Teresa in Berlioz's ill-fated *Benvenuto Cellini*.

7. Charles Hallé (1819–1895), Westphalian-born pianist and conductor. After the Revolution of 1848 he settled in England, where in 1857 he founded the orchestra bearing his name. He is also reputed to be the first pianist ever to present the cycle of all thirty-two Beethoven sonatas, in 1861.

8. Stephen Heller (1813–1888), Hungarian-born pianist. A prolific composer, his works were once very popular with amateurs.

9. Beethoven's Op. 69.

our purely musical excitement, even though bottles of champagne were already circulating around the room. Apropos of that, someone remarked that good beer was good but champagne was much better.

Oh, you indefatigable vagabond! When will you return and give us those musical nights over which you presided so handsomely? Just between us, there were too many people at your gatherings; they talked too much, they did not listen enough, they philosophized.[10] You were so lavish with your playing and ideas that it was enough to make a *few* of our heads swim, not counting all the *others*. Do you remember that evening at *Legouvé's* when the lamp was put out and you played the C-sharp Minor Sonata[11] with five of us lying on the floor in the dark—the magnetism in the air, the tears that *Legouvé* and I shed, *Schoelcher's* respectful silence, *Goubeaux's* astonishment?[12] My God, oh God, how sublime you were that night! Pardon me! I forgot that I belong to the school of the *indifférents*. And so, to continue my account.

This year the manufacturers' exhibition of their products took volumes of musical criticism to cover.[13] There was a lot of disagreement. People shouted pro and con about the pianos, pro and con about the organs. For a moment it appeared that a lawsuit would be filed over a flute stop, but an "adjustment" in the pressure forestalled the fray. I really did not understand all the infighting because we artists must in effect endure criticism every day that is at least as unjust and ridiculous as any that the instrument manufacturers would ever have to face, yet we let it pass without a word. Still we do not lack for self-esteem, our sensibility is not destroyed—far from it. And we could defend ourselves, but we do not do it. On those rare occasions, however, when a critic does have kind things to say about us, we thank him sincerely when the opportunity arises, without hurrying to knock on his door to do so, and all too frequently we even neglect the simple courtesy of sending him a little note. By contrast, the exhibitors who were praised have shown exemplary gratitude—visits, letters, gifts, they neglected nothing in their expression of it. Those, on the other

10. Evidently the "humanist" gatherings at the Hôtel de France in the latter part of 1836.

11. Beethoven's Op. 27 No. 2. Berlioz is referring to the Adagio movement and relates the same incident in greater detail in his "Quelques mots sur les trios et les sonates de Beethoven," *À travers chants*, pp. 63–67.

12. Ernest Legouvé (1807–1903), theater critic and writer; Victor Schoelcher (1804–1893), writer and politician; Prosper-Parfait Goubeaux (1795–1859), writer.

13. These exhibits, generally held every five years, lasted for several months and were well covered by the Paris press.

hand, who were overlooked or poorly spoken of could not understand why they couldn't chase after the critic and kill him on a street corner like a mad dog. Anyone can say what he thinks, or even what he fails to think, about the greatest artists, the most magnificent works, or even the more popular mediocre ones without causing much of a stir, but let someone fail to appreciate the price of a new peg for a double bass or to praise the bridge of a viola, and the clamor raised is loud and long.

The mystery behind this was finally explained to me: "Your *products*, the works you artists produce," they told me, "are not distributed *wholesale*, you sell them retail, if and when you can sell them at all. If you do not find buyers, your works serve *no real purpose*, because in the last analysis a talent that returns nothing is *worth nothing*, there is no disputing that. The men who manufacture instruments are *more serious*, their products are *far more important* because they are dealing in millions; and so you must understand that a newspaper article that will or will not move a hundred thousand francs worth of merchandise should not be regarded like one that only discusses a symphony by *Beethoven* or an opera by *Gluck*."—"Ah! yes, of course, it is a question of money; I hadn't thought of that."

Speaking of money, they have just found a way of saving it by not building a new hall for the Italian Opera.[14] The company at the Grand Opéra is going to find itself in direct competition with the singers from across the Alps, since they now want to merge both companies at the hall on Rue Le Pelletier [the Opéra]. It will be quite a melee: *Lablache* versus *Levasseur*, *Rubini* versus *Duprez*, *Tamburini* versus *Dérivis*, *Giulia Grisi* versus Mademoiselle *Nathan*, and the whole lot versus the bass drum. We will be there to point out the dead and the dying. The director, no doubt, will also take over the management of the London season, and he will perhaps make a lot of money, and that will be a wonderful thing, which is just fine with me. . . . I am one of the *indifferents*. It is up to the merchants to figure out how much income their musical commodities, utilized in this manner, will produce on average year in and year out. They are the ones who must concern themselves about how long their singing instruments will last. As for myself, if I were not one of the *indifferents* I would certainly say along with you, "I love music more than all that." *Duponchel*[15] will

---

14. The Salle Favart, home of the Théâtre-Italien, had been destroyed by fire the night of 14–15 January 1838.

15. Edmond Duponchel (1795–1868), scenery and costume designer, who was director of the Opéra from 1835 to 1841.

retain complete charge of the costumes, hence you need not be concerned—art and the artist will find themselves *well draped*.[16] In the meantime, Madame Stoltz[17] will not be joining the company; everyone is sorry about it, except the faction that pressured *Duponchel* not to rehire her.

Alizard,[18] a young singer who has come to the fore during your absence, is winning an ever-finer place for himself day by day in the opinion of connoisseurs and even with the general public; he sometimes sings very small roles in which he always finds a way to impress the audience. He was enthusiastically applauded at the Conservatory concerts last winter. He will succeed. Mademoiselle *Nau* has risen considerably; she is delightful in the role of a fairy that *Auber* has just written for her.[19] Many people are saying that the orchestra is getting tired or careless or disgusted with its role. The other day I heard some of the opera *habitués* complain that the instruments were not in tune; they claimed that the right side of the orchestra tended to rise in pitch until it was a quarter-tone higher than the left—an unconscionable claim, if you can believe them. "And you suffer this in silence?" one of them asked me . . . . "Me! I never said I was suffering; in the first place, because I haven't said a single word about it, and in the second. . . ."

Every now and then they perform *Don Juan* when they can't think of what else to do.[20] If Mozart returned to this world, he would perhaps say, along with the president Molière mentions, that he does

---

16. A pun: the phrase to be *dans de beaux draps*, literally "in fine drapes," usually means to be "in a fine mess, a pickle."

17. Rosina, actually Victoria, Stoltz (1815–1903), mezzo-soprano. She was so successful as Rosina in Rossini's *Barber of Seville* that she became known by that name. She had sung the role of Ascanio in Berlioz's *Cellini*.

18. Adolphe-Joseph Louis Alizard (1814–1850), bass-baritone.

19. Mademoiselle Nau's role was in Auber's *Le Lac des fées*, first performed at the Opéra, April 1839.

20. Sporting a French text by Castil-Blaze, Émile Deschamps, and Henri Blaze, Mozart's *Don Giovanni* reached the stage of the Paris Opéra in March 1834 as *Don Juan*. It was a lavish, five-act conflated version that presented Mozart's work as viewed through the then popular interpretation of it given in E. T. A. Hoffmann's tale "Don Juan." (For the reaction pro and con that this Mozart/Hoffman stage piece stirred, see Elizabeth Teichmann, *La Fortune d'Hoffmann en France*, pp. 133–43.) The preface to the libretto, moreover, informed the reader: "As for the dances, marches, final chorus, *entr'actes*, in short, all the accessory actions that are called for by the production of *Don Juan* at the Grand Opéra in Paris, they are drawn without exception, from the various masterpieces of the great composer: his symphonies, masses, *The Magic Flute*, *La Clemenza di Tito*, and the like. Thus, only Mozart's music is to be heard." In the finale, for instance, Don Juan goes mad as Donna Anna's funeral procession passes accompanied by the strains of the *Dies irae* from the Requiem. Such wholesale revi-

not want them to *play* it.[21] *Spontini*, on the other hand, did not want to be played, and that he has been. The people at the Opéra will not hear of reviving his early masterpieces. *Ambroise Thomas, Morel*,[22] and I were saying just the other day, however, that we would gladly give five hundred francs to hear a good performance of *La Vestale*. As we all know the score by heart, we sang it until midnight; we missed you at the piano to accompany us. *Spontini's* cause had been defended in a pamphlet written by our friend *Émile D.*, and several newspapers have joined him.[23] That cause was on the verge of winning out when *Spontini* felt the need to publish a letter on modern music and musicians that had already been published two or three years ago in Berlin. *Spontini's* enemies would have paid a thousand little gold pieces for the publication of that letter, and he gave it to them for nothing. All this does not keep *La Vestale* from being a masterpiece, but it does mean that we will never see it again. Madame *Giradin*[24] wrote an irate article about it, which irritated the management of the Opéra.

You saw in the most recent article by our learned collaborator H. B. [Henry Blanchard] that the professorship of composition at the conservatory, left vacant by the death of *Paër*, has just gone to *Caraffa*.[25] I am convinced that my system of indifference is beginning to be appreciated by the Ministry. The orange trees at the Jardin *Musard*[26] are already bearing fruit. *Théophile de Ferrière*[27] was attacked by an un-

---

sions, which border on vandalism in today's more literal musical climate, were fairly common in the first half of the nineteenth century. (Liszt, incidentally, probably had this production in mind when he wrote his *Réminiscences de Don Juan* in 1841.)

21. A purposely ambiguous phrase attributed to Molière: "*Tartuffe* ne sera pas joue: Monsieur le Premier President ne veut pas qu'on le joue" (*Tartuffe* will not be played: Monsieur the First President does not want them to play it [play him]).

22. Ambroise Thomas (1811–1896), composer and later the director of the Paris Conservatory; Auguste-Francois Morel (1809–1880), composer and writer.

23. Émile Deschamps (1791–1871), littérateur and translator. The spat, so typical of the Paris press, grew out of Duponchel's refusal to revive or produce any of Spontini's operas.

24. Delphine Gay de Giradin, the "Viscount de Launay" in the Letter to Pictet, chap. 4.

25. Ferdinando Paër (1771–1839), opera composer (with whom Liszt had briefly studied orchestration in 1825); Michele-Enrico Caraffa (1787–1872), Neapolitan-born opera composer. Berlioz himself had hoped to get the post.

26. Philippe Musard (1792–1859), extremely popular dance composer and orchestra leader, the "king of the quadrilles." His garden was one of Paris's finest dance halls.

27. Marquis Théophile de Ferrière de Vayer (died 1864), a diplomat and an amateur novelist writing as "Samuel Bach." He had been one of Marie d'Agoult's most devoted admirers in the years before she left with Paris with Liszt.

known assailant last week as he was leaving the Opéra-comique; he is recovering nicely. *Heine* is always spelled with an "e," and he lives on the Rue des Martyrs. Someone pilfered my copy of his delightful book on Italy. Have you seen his *Baths at Lucca?*[28] They are promising us "Venetian Nights" at the Casino [Paganini]. An orchestra of a hundred and forty performs there, except when some sixty of the musicians are hired to play at the same time at the Concerts Champs-Elysée. They have a *microscope à gaz* there;[29] I have seen lemons that looked as big as melons. I am giving you all my news just as it comes to mind. F. *Hiller* has sent me several pieces from his *Romilda* from Milan. They claim that *Rossini* is selling fish, the likes of which have hardly ever been seen before. I wager that he is as bored in his villa as his big fish are in their ponds. He always said, "What is that to me?" If he did not like his big fish so much, he would perhaps be well disposed to *absolute indifference*, etc. But I doubt it![30] Recently one of our enemies tried to throw himself off the Vendôme Column; he bribed the guard with forty francs to let him go to the top, but then he changed his mind. They are going to perform an opera by *Mainzer* at the Théâtre de la Renaissance.[31] It is a fine piece! A young tenor named *Ricciardi* has just made a successful debut there in *Donizetti's Lucia di Lammermoor*, given in a fine translation and production by A. *Roger* and *Vaës*. The manager of the Renaissance is making a tremendous effort to include music and musicians in the repertory there, but he has not received much help. The Opéra-comique is getting ready for several important debuts: two tenors and a soprano whom they say are quite remarkable; we shall take careful note of them. *Girard*[32] continues to conduct the small orchestra admirably, but one can only hope that the new hall

---

28. Heine's book *Die Bader von Lucca* (The Baths at Lucca) and its sequel *Die Stadt Lucca* (The City of Lucca), both wickedly satirical travel tales, were first published in 1829–30 as part of his *Reisebilder* (Travel Pictures) and soon translated into French.

29. A *microscope à gaz* was an optical device in which the image of an illuminated object was reflected through a series of mirrors and then projected enormously enlarged onto a screen.

30. Berlioz's point is not clear. Rossini spent the summer at a villa in Posillipo recovering from the depression brought on by the death of his father that spring. It was also rumored at the time, erroneously, that he had agreed to compose an *opera seria* for the Teatro San Carlo in Naples, and that perhaps is what Berlioz had in mind.

31. Joseph Mainzer. See p. 20n. His opera was *La Jacquerie*, which opened on 10 October 1839.

32. Narcisse Girard (1797–1860), violinist-conductor.

promised for the Opéra-comique will include an anteroom for the musicians, because the unhappy fellows—performing now at the Théâtre de la Bourse—are obliged to tune up *coram populo* before the curtain rises, and thus when the oboe and violins sound their *A*, the trombones growl their *B-flat*. Truly, one cannot be *indifferent* about something like that; it's terrible.

Kastner is hard at work. He is about to finish a treatise on orchestration considered in relation to harmonic and melodic expression, and it is due to appear soon.[33] I am very eager to read it. Last month *Wilhem* gave two public concerts; his five hundred vocal students were roundly applauded.[34] I did not consider their performance as a form of progress. All these young men and children have a hopelessly vulgar sense of rhythm. They hammer out every beat and turn just about everything into march time. The result, if we compare the laboring class's former ignorance with the knowledge they have today, is certainly a fine one, but *knowledge* is not everything in music; there must also be *feeling*, and I think that Parisians are much too fond of variety acts and drums. The opera by *Ruolz* has been in rehearsal for two and a half months.[35] Consequently, the singers do not know a note of it, but the costumes are ready, and *Duponchel* wants to give it this coming Friday. *Chopin* has not returned; he was said to be very ill, but it is alright.[36] *Dumas* has written an enchanting play,[37] but that is not my province. I have finished. There is no more news.

Adieu. For all my indifference, it is a little difficult for me to resign myself to your long absence. Come back, come back. It is high time for us, and for you too, I hope.

33. George Kastner (1810–1867), Alsatian composer and theorist. His *Cours d'instrumentation considéré sous les rapports poétiques et philosophiques de l'art* was published in Paris in 1839.

34. Guillaume-Louis Wilhem (actually, Bocquillon) (1781–1842). He was then general director of musical education in the Paris elementary schools and had instituted his concerts by school children in 1833. He, like Mainzer, also held singing classes for working men.

35. Count Henri de Ruolz-Montchal (1806–1887). The opera was *La Vendetta*.

36. Chopin had indeed been quite ill during his visit to Majorca with George Sand the previous winter. He was spending the summer at Nohant regaining his health and did not return to Paris until that October.

37. *Madamoiselle de Belle-Isle*, presented at the Théâtre-Française on 2 April 1839.

D

LISZT: RELIGIOUS MUSIC OF THE FUTURE[1]

The gods depart,[2] the kings depart, but God abides and the nations are surging upward. Let us, therefore, not despair for art.

According to a law passed in the Chamber of Deputies in 1834, music will soon be taught in the schools. We can congratulate ourselves on such progress and regard it as a pledge of even greater progress that will exercise a prodigious influence on the masses.

We want to talk about a regeneration of *religious music*. Even though that term normally refers only to the music performed in church during the ceremonies of worship, I am using it here in its broadest sense.

In an age when such worship both expressed and satisfied the beliefs, the needs, and the communal feelings of the people, at a time when men and women sought and found in the Church an altar before which to kneel, a pulpit that nourished their spirits, and a spectacle that refreshed and piously elevated their senses, religious music could confine itself to the mystical precincts and be content to accompany the magnificence of the Catholic liturgy.

But today, at a time when the altar creaks and totters, today when the pulpit and religious rites have become matters of doubt and deri-

---

1. *Gazette musicale*, 30 August 1835; *Pages romantiques*, pp. 65–67. When Ramann published this brief manifesto-like essay in Liszt's *Ges. Schriften*, 2:55–57, she presented it as a separate "Fragment (1834)" entitled "Über zukünftige Kirchenmusik." Presumably she did this with his consent, but its appearance in that form has misled a number of writers into thinking that it was a separate early article, when in fact it was first published as an insertion in the section discussing religious music in his "On the Situation of Artists."

2. "Les dieux s'en vont." This phrase—said to have been coined by the historian Josephus to mark the passing of the pagan age—recurs throughout this period as an allusion to the decadence, decline, and displacement of the *ancien régime*. Chateaubriand, Lamartine, Heine, and a number of others also cite it in their writings.

sion, it is essential that art leave the temple, that it stretch itself and seek to accomplish its major developments in the outside world.

As in the past, and even more so today, music must concern itself with PEOPLE and GOD, hastening from the one to the other, improving, edifying, and comforting mankind while it blesses and glorifies God.

And to bring this about, the creation of a new music is imminent. Essentially religious, powerful, and stirring, that music, which for want of another name we will call *humanistic* music, will sum up both the THEATER and the CHURCH on a colossal scale. It will be at once both dramatic and sacred, stately and simple, moving and solemn, fiery and unruly, tempestuous yet calm, serene and gentle.

The *Marseillaise*, which, more than all the legendary tales of the Hindus, Chinese, and Greeks, demonstrated the power of music to us, the *Marseillaise* and the wonderful songs of the Revolution were the awesome and glorious forerunners of it.

Yes, have no doubt about it, we will soon hear bursting from the fields, the hamlets, the villages, the suburbs, the workshops, and the cities, songs, canticles, tunes, and hymns which are patriotic, moral, political, and religious in nature, *written* for the people, *taught* to the people, and *sung* by the laborers, the workingmen, the craftsmen, the sons and daughters, the men and women who are the *people*.

All the great artists—poets and musicians—will contribute their proper share to the ever-renewed repertory of peoples' songs. The state will bestow honors, a public reward, on those who will have been triply crowned at the general competitions,[3] and ultimately *all classes of people* will be joined together in a common, religious, grand and sublime feeling.

That will be the FIAT LUX of Art.

Come, come then, oh age of glory, when art in all its forms will complete and fulfill itself, when it will raise itself to its ultimate heights by fraternally uniting all mankind in rapturous wonder. Come, too, the day when an artist will no longer have to dig arduously in sterile sand for the bitter, fugitive water that is his inspiration, but will see it gush forth like an inexhaustible life-giving spring. Come, oh come, hour of deliverance, when the poet and the musician will no longer speak of "the public," but of THE PEOPLE and GOD.

---

3. Clearly there is an error in the published text at this point, and in translating the passage I have followed Chantavoine's suggestion, *Pages romantiques*, p. 67, that the phrase "comme nous trois fois" should properly read "couronnés trois fois."

E

LISZT AS AUTHOR

Although Liszt died over a century ago, the question of his authorship of the literary and critical works published in his name is a matter which still continues to be discussed. It arises whenever the works
are mentioned because they are not the exclusive product of his own
pen, such as we know the writings of Berlioz, Schumann, and Wagner
to be, but the result of some form of collaboration with the two literary women in his life, Marie d'Agoult and, later, Carolyne Sayn-
Wittgenstein. Consequently, the nature of that collaboration has a decided effect on the credibility we can or should place in the articles
and monographs as authentic Lisztiana. Did he, the accommodating
lover, simply sign his name to the articles? Did he write some of them
independently and they the others? Or did the women produce the
writings to order, as it were, working under his supervision? Questions such as these, which have been raised and disputed over the
years, require some form of answer when presenting Liszt as an author vis-à-vis Madame d'Agoult.[1]

The issue of who wrote the *Lettres d'un bachelier* and the other
early articles is not a new one; it first surfaced in 1838 when the *Gazette musicale* ran the following notice:

> The *Pariser Zeitung*, a German newspaper published for the
> past several days in Paris, contains the following news item in its
> third issue [2 October].
> "A French journal attributes the letters of the celebrated pi-
> anist Franz Liszt—published recently in the *Gazette musicale* and
> prior to that [sic] in *Le Monde*—to a clever woman, the Countess

---

1. Liszt's literary activities at Weimar (1848–61) and his collaboration with Princess Carolyne reflect a totally different set of circumstances and need not concern us
here.

d'A——. It claims that Liszt only lends his name to these literary works. This assertion seems a risky one to us. These works probably have two authors. Liszt, moreover, would do better to be satisfied with his success in music."

That the letters of Liszt are not to the German paper's taste is surely a great pity, but we wish to affirm that they are really by him, and as proof of that, anyone who cares to may examine the autographs in our possession. (7 October 1838)

The *Gazette*'s unequivocal statement evidently satisfied the sceptics, and the paper simply continued to publish the articles as Liszt's own work. No doubts whatsoever.

Or none, that is, until the earlier decades of this century, when Liszt's grandson Daniel Ollivier (1862–1941) decided he could with impunity finally make some of his grandparents' archival papers public. In 1927 he published Marie d'Agoult's *Mémoires, 1833–1854*, a volume he compiled and edited from her manuscripts and miscellaneous notes and which was to serve as the continuation of her own *Mes Souvenirs, 1806–1833*, published in 1877. In 1933 and 1934 he also edited and published the correspondence between Liszt and Madame d'Agoult. Needless to say, these publications, by bringing to light her notes and hundreds of the couple's hitherto unknown letters, sparked a thorough reexamination of the relations between them.

It was in this connection that the Liszt scholar Emile Haraszti challenged the assumption that Liszt was ever, in fact, an author. Everything about his published writings, Haraszti declared, was a "mystification."[2] Building his case, he noted first that no manuscript copies of Liszt's articles could be found; second, that a number of passages in the travel articles were taken almost word for word from the *Mémoires*; and third, that Liszt when writing to Marie not only referred to "our" articles, but had even asked her to prepare one for his signature. All this fresh evidence, which will be reviewed shortly, led Haraszti to conclude that everything published in Liszt's name during the d'Agoult years "was not his work, but hers."[3]

---

2. Emile Haraszti, "Franz Liszt—Author despite Himself. The History of a Mystification," The article published in *The Musical Quarterly*, 1947, is the English version of the same basic article published in various other languages during the previous decade, and listed in it.

3. Haraszti, "Franz Liszt," p. 505. He was not the only one to maintain that the countess wrote the articles. Her biographer, Jacques Vier, for instance, was of the same opinion and included all of the articles signed by Liszt as part of her list of works (Vier, *La Comtesse d'Agoult*, 6:139–40).

This unprecedented, sweeping challenge to Liszt's authorship could not and did not go unanswered. Several scholars—Marix-Spire, Guichard, and others[4]—came to his defense with a series of rebuttals (some more effective than others), which have led in turn to the current consensus that the articles were not written exclusively by either Liszt or Marie d'Agoult but, as the *Pariser Zeitung* had suggested, by some combination of the two working together.

That conclusion is fine as far as it goes. Still, a collection such as this which presents the writings as Liszt's work has an obligation to explore the nature of that collaboration—even while admitting at the outset that the problems inherent in the joint, collaborative effort do not admit of a neat, precise solution, since we are dealing with a body of documentary evidence that is both fragmentary and contradictory, an intimate living and working relationship between Liszt and his literary companion, a group of sixteen articles written under various circumstances over a period of six years, and that ambiguous verb "to write." If "to write" means putting a literate and effective version of another's ideas on paper, such as a ghost writer or a professional speech writer is expected to do, that is one thing; but if the verb also includes the choice of subject and the conceptualization of the content, that is quite different—and therein lies much of the whole problem.

The following review is, in a sense, a journey round Robin Hood's barn to arrive back at the conclusion that Liszt and Marie "collaborated." Yet a general reassessment of the evidence to be gleaned from the manuscripts, the countess's *Mémoires*, and the correspondence of these years can go some way toward characterizing the interaction between the two when writing the Letters. Haraszti, in this respect, provides a good point of departure, because he by marshaling the evidence to support his claim of Marie's authorship has actually given us a fairly good indication of her part in the collaboration.

The manuscripts. As the question of surviving Liszt manuscripts is more directly concerned with his authorship of the writings than with the joint effort that produced them, it can be disposed of first. Haraszti had unequivocally stated that none of the manuscripts of Liszt's articles could be found, but that is no longer the case. In recent decades scholars have discovered two pertinent Liszt holographs

---

4. Marix-Spire, *Romantiques*, pp. 625–26; Guichard, "Liszt et la littérature français," pp. 15–21. Also see Serge Gut, *Franz Liszt*, pp. 29–42; Eleanor Perényi, *Liszt*, pp. 175–78; and Walker, *Franz Liszt*, 1:20–23.

in library collections, and even if neither of them is the manuscript of a Letter—all of which are evidently lost—they do at least date from the d'Agoult years: they are a section of "On the Situation of Artists"[5] and a copy of his 1840 essay "On the Death of Paganini." By contrast, d'Agoult scholars who have gone through her papers have yet to find a single autograph draft or copy of any of the articles published during their years together. Thus the documentary evidence of the manuscripts, scant as it may be, points to him, not her, as the one who produced the articles.

The Mémoires *journal.* Incorporated into the countess's published *Mémoires* is the journal that she kept during the travels,[6] especially in Italy, and since it gives a parallel account of the journey as reported in the travel articles, a comparison of the two sources provides some instructive insights into her literary partnership with Liszt.

First, it is undeniable that some passages in the articles are taken word for word from the journal. Haraszti cited them to support his claim that d'Agoult was the sole author of the Letters. He neglected, however, to add that the passages in question are few and far between, amounting at most to a dozen excerpts which account for only a tiny fraction of the articles' published text, and that they are mostly brief descriptive passages recounting such travel tidbits as the ascent to the *Grande Chartreuse*,[7] night fishing on Lake Como, and the like.[8]

5. See Edward N. Waters, "Sur la piste de Liszt"; also, Maria P. Eckhardt, "New Documents on Liszt as Author," for a summary of all the Liszt literary holographs now known to survive.

6. The journal—begun at Nohant in June 1837 and kept sporadically all during the travels in Italy—is the most trustworthy portion of the *Mémoires*. The other sections, which differ markedly in places from independently ascertainable facts, are, from all appearances, less of a contemporaneous record of the events as they occurred than a revised and occasionally highly colored version of them written at some later but unknown time. When presenting the volume, Ollivier noted, "Such as they are, despite the lacunae, these fragments of memoirs, these notes, this journal did seem to us worthy of being published" (d'Agoult, *Mémoires*, p. xii).

7. As an example, Haraszti, "Franz Liszt," p. 496, prints the passage describing the climb to the *Grand Chartreuse* from the *Mémoires* and from the Letter to Ronchaud (chap. 5) in parallel columns. The texts "We climb a rather gentle slope . . . *omnes qui laboratis*" are virtually identical.

8. Vier, *La comtesse d'Agoult*, 1:409–10, gives a list of the places where the articles are beholden to the journal. For the record these include: the paraphrase of Schubert's "Erlkönig" [and bits of the scene on Sand's terrace] in the Letter to Pictet (chap. 4); the ascent to *Grande Chartreuse*, and the passages about Isola Madre and Sesto Calende in the first Letter to Ronchaud (chap. 5); the passages about the Dante statue, Liszt's adventures with the urchins, the village festival, and night fishing in the Letter to Ronchaud about Lake Como (chap. 5); and some remarks about Countess

In other words (pace Haraszti), the passages that were copied from the journal to the articles do not really amount to much, and they are not very substantive in nature.

A different method of comparison is to see the journal as a source for Liszt's remarks in the articles, since there are many instances in it where Marie writes "Franz said," or "Franz thinks." During their visit to the *Grande Chartreuse*, for example, she noted in the journal that "Franz, fundamentally more Catholic than I, told me that a skillful pope could have derived enormous profit from the monasteries . . . by converting them to intellectual enterprises or even to industrial use. A new Gregory . . . could have erased the stain of greed which has made monasticism so odious to the people."[9] One need only turn to the letter to Ronchaud (chapter 5) to see that these are not only the same opinions, but almost exactly the same words that appear there. The countess, in effect, was writing as a Boswell to Liszt's Johnson.

A further and more crucial measure of the literary collaboration is to look at the matters about which the two disagreed. The two most important of them have already been mentioned in passing in the annotations of the text, so they need only be recalled here. One is the article about Raphael's *Saint Cecilia* in chapter 8. Madame d'Agoult, as noted, had been unimpressed by the painting, yet the published account of it is a paean to its sublimity both as a work of art and as an "admirable and perfect symbol" of music. The other is Liszt's trip to Vienna. Here again the two disagreed: she was against it,[10] but the account given of it in the letter to Massart (chapter 7) is long and glowing and written entirely from Liszt's point of view. (Are we to assume that she would write so emotionally about things with which she disagreed?)

To the extent that one can generalize about the active partnership on the basis of the journal, then, it is clear that it is at most a partial and in many respects an incidental source for the text of the articles.

The correspondence. Liszt's correspondence with his collaborator

---

Samoyloff in the Letter to Massart (chap. 6). To these, I have added a note about the discussion of Christian and pagan art in the article on Venice (chap. 7).

9. d'Agoult, *Mémoires*, p. 104.

10. d'Agoult's account of Liszt's trip is given in the *Mémoires*, pp. 143–50, as an "Episode de Venise." There is every reason to suspect, however, that it is a later (1840?) and partially fictionalized retelling of the story.

presents much the same picture as that just sketched for the *Mémoires*, in that there is ample proof that she did some of the writing, while he was responsible for the content.

This is a distinction Haraszti failed to make when he claimed that d'Agoult was the author of the writings. To give him his due, the argument he advances centers on the events of February 1837 and the publication of the "Letter to a Poet-Voyager" (chapter 2). Marie was then visiting Sand at Nohant, and Liszt's correspondence with her does indeed contain a number of references to her efforts.[11] He writes, for instance that he has just revised "our letter in order to give it on Sunday to *Le Monde* and to the *Gazette*. I expect it will have a great success. I shall be grateful to you for keeping half the secret, at least with George." In another, he reports that "The *lettre d'un bachelier* appeared yesterday. . . . Unless I am mistaken, it should have much success. When I come to Nohant I shall give you an order for one or two articles. Little Zyo [Marie] is decidedly a great writer." Further, when asking her to write the article he had outlined about his Beethoven series,[12] he adds: "The article ought to be written in my personal name. This is an important matter for me. I am asking you for a real service. Try to let me have it within five or six days so that I can have it printed in the *Gazette* of Sunday, 26 February, and also in *Le Monde*."

Unquestionably, Liszt was looking to his lover for a service; but before we make too much of the nature and urgency of his requests, as Haraszti did, it is well to recall that these notes to Marie were written at the height of the Thalberg affair, a time when he seemed to be reaching out for anything that would keep his name favorably before the public. Furthermore, even if Liszt did "order" the articles from his collaborator, he most certainly specified what they were to say.

Granting that his later letters to Marie also refer at times to "our" articles, it is also true that as far as the rest of the world was concerned, Liszt assumed full responsibility—proprietorship, if you will—for the writings. In all his personal correspondence of this period with his mother, close friends, and professional colleagues, he never once refers to the articles as anything but his own work. It is difficult to believe, therefore, that he would be deliberately deceptive when he writes to a respected friend like d'Ortigue, for instance, and

11. The following quotations, cited by Haraszti, are taken from *Corres. Liszt–d'Agoult*, 1:180–201.

12. See "To George Sand," p. 33, n. 7.

tells him that he was pleased with his reaction to the Letter on *Saint Cecilia*;[13] or when he, in a lighthearted mood, writes to Sand, (addressing her in masculine form as he typically did) and remarks: "As to that illustrious being [Sand herself], I must tell you that an impertinent fellow, one F. Liszt by name, has had the audacity to cite him (in a completely harmless manner, it is true) in an article discussing Berlioz, the *man of genius*. If, by some unlucky accident, said article falls into your hands, please forgive me the very great liberty";[14] or when he tells Cristina Belgiojoso apropos the Letter to Berlioz that "I have just worn myself out trying to describe the forest in which I have been living for nearly a month (see the *Gazette musicale* No.——, I don't know which yet)."[15] In all these instances Liszt implies that he did the writing himself. With Marie's help? There is no way of telling; theirs was an active and fluid literary partnership.

The nature of their collaboration, therefore, can only be characterized in the most general of terms—mostly Liszt's ideas as expressed in d'Agoult's words—with a caveat that the precise mix of this general formula cannot and need not be specified further, especially in light of all the equivocal points just mentioned when reviewing her *Mémoires* and his correspondence. She, though, was probably the "writer" responsible for the final, published texts of the articles.[16] Liszt was sensitive about his lack of formal education, and French was not his native language, thus he would naturally defer to her greater facility with words.

The basic, underlying substance of the articles, on the other hand, can only be attributed to Liszt. He, for one thing, was the force behind the literary partnership, if only in the sense that it is virtually impossible to believe that Marie d'Agoult would have written anything like the articles in question without him. For another, it is difficult to imagine that Liszt, who was extremely sensitive about his reputation,

13. See "The *Saint Cecilia* of Raphael," p. 162, n. 1.

14. Letter [27 June 1835] in Marix-Spire, *Romantiques*, p. 610. Liszt cites the phrase "*Berlioz, homme de génie*" in the fourth installment of his "On the Situation of Artists," *Gazette musicale*, 26 July 1835.

15. Letter of October 1839, in Daniel Ollivier, *Autour de Mme d'Agoult et de Liszt*, p. 158.

16. Reviewing her literary aspirations, Madame d'Agoult told Georges Herwegh, perhaps a bit disingenuously: "For a long time I was extremely diffident, and I did not dream of doing anything with my pen except to help Liszt write musical articles. A modest ambition" (letter of October 1844 in Marcel Herwegh, *Au printemps des dieux*, p. 110).

would allow anything that he did not believe or endorse to appear in print. He signed the articles. He assumed full responsibility for them, and even when they provoked controversy it was he who leapt to their defense. Furthermore, the basic philosophy behind them reflects all the ideas about the nobility and social function of art, the humanistic Romanticism that he had absorbed from the Saint-Simonians, Lammenais, and others, independent of the countess. That the wide range of subjects discussed and the opinions expressed would perhaps occasionally reflect her particular interests more than his is a natural outcome of six years' collaboration, but it does not alter the fact that the "author," the person responsible for these articles is Liszt.

BIBLIOGRAPHY

Agoult, Comtesse [Marie] d'. *Mémoires 1833–1854*. Edited by Daniel Ollivier. Paris, 1927.

Altenburg, Detlef. "Die Schriften von Franz Liszt. Bermerkungen zu einem zentralen Problem der Liszt-Forschung." In *Festschrift Arno Forchert*. Kassel-Basel-London-New York, 1986.

Asow, E. H. M. von. "Hermann Cohen. Ein Lieblingsschuler Franz Liszts." *Oesterreichische Musikzeitschrift* 9 (1961): 443–52.

Attardi, Francesco. *Roma musicale nell'800, dalla musica vocale alla strumentale*. Padua, 1979.

Bailbé, Joseph-Marc. *Le Roman et la musique en France sous la Monarchie de Juillet*. Paris, 1969.

Ballanche, Pierre-Simon. *La Théodicée et La virginie romaine*. Presentation and analysis by Oscar A. Haac. (*Textes littéraires français* 88) Geneva-Paris, 1959.

Bénichou, Paul. *Le Temps des prophètes: Doctrines de l'âge romantique*. Paris, 1977.

Berlioz, Hector. *À travers chants*. Paris, n.d. First pub. 1862.

———. *New Letters of Berlioz 1830–1868*. Translated and edited by Jacques Barzun. New York, 1954.

———. *The Memoirs of Hector Berlioz*. Translated and edited by David Cairns. London-New York, 1969.

———. *Correspondance générale*. Edited by Pierre Citron et al. 4 vols. to date. Paris, 1972-.

Blanc, Louis. *The History of Ten Years, 1830–1840*. 2 vols. London, 1845. Reprint. New York, 1969.

Bory, Robert. "Diverses lettres inédites de Liszt." *Schweizerisches Jahrbuch für Musikwissenschaft* 3 (1928): 5–25.

———. *Une Retraite romantique en Suisse. Liszt et la comtesse d'Agoult*. 2d augmented ed. Lausanne-Paris, 1930.

Brombert, Beth Archer. *Cristina: Portraits of a Princess*. New York, 1977.

Butler, Eliza Marian. *Heinrich Heine*. New York, 1957.

Cambiasi, Pompeo. *La Scala 1778–1906: Note storiche e statistiche.* Milan, 1906.

Carr, Philip. *Days with the French Romantics in the Paris of 1830.* London, 1932.

Castelot, Andre. *The Turbulent City: Paris, 1783–1871.* Translated by Denise Folliot. New York-Evanston, 1962.

Chantavoine, Jean. "La comtesse d'Agoult: Lettres à Ferdinand Hiller." *Revue (Bleue) politique et littéraire* 51 (8 November 1913): 577–81 and (15 November 1913): 613–19.

———. *Liszt.* New ed. Paris, 1950.

Chantavoine, Jean and Jean Gaudefroy-Demombynes. *La Romanticisme dans la musique européenne. (L'évolution de l'humanité* 76.) Paris, 1955.

Chopin, Fryderyk. *Selected Correspondence.* Translated and edited by Arthur Hedley. London, 1962.

Crosten, William L. *French Grand Opera: An Art and a Business.* New York, 1948.

Derré, Jean-René. *Lamennais, ses amis et le mouvement des ideés à l'époque romantique.* Paris, 1962.

Deutsch, Otto Erich, ed. *Schubert: Memoirs by his Friends.* New York, 1958.

Donakowski, Conrad L. *A Muse for the Masses: Ritual and Music in an Age of Democratic Revolution, 1770–1870.* Chicago, 1977.

Duverger, J. *Notice biographique sur Franz Liszt.* 2d ed. Paris, 1843.

Eckhardt, Maria P. "Diary of a Wayfarer: The Wanderings of Franz Liszt and Marie d'Agoult in Switzerland, June-July 1835." *Journal of the American Liszt Society* 11 (June 1982): 10–17, and 12 (December 1982): 182–83.

———. "New Documents on Liszt as Author." *New Hungarian Quarterly* 25 (Autumn 1984): 181–94.

Evans, R. L. *Les romantiques française et la musique.* Paris, 1934.

Fragapane, Paolo. *Spontini.* Bologna, 1954.

George, Albert Joseph. *Lamartine and Romantic Unanimism.* New York, 1940.

———. *The Development of French Romanticism: The Impact of the Industrial Revolution on Literature.* Syracuse, 1955.

Guichard, Léon. *La Musique et les lettres au temps du romantisme.* Paris, 1955.

———. "Liszt et la littérature française." *Revue de musicologie* 56 (1970): 3–34.

Gut, Serge. *Franz Liszt. Les Éléments du langage musicale.* Paris, 1975.

Hankiss, Jean. "Liszt écrivain et la littérature européene." *Revue de la littérature comparée* 17 (April-June 1937): 299–323.

Haraszti, Emile. "Franz Liszt—Author despite Himself: The History of a Mystification." *The Musical Quarterly* 33 (1947): 490–516.

———. *Franz Liszt.* Paris, 1967.

Heine, Heinrich. *Historisch-kritische Gesamtausgabe der Werke. (Collected Works,* the "Düsseldorfer Ausgabe.") Edited by Manfred Windfuhr et al. Hamburg, 1973-.

Herwegh, Marcel. *Au printemps des dieux: Correspondance inédite de la comtesse Marie d'Agoult et du poéte Georges Herwegh.* Paris, 1929.

Huneker, James. *Franz Liszt.* New York, 1911.

Isenburg, W. K. von et al. *Europäische Stammtafeln.* Vol 3. Marpurg, 1955.

Joubert, Solange, ed. *Une correspondance romantique: Madame d'Agoult, Liszt, Henri Lehmann.* Paris, 1947.

Kapp, Julius. *Franz Liszt.* Berlin and Leipzig, 1909.

Keeling, Geraldine. "Liszt's Appearances in Parisian Concerts, 1824–1844." *Liszt Society Journal* 11 (1986): 22–34; and 12 (1987): 8–22.

Kling, Henri. "Franz Liszt pendant son séjour à Genève en 1835–1836." *Le Guide musical* 43 (1897); 123 ff. (six installments).

Kroó, György. "Ferenc Liszt: dall'Album alla Suite." *Musica/Realtà* 19 (April 1986): 117–37; and 20 (August 1986): 149–69.

La Fontaine, Jean de. *The Best Fables of La Fontaine.* Translated by Francis Duke. Charlottesville, Va., 1965.

Laforet, Claude [Flavien Bonnet-Roy] *La Vie musicale au temps romantique (Salons, Théâtres et Concerts).* Paris, 1929.

Lamennais, Felicité. *Paroles d'un croyant.* New ed. Paris, 1866.

Legány, Dezső. *Franz Liszt: Unbekannte Presse und Briefe aus Wien 1822–1886.* Budapest, 1984.

Liszt, Franz. *Gesammelte Schriften.* Edited by Lina Ramann. 6 vols. Leipzig, 1880–83. Reprint. Hildesheim-New York, 1978.

———. *Briefe.* Edited by La Mara [Marie Lipsius]. 8 vols. Leipzig, 1893–1905.

———. *Letters.* Edited by La Mara. Translated by Constance Bache. 2 vols. London-New York, 1894. Reprint New York, 1969. Vols. 1 and 2 of the *Briefe.*

———. *Pages romantiques.* Edited by Jean Chantavoine. Paris-Leipzig, 1912.

——. *Briefe an seine Mutter.* Translated from the French and edited by La Mara. Leipzig, 1918.

———. *Correspondance de Liszt et de la comtesse d'Agoult.* Edited by Daniel Ollivier. 2 vols. Paris, 1933–34.

———. *Divagazioni di un musicista romantico.* Edited by Raoul Meloncelli. Rome, 1979.

———. *Piano Transcriptions from French and Italian Operas.* Selected, with an introduction by Charles Suttoni. New York, 1982.

Locke, Arthur Ware. *Music and the Romantic Movement in France.* London, 1920.

Locke, Ralph P. "Liszt's Saint-Simonian Adventure." *Nineteenth-Century Music* 4 (1980–81): 209–27 and 5 (1981–82): 281.

———. *Music, Musicians, and the Saint-Simonians.* Chicago, 1986.

Lutyens, Mary, ed. *Effie in Venice: Unpublished Letters of Mrs. John Ruskin written from Venice between 1849–1852.* London, 1965.

Maier, Hans. *Revolution and Church: The Early History of Christian Democracy, 1789–1901.* Translated by E. M. Schlossberger. Notre Dame, Ind., 1969.

Main, Alexander. "Liszt's *Lyon:* Music and Social Conscience." *Nineteenth-Century Music* 4 (1980–81): 228–43.

————. "Liszt and Lamartine: Two Early Letters." *Liszt-Studien 2.* (Report of the 2nd European Liszt Symposium. Eisenstadt 1978.) Edited by Serge Gut. Munich-Salzburg, 1981.

Marchand, Leslie A. *Byron: A Biography.* 3 vols. New York, 1957.

Marix-Spire, Thérèse. "Bataille de dames. George Sand et Madame d'Agoult (d'après des documents inédites)." *Revue des sciences humaines* (April-September 1951): 224–43.

————. *Les Romantiques et la musique. Le Cas George Sand, 1804–1838.* Paris, 1954.

Nani-Mocenigo, Mario. *Il Teatro La Fenice: Note storiche e artistiche.* Venice, 1926.

Ollivier, Daniel, ed. *Autour de Mme d'Agoult et de Liszt (Alfred de Vigny, Émile Ollivier, Princesse de Belgiojoso).* Paris, 1941.

Ortigue, Joseph d'. "Études biographiques I: Franz Liszt." *Revue et gazette musicale* 2 (14 June 1835): 197–204.

Pascal, Blaise. *Pensées.* Translated and edited by H. F. Stewart. New York, 1950. Bilingual edition.

Perényi, Eleanor. *Liszt: The Artist as Romantic Hero.* Boston and Toronto, 1974.

Photiadès, Constantin. "En Avignon, avec Liszt et Berlioz." *Revue musicale* 9 (May 1928): 18–32.

Pincherle, Marc. *Musiciens peints par eux-mêmes: Lettres de compositeurs écrites en français (1771–1910).* Paris, 1939.

Poisson, Jacques. *Le Romantisme social de Lamennais: Essai sur la métaphysique des deux sociétés 1833–1854.* Paris, 1931.

Pleasants, Henry. *The Great Singers, from the Dawn of Opera to Our Own Time.* New York, 1966.

Prod'homme, Jacques-Gabriel. "Les Oeuvres de Schubert en France." *Mercure de France* 208 (15 November 1928): 5–37.

Quicherat, Louis-Marie. *Adolphe Nourrit, sa vie, son talent, son caractère, sa correspondance.* 3 vols. Paris, 1867.

Ramann, Lina. *Franz Liszt: Artist and Man, 1811–1840.* Revised ed. Translated by E. Cowdery. 2 vols. London, 1882.

————. *Lisztiana: Erinnerungen an Franz Liszt in Tagebuchblättern, Briefe und Dokumenten aus den Jahren 1873–1886/87.* Edited by Arthur Seidl. Text revised by Friedrich Schnapp. Mainz, 1983.

Sallès, Antoine. *Le Centenaire de Liszt: Liszt à Lyon.* Paris, 1911.

Salvioli, Giovanni. *La Fenice: Gran teatro di Venezia.* Milan, 1878.

Sand, George. *The Intimate Journal of George Sand.* Edited and translated by Marie Jenny Howe. New York, 1929.

————. *George Sand: In her own Words.* Translated and edited by Joseph Barry. Garden City, N.Y., 1979.

————. *Lettres d'un voyageur.* English translation by Sacha Rabinovitch and Patricia Thomson. Harmondsworth, 1987.

Searle, Humphrey. *The Music of Liszt.* 2d revised ed. New York, 1966.

————. and Sharon Winklhofer. "Liszt." In *The New Grove Early Romantic Masters 1*. New York, 1985.

Spencer, Philip. *Politics of Belief in Nineteenth-Century France*. London, 1954.

Suttoni, Charles. "Liszt à Milan." In *Actes du colloque international Franz Liszt. Revue musicale* nos. 405–07 (1987).

Tappolet, Claude. *La vie musicale à Genève au dix-neuvième siècle (1814–1918)*. Geneva, 1972.

Teichmann, Elizabeth. *La Fortune d'Hoffmann en France*. Geneva-Paris, 1961.

Tinti, Mario. *Lorenzo Bartolini*. 2 vols. Rome, 1936.

Trollope, Fanny. *Paris and the Parisians*. London, 1836. Reprint. Glouchester-New York, 1985.

Valery [Antoine-Claude Pasquin]. *Historical, Literary and Artistical Travels in Italy, a Complete and Methodical Guide for Travellers and Artist*. Translated from the second corrected and improved edition by C. E. Clifton. Paris, 1839.

Viala, Claude. "Franz Liszt au Conservatoire [de Genève] (1835–1836)." *Revue musicale de Suisse-Romande* 38 (1985): 122–29.

Vidler, Alec R. *Prophecy and Papacy: A Study of Lamennais, the Church and Revolution*. New York, 1954.

Vier, Jacques. "Liszt et Lamartine." *La Table Ronde*. New series, vol. 2 (1946).

————. *Franz Liszt: L'artiste-Le clerc: Documents inédites*. Paris, 1950.

————. *Marie d'Agoult: Son mari-Ses amis: Documents inédites*. Paris, 1950.

————. *La comtesse d'Agoult et son temps*. 6 vols. Paris, 1955–1963.

Walker, Alan. *Franz Liszt*. Vol. 1: *The Virtuoso Years, 1811–1847*. New York-London, 1983.

Waters, Edward N. "Sur la piste de Liszt." *Notes* 27 (1970–71): 665–70.

Weinstock, Herbert. *Rossini: A Biography*. New York, 1968.

Williams, Adrian. "Liszt's British Tours (II)." *Liszt Society Journal* 9 (1984): 2–15.

Winklhofer, Sharon. "Liszt, Marie d'Agoult and the 'Dante' Sonata." *Nineteenth-Century Music* 1 (1977–78): 15–34.

INDEX

Aesop, 211
Agoult, Marie d', ix–xii, xiv, xxiiin,
 xxvii, 3, 11–12, 25–27, 33n, 38n,
 39–40, 41n, 51, 53–54, 62n, 72–
 73, 84n, 92n, 100, 101n, 107n,
 140n, 145–47, 159n, 163n, 167,
 181–82, 189n, 191, 198n, 200, 201,
 206n, 207n, 215, 233n, 238–45
Alberti, Leon Battista, 188n
Alizard, Adolphe-Joseph Louis, 232
Allegri, Gregorio, xxiv, 179, 186; *Mi-
 serere,* 179n
Amadé, Thaddeus d', 139n
Amadeus VIII (duke of Savoy), 60n
Arago, Emmanuel, 215
Aristotle, 135
Artôt, Alexandre, 229
Auber, Daniel François Esprit, 8n,
 232

Bach, Johann Sebastian, 44, 150, 182,
 193, 195
Badiali, Cesare, 82
Ballanche, Pierre Simon, xiv, xvi,
 xviii–xix, xx, xxi, 104, 221; *Palin-
 génésie sociale,* xviii, 102, 221n
Balzac, Honoré de, xiv, 14, 43, 228
Bandinelli, Bartolomeo, 155
Barchou de Penhoën, Auguste-
 Théodore-Hilaire, 13, 44
Bartolini, Lorenzo, 158–62, 188–89
Bassano (Jacopo da Ponte), 120

Batta, Alexander, 25, 26, 32n, 33n,
 207, 228, 229
Beato, Fra (Guido di Pietro), xxiv,
 186
Beauharnais, Eugène de, 116
Beethoven, Ludwig van, xxiv, xxv,
 17, 19, 25, 31–32, 46, 48, 77, 90,
 135n, 141, 183n, 186, 187, 188–89,
 231; Quintet Op. 16, 26; Piano
 Sonata Op. 26, 141n; Piano So-
 nata Op. 27, no. 2, 141n, 230n;
 "Adelaide," Op. 46, 141n; Violin
 Sonata Op. 47, 32n, 187n, 194;
 Symphony Op. 55, xxiv, 186, 193;
 Cello Sonata Op. 69, 229; *Fide-
 lio* Op. 72, 193n; Fantasy Op.
 80, 193; Trio Op. 97, 12, 32n;
 Piano Sonata Op. 106, 24n
Beethoven Committee (Bonn), 189n
Belgiojoso, Cristina, 7n, 26, 38n,
 39n, 71n, 181n, 222n, 244
Belgiojoso, Emilio Barbiano, 7, 8n,
 9
Belgiojoso, Pompéo, 84, 94
Belgiojoso, Tonino, 84
Belgiojoso family, 71, 176
Bellatella, Salvatore, 61
Bellini, Vincenzo, 9, 90, 93, 173; *La
 Sonnambula,* 8n, 79, 161n; *I Pu-
 ritani,* 39n
Benedict, Julius, 229
Béranger, Jean Pierre, xiv